Frontiers in Birding

Frontiers in Birding

by Martin Garner and friends

Published in 2008 by BirdGuides Ltd,
PO Box 4104 Sheffield S25 9BS. Tel 01909 560992
email sales@birdguides.com, www.birdguides.com

Printed in 2008
10 9 8 7 6 5 4 3 2 1

Emily Garner	Eiders, Blue-winged and Cinnamon Teal
Martin Garner	Brent Geese, Common and Black Scoter,
	White-fronted Geese, Redhead, Canvasback and
	Pochard
Mick Cunningham	Moorhens, Kites
John Martin	Northern Harrier and Hen Harrier
Richard Millington	Cormorants
Rob Hume	Herring, Yellow-legged and Armenian Gulls
Jimmy Steele	Newbiggin map

Cover image: Northern Harrier by Ian Lewington
www.ian-lewington.co.uk

Vignettes by Ian Lewington unless otherwise stated in the text.

ISBN 978-1-898110-47-7

Printed and bound in Great Britain by J.H. Haynes & Co. Ltd, Sparkford.

Contents

Acknowledgements

Anyone who has ever had to write an acknowledgments page knows, I guess, how daunting it is! We all build on the work of others who have gone before, blazing a trail. So many top-quality people have inspired me, informed me and mentored me, it would simply be impossible to name them all. I am still, to this day, learning from others almost every time I go out in the field, pick up a bird book or log on to the Internet. For all those people... thank you!

Frontiers of Bird Identification (published 1980) is a collection of pioneering identification papers published in *British Birds*. It was a milestone publication and one of the inspirations along the road for this book.

In the delivery of this particular project, I want to express gratitude to a host of contributors who quickly and faithfully did exactly what was asked for. Specifically these are Richard Millington, John Martin, Rob Hume, Stuart Bearhop, Steve Votier, Andy Stoddart, Martin Collinson, Ken Shaw, Keith Clarkson, Jimmy Steele, Paul Hackett, Stuart Rivers, Ian Wallace, Dave Farrow, Keith Vinicombe, John McLoughlin together with past and present members of the British Birds Rarities Committee, from whom I learn so much. Originally I thought I could do this by myself, but with the breadth of subjects I desired to cover I quickly knew I was out of my depth. Pioneer Birding is ultimately best expressed as a community experience. I can't believe your work in these pages won't inspire many; I hope you think it was worth it! As well as those whose artwork accompanied their texts a big thank you to artists Ian Lewington (how does he do it?) and, for the first time in print, Mick Cunningham and Emily Garner: an amazing job from some very special people! Abigail Garner, you are great at typing, I would never have finished it without you! To the guys at BirdGuides, especially Russell Slack and Fiona Barclay, thank you for cajoling, encouraging and believing. Jason Crook, I really appreciate you. Awesome job on the proof reading, can't believe you missed anything. Stuart Winter, you conceived something like this a long time ago; thanks for the ongoing encouragements along the road.

To Mum and Dad Hanna, you and Glendale provided a real writing sanctuary. You are one of the biggest blessings in my life. To my amazing wife Sharon, no you are pure gold. I love you.

Finally I dedicate this book to my lovely Mum and Dad. This is for you. I finally got there!

Martin Garner Sheffield, UK

Frontiers in Birding – an introduction

Martin Garner

What is it exactly? What is it that inspires us about birds?

At 11 years old, my bedroom (box room) was the smallest in the house. It had just enough space for a bed and small bookcase, at the bottom of which were my prized YOC magazines and set of 'Ladybird Guide to Birds'. Brushing the window of that tiny room were the branches of a large flowering cherry and it was here that I encountered, less than ten feet away, my first-ever Bullfinch. A male. No binoculars needed and mesmerizing in its beauty. I recently asked a group of friends about what gave them a sense of 'wonder' in birding. One of them (who is not especially religious) felt that there were times when watching birds was a spiritual experience, a connection with something much greater. I think I know what he means.

Many years after my first Bullfinch encounter, I moved to within reasonable proximity of Britain's east coast. The possibility of regular coastal trips helped conceive the notion of finding an example of the irruptive 'Northern' Bullfinch. A gestation period of about two years involved careful scrutiny of Bullfinches of the British form in all circumstances combined with thoughtful literature study and ended on 30th October 2003. Having identified my first Scandinavian Treecreeper nearby, and with both Pallas's and Yellow-browed Warblers in evidence, the scene was set. A female Bullfinch in South Landing, Flamborough appeared rather more ghostly pallid than the British females with which I was now so well acquainted. Struck by the paleness of this Bullfinch, combined with significant 'plumpishness' and seemingly extra white below, I quickly exclaimed to my colleagues "it's a Northern, it must be a Northern"!

The bird then dutifully flew straight into a mist net. My euphoria was momentarily suspended as I imagined having to backtrack when the in-hand biometrics showed it to be just a local breeder. But no! Mike Pearson, suitably grinning, announced that its wing length of 93 mm meant only one thing: it was indeed a Northern, its wing nearly a centimetre longer than the longest British females. I had done it! Here was yet another little discovery that brought the same kind of 'wow' factor which I had so relished with my very first Bullfinch. Despite many 'sight' records, it was also only the second ever at Flamborough to be confirmed through trapping.

The Bullfinch theme was not exhausted however. Autumn 2004 brought an unprecedented invasion of Northern Bullfinches to Britain and, with it, an unknown trumpet call which elicited much interest and furious debate in the birding fraternity. We were learning together. I was fortunate to find three birds in late October 2004 at Whitby, one of which, a male, had 'extra' white running up the outer edge of the greater coverts, creating U shapes in the large wing bar. This pattern is usually found on birds from eastern Siberia! I don't yet have an answer to the questions this individual has posed, but the discovery and adventure continues unabated! As the commentary in 'The 'Northern Bullfinch' invasion of autumn 2004' (Pennington and Meek 2006) reads, "...there are still many things to discover even about a common and familiar species such as the Bullfinch".

Same birds, different perspectives

In late April 2007, I headed out to a local wetland near Sheffield for a couple of hours birding. A quick count of over 60 Common Swifts heralded the arrival of the first big wave of this awesome aerial master that had last graced Yorkshire skies the best part of eight months ago. My family and I had raised three orphaned young swifts the previous summer and knew well that once released these birds may never land again for another two years! While pondering the wonders of the Common Swift, it was not long before I came across a red male and two female-type Bar-tailed Godwits. These were stunning waders en route to breeding grounds in the arctic tundra, and a rare and special sighting of them so far inland. As I finished my small circuit, a male Greenland Wheatear fed at close range. This is one of the marvels of bird migrations, being possibly the only small migratory song bird in the world that chooses to cross an ocean to order to breed. Up until a few weeks ago it had been wintering in Africa but was now en route to North America via Yorkshire. In awe once again at the wonders of the avian world, and having found some good 'unexpecteds', I came to the end of my morning walk. As I did so, I came across a fellow birder and enquired with the usual tribal greeting "'ave ya seen much?" to which he tersely replied "it's crap today". Well, I could scarcely think of the words to respond. Afterwards I felt I should have suggested he really ought to give up birding and take up another hobby. Where had the awe, the wonder, and the wow factor gone for this guy?

Birding, I propose, is the opportunity not only to delight in what is already known but also to seek out continuous discovery, whether it's in your garden, on a local patch or in some far-flung corner of the world. It's an invitation into a world that should continuously inspire us with the promise of more discoveries. This book is an attempt to recapture some of that wonder and 'pioneering spirit'. It comes in two parts. One is more about inspiration with stories and thoughts written by friends who enthuse about their particular areas of interest and expertise. I hope some of their words inspire you. The second part is new information covering a number of species or subspecies where there are new identification criteria and where I think there may be opportunities for pioneering discoveries yet to be made. These cover about 20 species/groups of a large group of about 60, the rest of which may be covered in future volumes. Some of the material and ideas need further testing, challenging and adapting. I invite you never to lose your ability to enjoy the wonder of birds and to stir up your pioneering spirit to go and discover new things for yourself and others.

Soli Deo Gloria.

Martin Garner February 2008

Discovering new skills

Discovering skills and equipment

Discovering note-taking

Note-taking, they say in the day of the digital revolution, may be a dying art. Something else, however, will also be lost: perceptive observation. The process of learning, according to educationalists, involves observation, reflection and discussion, together with plans and actions to take into the next learning experience. Some kind of note-taking in whatever form provides the clearest means of accurate observation, and a period of careful reflection while 'logging down' can produce the questions that take you into the next birding, learning experience. I reckon all the most skilful observers of birds have honed their discipline in some fashion through careful logging of observations. Now, personally, I'm an extrovert when it comes to processing information. To some, I guess, it means I can end up speaking before I think! I like to process ideas and observations by talking about them and chewing them over with others. Note-taking for me is a much more messy and unstructured art form than it is for someone who is more of an introvert processor. Introvert processors take time to think more before speaking. They also make much better and much neater writers! Nevertheless my own poor and inconsistent scribbles are still the core means of learning, helpfully backed up with all the new fangled digital and computer stuff.

Here in Ian Wallace is perhaps the ultimate note-taking enthusiast, the only contributor to the mighty BWP who appears as both author and artist. I hope he inspires you, as he has me, to leave behind the tardy crowd…be a learner with a clear process of recording your observations that will maximise your learning, discovery and enjoyment of birds.

Martin Garner

Paddyfield Warbler   Hartlepool   18th Sept '94

wings usually hold slightly drooped with the tail cocked & slightly spread

Generally quite a pale bird but not as pale as a Booted Warbler!

dark lateral crown stripes

super fading off behind eye

warmer rufous brown

short primary proj

dark centred tertials with broad pale fringes

bill not too blunt tipped - pinky base to lower mandible

pale wedge on neck side

100 notebooks later and still going...
Ian Wallace

My kind of ornithological record is in its seventh decade. I made my initial diary entry in 1943, my earliest dated drawing in 1948 and my first rarity description (written on the fly-leaf of Volume 4 of the Witherby *Handbook*) in May 1950. Looking in three of my study's cabinets, I can see nearly 100 diaries, loose-leaf folders and identification files, most in A4 format, all bulging and increasingly dog-eared from repeated use. How many words? It has to be a seven-figure sum and counting. And why such an archive? Because in terms of my odyssey after and perception of birds, I soon realised that my own records were making up the core intelligence. Not free of error, of course, but none-the-less a growing treasure, uniquely valuable.

Looking back through the tatter and many associated publications, I can experience afresh the pain of having my first rarity misidentified by my second French master/ornithological tutor in 1948. Adding another set of annotated sketches, I can log yet another Caspian Gull from the Dove floodplain, fellow-travelling into my patch with Lesser Black-backs yet again. With an increase in discipline, I can see how excited scribbles became decent descriptions. I based them particularly on the published models in *British Birds*, my lifetime mentor journal. Furthermore mere lists of names and numbers were adorned with purple prose if the bird or spectacle was exceptional.

One particular penchant of mine is to watch for birds' individual signals in movement. Thus years after I had written off a glimpsed Red-flanked Bluetail on St. Agnes in the magic October of 1971, I found out that this lovely chat has a habit of jerking its tail downwards. Referring back to my tales of the days, there it was, the very same behaviour incorporated into the written record of the second view of the St. Agnes bird. Still not enough for the claim but more importantly, I knew that as an observer I had passed a real test and perceived a crucial field mark.

So do not be seduced by the magic of modern optical recording. Not one snapped image using the amazing technology can match the constant argument of your eye and mind and to exercise the latter fully you must practise. "Look, really observe, draw, describe, and finally see" is the course. You will not find it or its product of perception in a video grab or on a digital retina. They provide excellent, at times miraculously captured, clues but the only way to see the whole bird and its way of life is to pile observation upon observation and to question constantly their content. We have hardly begun to write the specific litany of essential identity signals and their discovery remains one of the great quests open to young birdwatchers.

What kind of notebooks should you use? In his classic *Birders: tales of a tribe* (2001) Mark Cocker discussed several. The classic brand was the Alwych. Complete with black 'all-weather cover' and used by many as a "for-all-time" repository for dates, places, weathers, bird lists and numbers, descriptions, drawings and outbreaks of narrative. The larger model needed a poacher's pocket for easy accommodation, but it and its smaller version did make for "one-stop" recording and archiving devices. Regrettably in recent years Alwych sturdiness has lessened and its continuity of use even by lifelong fans (like Richard Porter who to date has put 146 field note books and 45 record books onto his book shelves) is threatened.

Nowadays, I observe that the types of notebooks vary considerably. Really dutiful observers still use true pocket-sized 'policeman notebooks', complete with elastic page holders/markers. Many then fair-copy their field scribbled contents into a more considered form and enter records in diaries or logs, recreated within hours once home. I am one of the compulsive re-writers but oddly, even after 64 years, I still have not finally ended my debate on "foolscap diary versus loose-leaf folder". Indeed recently my obsessive patchwork has demanded the use of both, always using faintly ruled narrow-spaced writing sheets and allowing the folder to expand to harbour maps, habitat registers, count schedules (on 5mm squared sheets), survey results and even an annual patch report. I begin the last in December and finish in January, one copy to my cabinets and others to my local recorders in Staffs and Derby. For me, just as any unusual bird gets precise address on the night of its discovery, each year deserves a full review while its impressions are fresh. Any lapse from either rule leads to regret. Making anything up from memories is pointless; they always jumble and tend to get better! As Mark Cocker rightly observed, if you want to create a valuable 'cave wall' of perceptions you have to be a scribe and/or artist. Not to do your homework is to be a dilettante.

For 25 years up to the early 1980s I kow-towed completely to the national rarity discipline, only out of necessity breaking the rule of 'description before reference' and usually writing a full narrative of every bird claimed. However crucial my field sketch was to the retention of the bird, I slogged through the compulsory written elements set out in the BBRC model. Regrettably for the last 25 years I have been a very fitful adherent and for instructions on how to do an electronic submission, please see elsewhere. My last advice is stick to the rules and let your critical path to the bird's identity be clear. I have learnt that committees do not enjoy narrative. It's best kept in one's own log.

Recently I hear many moans about the decline of note-taking in the field and diary or log-writing at home. Certainly when I looked down the ranks of hundreds of twitchers collecting the Taiga Flycatcher at Flamborough Head on 27th April 2003 I was not blinded by the glints of moving pens or pencils. "None taking notes?" I challenged. Embarrassed silence followed and then came a muttered "It's already been caught and photographed. What's the point?" True in terms of the national discipline, the charmer was a 'done deal' but I found the lack of individual interest in its structure and behaviours astonishing. It was not just an odd Red-breasted; it was another species, worthy of full regard. How many birders left it, actually uninformed of its being and with only a tick to show for their attendance? They had missed a chance for adventurous perception, something no committee ever supplies.

Taking on the challenge of bird recognition was soon my first defined purpose as an amateur. Along with the task of being a full patch worker wherever I lived it has remained a recipe for constant recreation and occasional utter joy. Mark Cocker opined that a birder's greatest asset is his optics but at my time of life, what really scares me is the thought of losing my utmost singular possession, those 100 tattered diaries and folders. My bins I can replace; my past times with birds I cannot.

Note-taking and record-keeping is the most essential investment for anyone wanting to contribute to pro-active purposeful birdwatching. Don't hold back!

THE ASCENT OF FIELD SIGHTING TO NATIONAL ORNITHOLOGY

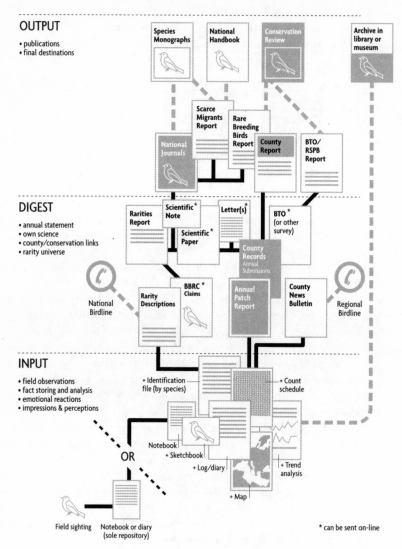

OUTPUT
• publications
• final destinations

Species Monographs
National Handbook
Conservation Review
Archive in library or museum

Scarce Migrants Report
Rare Breeding Birds Report
National Journals
County Report
BTO/ RSPB Report

DIGEST
• annual statement
• own science
• county/conservation links
• rarity universe

Rarities Report
Scientific* Note
Letter(s)
BTO* (or other survey)
Scientific* Paper
County Records Annual Submissions

National Birdline
Rarity Descriptions
BBRC* Claims
Annual Patch Report
County News Bulletin
Regional Birdline

INPUT
• field observations
• fact storing and analysis
• emotional reactions
• impressions & perceptions

+ Identification file (by species)
+ Count schedule

Notebook
+ Sketchbook
+ Log/diary
+ Trend analysis

OR

+ Map

Field sighting   Notebook or diary (sole repository)

* can be sent on-line

Diagram by DIM Wallace
Rendered by Ian Durman, FrankCreative

14

Discovering the skills of rare bird hunting

Last winter a Waxwing stayed in my garden, my own garden…for a whole week. This was a mere 30 years after my hunt for a garden Waxwing tick had begun. A disciple initially of the 'Ladybird Guide' (no laughing!), I followed its counsel by regularly checking the cotoneaster bushes at the front of our family home, but all to no avail. Last winter I finally got one in my own garden. Common, scarce or rare are all relative terms in regard to birds. It just depends where you are. The thrill of finding that Waxwing was just as good as that of some of the rarer birds I have found. Like most of us I have not found enough yet and want to keep improving my skills. I am discovering there are lots of useful tips and gems of advice to be had. Here, top rare bird finder, Ken Shaw, who is the epitome of contagious enthusiasm, brings some inspiring wisdom and encouragement. It has left me with new targets, new reading and new ideas. Whether I find any new birds remains to be seen! *Martin Garner*

Bird finding - from your window to St Kilda
Ken D Shaw

From the window of my tiny flat in Whitley Bay, Tyne & Wear, I used to watch the weather. Two streets and nine minutes away was Cullercoats, my local seawatching point. My wind gauge was the leaves on the trees up the street and almost every day decisions were made about when and where to go birding, based on the information gleaned from this 'window' to the rest of the world. I spent six happy years in Tyneside, 1981-1987, and fell in love with the Northumberland coast, from the magic, bird-filled, autumn days in Tynemouth to the early spring mornings on Holy Island with Hoopoes and Great Grey Shrikes.

It was, however, a mid-July day that brought a significant change to my outlook. Mike Watson and I worked our way up the coast on 13th July 1985 visiting all the 'wader spots'. At Hauxley we entered the top hide and, about 200 metres away, in front of the other hide was a pale, elegant, leggy, *Tringa* wader. Greenshank and Wood Sandpiper were dismissed and pretty quickly the possibility of Marsh Sandpiper took centre stage. As we walked hurriedly to the other hide I felt the thrill of the hunt, something I had felt before and I was to feel many times again. We quietly opened the hide windows and there it was, right in front of us: Northumberland's second-ever Marsh Sandpiper! Phone calls were made and over the next few days the bird was observed by hundreds of birders from the north of England. We had found rarities before but this was a big county bird and, in a way, we had been searching for it. You see, we had 'targeted' rare waders for that day and it was this focusing of our efforts that I believe had yielded such a positive result. . The memory would stay with me, a real 'top tenner'.

Some of the lessons I learnt that day have stayed with me too. Firstly, July is a good month for finding rarities. Gull-billed Tern, Least Sandpiper, Ferruginous Duck, Lesser Scaup and Surf Scoter were all to be July finds. Secondly, don't give up when there are few birds around. Thirdly, it CAN happen on your local patch. However, the biggest lesson was that bird finding is a sport and at the same time an intellectual challenge. You have to be up for it but you have to work out the best ways to do it.

'Bird projects are everywhere'

One of the great things about birds is they are everywhere. In a way every bird or record can be significant: the first Green Sandpiper along your patch of river, the highest Siskin count in your garden, the furthest north we can see Nuthatch in Scotland, the furthest south we can see Hooded Crow in England. I always remember my ex-boss Frank Hamilton telling me that he used to count the Common Gulls every day from the bus on his way to work in Edinburgh. A bird project is always available. There are always questions too. How far from your house are the nearest breeding Long-eared Owls or Goshawks…or Honey Buzzards? All probably closer than you think!

Bird finding fills many of our basic instincts, but not all of them…obviously! The hunter in us, the need to be part of a team, to be successful, to contribute, and the need to learn more and more ways of doing something we are already good at. We can do it anywhere, from our back window to St Kilda and from our family holiday in France to our expedition to Panama, Chile or Yemen.

I now live near the Kinross/Fife border. From my house in Kinross I can see the Lomond Hills, partly in Fife and partly in Perth & Kinross. These isolated hills reach 1731 ft at the summit of West Lomond. Fife is flat country in general terms, so any hill ground is of special interest to the bird finder. Breeding Long-eared Owl, Raven, and occasionally Goshawk, all occur there. It is also the place of all those unsuccessful attempts to find Dotterel on passage!

On 22nd October 2006 I went walking in the Lomonds. I have several routes in the hills but on that day I chose Glen Vale, one of the most beautiful and romantic glens and one of the last places Whinchat breed in Fife. Near the top of the glen I spotted a sub-adult Golden Eagle. This was a big bird, in more ways than one! After phoning 'the boys' I returned and went straight to the record books and read that the last records were in the fifties. Smout (1986) quoted three records from that decade.

"You will never use THAT book" was my wife's, or should I say my significant co-observer Kathy's, comment when I bought *Birds in Counties: An Ornithological Bibliography* by David Ballance. Nothing could be further from the truth. This amazing piece of work lists all the books and papers relevant to the ornithological history to each county providing an important tool for the bird finder. Within these historic documents are a thousand secrets of where to look for birds today. In Fife, for example, Hawfinch, now a very rare bird, used to breed in Newport at the turn of the century but there has not been a Fife breeding record since the '20s. Hawfinches are doing a little better again in surrounding counties and there are still mature gardens in Newport. It may be worth a check in late winter.

I like to walk the line between ornithological contribution and adventure in a project-led fashion. Over the last four years, working with Martin Scott, Alan Lauder, Andy Carroll and others, I have changed the status of Yellow-billed Diver in Scotland. It is a perfect project for me, combining a small contribution to our knowledge of Scottish birds with the chance to visit islands and headlands throughout northwest Scotland. The project approach is a good one because it keeps me motivated and it has an output.

What it takes to be a bird-finder

There are some birders who more than exemplify the qualities that are needed to become a modern bird finder and I am a fan of all of them. There is Ian Wallace, a real pioneer. I often wonder where we would be without the likes of Wallace and Roy Dennis who in so many ways have 'led the line'. We owe them so much. Then there is Keith Vinicombe and his writings. Keith is the thinking man's birder. He is top at explaining identification technique in a user-friendly way, inventive in describing rare birds, and expert in questioning why ornithological events happen. Lastly, there is Alan Dean. The most solid birder I have ever known, immersed in detail, loyal to his local patch, steady as she goes. I remember spending hours studying an Isabelline Wheatear with him on St Agnes.

The modern bird finder needs to be one-third of Wallace, Vinicombe and Dean and they must have a copper-plated arse…and a camera! He or she must see the world in terms of layers of opportunities depending on location. The garden, the local walk, the local patch, the county, the islands, the holidays in Cornwall. They all provide opportunities for finding relatively unusual birds, any day of the year. Strangely, when you are looking for something that is not routine, getting into a routine is part of the secret. Your regular walk round the country park WILL turn up a Lesser Scaup if only because everywhere else has had one! When I see a flock of 500+ diving duck on Loch Leven I go through them judging I have a fifty-fifty chance!

How to find 10 "*BB*" rarities a year

If you want to find ten "*BB*" rarities a year you need to plan. You need to create time at the right time of year and you need to visit as many islands as possible. You also need to be in the right place at the right time with no other birders there. That may sound a bit daft but it is possible. The trick is to go to well-trodden islands just off the 'main time' (whatever that is!) and also to visit islands that have been ignored at any time of year. The list is not exclusive but would include St Agnes in the last week of September, Fair Isle during the first ten days of June, Barra in the first week of November and any time for Sanday, Westray, Hoy, Yell,

Fetlar, Bressay, Canna, Bryer, St Martins, North Ronaldsay and my two favourite bets for the future, Papa Stour and Mingulay. Two of the big Scottish rarity-finding crews have proved that Foula and Barra 'work', therefore Papa Stour and Mingulay must surely 'work'.

Birdwatchers have always been drawn to islands. The remoteness, the breeding seabirds and the chance of migrants are all attractions. For me, the inspiration for bird finding in these places has come from reading about not only two of the most remote islands, St Kilda and Foula, but also from the more generic writings of Williamson and Morton Boyd in their *A Mosaic of Islands* and Atkinson in his *Island Going*. Some of the Scottish islands are more accessible than they once were and *Scottish Island Hopping* by Jemima Tindall is worth a read.

Birds can turn up anywhere

In 1993, I was living in the small coastal village of Newtonhill in Aberdeenshire. Our garden was tiny, basically a small lawn with a flower border a foot wide with a few flowers and shrubs. On the morning of 23rd October I was helping my three-year-old daughter to put on her little boots, when I looked out of the window and there, feeding on the ground, was a Booted Warbler. It was the first for mainland Scotland. We had just joined the ever-growing ranks of birders who have had a rarity in their garden.

The next two days were a lot of fun with many visiting birders. However, it got a bit dull after that. I can understand observers who find a big rarity on an island they have to themselves and pass on the information for a couple of days but not thereafter so they can enjoy at least part of their break. We were never sure how many birders visited us but luckily Lee Evans was on hand to give us an accurate count!

The inevitable then happened. A couple of Scottish birders turned up an Icterine Warbler nearby, a very late date for that species on mainland Scotland. It is amazing how often this happens; a rare bird turns up then bingo another is found at the same site. I am a bit of a believer in micro falls. An example is the arrival of at least 23 Pallas's Warblers during October/November 1994 to one small area of Aberdeenshire. This phenomenon does, however, seem to beat statistics.

Thinking about it, the rarity-finder must ask one obvious question: just how many rarities arrive in Britain each year? You flick through the rarities report year after year and there are more and more. I remember once on Fair Isle we discussed what percentage of rare birds were found on that fine island in September/October. The consensus was about 80 percent. So if it's 80 percent for Fair Isle, less for mainland Shetland and less still for an east-coast Scottish county, how about a coastal county in Wales (for example)? The percentage must be small. That illustrates just how big an opportunity remains for the modern rarity finder.

But I digress. Back to the Icterine Warbler in Newtonhill. It duly appeared in the sycamores I could see from my garden. I am very keen on my garden list. Okay I have lived in some great birding houses, at Tynemouth and Newtonhill especially, but I believe wherever you live there is interest. It might be the flashing Merlin, the group of Waxwings on your only tree or the thrill of a Redstart or Pied Flycatcher stopping off for a day on migration. My target for my present house is one hundred species, with a very tough ten to go.

How to find 400 species in Britain

I remember when Ron Johns reached the personal listing total of 400 birds seen in Britain. A great achievement then. The challenge now is to FIND 400 species in Britain and, with several bird finders approaching 350, I think it is on! But it is a huge mental challenge, not to mention a test of resilience and leg power.

Finding 400 species in Britain is about gap-filling, identifying targets and then working out a strategy for finding that species. Recently I wrote an article in *Birding Scotland* in which I split the rarities that have occurred in Britain into three groups: those of predictable occurrence (Greenish Warbler, Yellow-breasted Bunting, Pallid Swift, Ross's Gull, Lesser Scaup, etc.), those of totally unpredictable occurrence (Franklin's Gull, Roller, Little Bustard, Little Crake, Killdeer, etc.) and importantly the 'middle group' which has a large number of species (Red-flanked Bluetail, Red-eyed Vireo, Alpine Swift, Isabelline Wheatear, etc.). It is the latter group of species that have both predictable and unpredictable elements to their occurrence. The bird finder who is young enough and can 'crack' this middle group is the one who will achieve a 'find list' of 400.

The joy of a find

On 1st November 2002 I was staying on St Agnes, Isles of Scilly. All the birders had gone and it was a 'drifty' kind of a day, perfect conditions for the bird finder. I walked back from Gugh a little disappointed in the lack of birds but driven on by the atmospheric pressure, two House Martins and a couple of cheap Tim Cleeves philosophies: 'the big one always travels alone' and 'the later it is, the further it has come'.

The warbler got up almost at my feet. It was an *Acro*, pale, short-winged and with a strong face pattern. Paddyfield? It disappeared into some thicker scrub. What to do? Well, I was not absolutely alone. I got Doug Page from the shop. This was not the first or last time he has acted as my 'safety net'. A quiet, 'drifty' day on an island with a great history. Two observers and a Paddyfield Warbler. The bird finder lives for moments like these.

Recently, I met Martin Garner at an open BBRC meeting. 'What makes a good rarity finder then Ken?' was his first question. 'Good co-observers' I replied. Good hunting!

References

Atkinson, R. 1949. *Island Going*. Collins, London

Balance, D. K. 2000. *Birds in Counties, An Ornithological Bibliography for the Counties of England, Wales, Scotland and the Isle of Man*. Imperial College Press

Scott, M. S. & Shaw, K. D. *The Status of Yellow Billed Diver in NW Scotland* (in prep.)

Smout, A-M. 1986. *The Birds of Fife*. John Donald, Edinburgh

Shaw, K. D. 2006. *How much further can we focus our rarity finding? Birding Scotland* 9 (1)

Tindall, J. 1981. *Scottish island hopping. A handbook for the independent traveller*. Mc Donald, London

Williamson, K. & Morton Boyd J. 1963. *A Mosaic of Islands*. Oliver and Boyd,

Discoveries in science and birding

In recent years, field ornithology and professional avian biology have not always been comfortable bedfellows. The laboratory-based crowd cries, "you just don't know enough" and the field-based crowd replies, "you just don't get out enough". Of course both are, and always have been, essential to a holistic advancement in our understanding of the world of birds. The fools who think their 'wing' of ornithology is the only one that matters will find themselves flying around in circles! As fortune would have it, some of the science has come much closer to the field birding community and some very good birders also happen to be avian biologists. One such is Steve Votier who gripped me off by finding Caspian Gull in Sheffield before me and also knows all about "The ratio of the heavy hydrogen isotope 2H to the light isotope 1H (expressed as δ2H or δD)"! The science that Steve, Stuart and Martin write about clearly has the capacity to open our understanding about bird identification, movement and vagrancy in areas that would otherwise elude us. We are already familiar with using such science to identify Swinhoe's Petrels and 'Southern' Skuas in the UK. Orphean Warbler and Lesser Whitethroat taxa are coming under its gaze and for some, maybe the only way to nail the Somerset Yellow-nosed Albatross (July 2007) to species (Atlantic or Indian) will be through analysis of its excrement. How exciting can birding get! Read and learn. *Martin Garner*

Forensic birding: Using molecular and stable isotope techniques to establish identification and origin of vagrants

Stephen C Votier, Stuart Bearhop
& Martin Collinson

Birders are no strangers to developing technologies. Over the past 100 years or so everything from guns to radar, microphones and mist-nets to satellite tags have been employed to establish the origins of migrants or used to unravel identification mysteries. More recently, analysis of DNA sequences or ratios of stable isotopes have been used to resolve identification headaches or to establish the origins of vagrants. Although these techniques are widely used by the scientific community, they can be esoteric and remain unfamiliar to many birders. Here we provide insight into these two state-of-the-art technologies and consider the effectiveness, shortfalls, and growing potential of these two approaches to a truly pioneering branch of forensic birding.

Stable isotopes

What are stable isotopes and why are they useful to birders?

Firstly, you may rightly ask, what exactly is a stable isotope? All chemical elements occur as a number of isotopes; that is to say their atomic nucleus contains a variable number of neutrons, which are in addition to the number of protons that uniquely defines them. Some isotopes (known as radioactive isotopes) are chemically unstable and release radiation as they decay, while others (stable isotopes) do not break down as they decay. Because of their differing masses, different stable isotopes of a single element such as hydrogen behave slightly differently to one another during chemical and biochemical reactions. This means that different habitats and regions of the world tend to have different stable isotope ratios associated with them, for example because of different sources of their rainfall or maybe their different geologies. Most importantly, because all 'animals are what they eat' the growing tissues of animals living in these habitats or regions tend to have isotope ratios that are similar to those of their environment. Hence we can analyse the isotope composition of these body tissues to infer the origins of birds.

Analysing the ratio of stable isotopes in bird feathers, claws or blood can be a powerful tool for biological study. A key point here is that feathers and claws are effectively dead once they are grown and as a consequence these tissues retain a record of the habitats and geographical location used by an individual bird, i.e. once these tissues are made, their isotope composition is assumed to be frozen in time and remains constant no matter how far the bird migrates. Until recently, the only way of tracing the movements of individual migrants was via ringing or via the attachment of satellite tags. While the former has provided us with excellent data on the movements of some species, it requires that the animal is captured twice and, once ringed, the chances of a recovery are usually very small. The only exception to this is the use of coloured rings which enables the identity of an individual in the field subsequent to the initial marking and without the need to recapture. Satellite tag technology has also given us some remarkable insights, but it is expensive and much too bulky for smaller species. One of the beauties of the stable isotope approach is that every capture is effectively a recapture. This is because, if we measure the stable isotope ratios in the tissue of a migratory bird and combine this with some knowledge of how these ratios change across regions, we can infer where those tissues were grown and, from this, where the bird is likely to have originated. This means that stable isotope approaches may be able to tell us a great deal about the evolution of migration, the origin of migrants or even provide insight into the identification of a vagrant, which is why it has generated so much interest both among scientists and in the wider birding community.

Stable isotopes and migration

The most commonly used isotopes for studying bird migration are hydrogen, oxygen, carbon and nitrogen. With hydrogen we can measure the ratio of the heavy isotope 2H to the light isotope 1H (expressed as δ2H or δD) and we can also compare the stable isotope ratios of oxygen (δ18O). These vary, in different parts of the world, according to how much rain falls and where that rain comes from (Hobson *et al.* 2004). 2H tends to precipitate in rainfall before 1H, because it is heavier. Therefore, areas with lots of rainfall will often have higher δ2H ratios than continental areas in a rain shadow, from which the 2H has already been lost before the rain gets there. Hence the isotope ratios show gradients, which have been mapped across continents and offer the potential to distinguish the origin of birds over a relatively large spatial scale. For example, weather in the UK is dominated by heavy rainfall compared to the Iberian peninsula. As a consequence, there are marked differences in the δ2H patterns between these areas making it possible to differentiate between Blackcaps *Sylvia atricapilla* wintering in Spain and those wintering in the UK (Bearhop *et al.* 2005). Recently the same principle was applied to provide the birding community with the first evidence that Siberian wildfowl may occur here as genuine vagrants. A first-winter Baikal Teal *Anas formosa*, mistakenly shot as a Eurasian Teal *A. crecca* in Denmark during November 2005, had a mixture of juvenile feathers, grown in the nest, and freshly moulted first-winter feathers. By analysing the stable isotope composition of these feathers, Fox *et al.* (2007) found that the juvenile feathers had very low δ2H and δ18O values. These values were much lower than would be expected for feathers grown in Western Europe and much more consistent with them having a distant continental origin, for example in western Siberia within the breeding range of Baikal Teal. Furthermore, their values were in marked contrast to those of the recently replaced first-winter feathers, which had a signature consistent with the maritime climate of Western Europe. The simplest explanation for this is that the bird must have hatched in Siberia and found its way to Denmark in time to undertake a partial post-juvenile body moult before its date with destiny. Establishing the provenance of vagrants (particularly wildfowl and far-eastern vagrants) has long proved problematic and here stable isotopes seem to offer some hope for resolution of this thorny issue. However there are a number of important caveats to bear in mind, which we will cover later.

In addition to unravelling the origins of individual migrants, stable isotope ratios also have the potential to provide insight into the migratory behaviour of populations or whole species. Among the three subspecies of Willow Warbler *Phylloscopus trochilus*, there are two races, nominate *trochilus* and *acredula*, which breed in Europe and winter in Africa (Cramp *et al.* 1988, Svensson 1992). These two taxa have different breeding ranges and subtle plumage differences, as well as genetic differences. Analyses of a small number of ring recoveries indicated that they may have different wintering ranges and therefore different migratory behaviours, but the data were too sparse to be certain. To overcome this problem, Chamberlain *et al.* (2000) collected birds of both taxa in their Scandinavian breeding areas and analysed the stable isotope ratios of feathers grown in their wintering grounds. The results strongly supported the idea that *trochilus* and *acredula* wintered in separate regions because of significant isotopic differences between the two. In this instance, stable isotopes have important implications for understanding migration in general but may also be of interest to understanding taxonomy. Differences in migratory behaviour are likely to be related to genetic differences, which may reveal more about the taxonomic status of a particular form than morphological differences alone.

The stable isotope technique has also enabled researchers to discover new breeding areas of some relatively well-known species. Bicknell's Thrushes *Catharus bicknelli* undergo a post-breeding moult close to the breeding grounds. When analysing the $\delta 2H$ ratios in the feathers of Bicknell's Thrushes wintering in the Caribbean, Hobson *et al.* (2004) realised that some of the isotope values were not consistent with those of the known breeding range. Using isotopic maps they narrowed down the potential areas that these birds could have come from and subsequently found two previously unknown breeding populations in the hills of Quebec.

Stable isotopes and identification

It may also be possible to use stable isotopes to distinguish between very closely related and morphologically similar birds. The Lesser Whitethroat *Sylvia curruca* complex is a species, or group of species, which shows a striking degree of variability that has defied attempts to produce an acceptable taxonomy with clearly defined taxa (Shirihai *et al.* 2002). Although the forms within this group are very similar in plumage characters, vocalisations and mitochondrial DNA (mtDNA) they might segregate according to habitat as follows: *S. c. curruca* to northern temperate regions, *S. c. minula* to the deserts, *S. c. halimodendri* to the steppes and *S. (c.) althea* to the mountains. Ordinarily this would be of no value in terms of identifying a vagrant. However, there are often pronounced isotopic differences between habitats, for example in very arid regions (the origin of 'Desert' forms such as *minula*) compared with areas with higher rainfall (e.g. *curruca*) or mountain habitats (e.g. *althea*). In this way, stable isotope signatures may prove a powerful tool to identify these forms when they occur away from the breeding grounds (Votier & Bearhop *unpublished*).

Limitations and considerations

Although there is great potential in using analysis of stable isotopes to answer questions about vagrancy patterns, migration or perhaps identification, it is not a magic bullet. Firstly, this approach only works where species occupy isotopically distinct habitats at different stages in their lives. Those differences in turn need to be integrated into body tissues. A starting point for any investigation must include an assessment/measurement of the isotopic variation in the putative regions that birds may have come from. Even once habitat/regional differences are characterised, it is important to recall that these differences might occur over variable spatial scales and that other phenomena may add noise to the patterns. Such complicating factors may include altitude, geology, seasonal/annual variations in weather, unusual hydrological systems, localised use of groundwater (as opposed to rainfall) or the artificial provision of food sources that may have been transported a long way from where they grew. It is also essential that the bird in question should be examined in detail in the hand to establish age, sex and moulting status, where this is possible. Knowledge of the moult strategy for that particular age/sex is fundamental so that differences or similarities in isotopic signatures can be linked to particular time periods, allowing inferences about recent movements or habitat occupancy to be made. Ecologists who are familiar with the approach are important in data analysis as they are probably the people that are most acutely aware of its shortcomings. Analysis of stable isotopes by itself will be suitable for establishing the identification or provenance of only a small subset of vagrants, and is never going to be within the toolbox of even the most sophisticated amateur birders. It does, however, provide another option at the interface of science and birding for unravelling the mysteries presented by migrant birds.

Molecular approaches

Background and basic principles

The familiar helical chain of deoxyribonucleic acid (DNA) is the blueprint for protein construction and forms the molecular basis of heredity. Variation in the sequence of bases ('letters') within the DNA genetic code occurs as a function of mutations and these mutations are maintained or lost partly by the process of natural selection. Individuals within interbreeding populations usually have reasonably similar DNA, but if two populations diverge so they no longer interbreed, differences in DNA tend to be built up between the two over time. Should inbreeding occur, then these differences are reduced as genetic material flows between the two. By analysing differences in DNA, biologists can infer much about the level of interbreeding between populations of birds and this can inform studies of their taxonomy. This is the basis of molecular approaches to birding.

Taxonomy

Perhaps the most familiar application of molecular techniques to birders is taxonomy. Phylogenetic arrangements are made on the basis of differences in DNA in much the same way as traditional phylogenies based on plumage, song, behaviour, etc. Via the analysis of molecular data, the taxonomic landscape has changed considerably in recent times. For example, we are gradually beginning to understand the true relationship between the large white-headed gull complex (e.g. Crochet *et al.* 2002, Liebers *et al.* 2004) as well as the true relationships within the Branta goose complex (e.g. Paxinos *et al.* 2002). These examples represent the tip of the iceberg in terms of molecular taxonomy and will not be considered further in this chapter (Maclean et al. [2005] provides a digestible review of this process).

Identification

Recently birders have realised the value of molecular techniques in identifying taxa which are morphologically extremely similar, or whose characteristics are insufficiently understood. Two large skuas found storm-driven in the UK (on the Isles of Scilly during October 2001 and in South Wales in February 2002) could not confidently be identified on the basis of the current knowledge of plumage and therefore feather samples were taken for molecular analysis. On the basis of two mitochondrial genes, these two birds were found not to be Great Skuas *Stercorarius skua*, as seemed most likely, but were instead consistent with one of the Brown Skuas *S. antarctica* group, most likely Falkland Skua *S. antarctica antarctica*. This represented the first confirmed occurrence of southern hemisphere skuas for Europe (Votier *et al.* 2004). Without this molecular evidence, it is unlikely that these two skuas would have had their identity confirmed as belonging to southern-hemisphere taxa and a vital piece in the jigsaw in the identification of immature large skuas would have remained missing.

Perhaps the first time DNA was used to resolve the identification of a vagrant was when three all-dark *Oceanodroma* petrels were caught at Tynemouth, Northumberland during the summers of 1989 to 1994. The identity of these remained the matter of much debate until samples of DNA were analysed and found to be comparable with Swinhoe's Petrels *O. monorhis* sampled in Russia and Korea (Bretagnolle *et al.* 1991). It is not only seabirds that have been identified using DNA. The subspecific status of an Orphean Warbler *Sylvia hortensis* trapped at Portland Bill in September 1955 had been the subject of intense debate.

Plumage and measurements provided some evidence but, fortunately, a feather was retained from the time of trapping and was available for analysis. It revealed that this bird had DNA consistent with the western subspecies *hortensis* (which has now been elevated to the status of full species). Once again without this molecular evidence the identification would have remained equivocal. More recently, genetic analysis of a Lesser Whitethroat in Aberdeen in December 2004 showed it to have an mtDNA sequence typical of *S. c. halimodendri* from Khazakhstan (*Birding Scotland* 8. 2 : 87-92) It may also be possible to test the identity of museum specimens of eastern Yellow Wagtails to confirm whether the subspecies *Motacilla (flava) tschutschensis* has been recorded as a vagrant in Western Europe, or confirm the provenance of any future claims of Least Tern *Sternula (albifrons) antillarum* by genetic analysis of feathers.

Limitations and drawbacks

Although the use of DNA can be a powerful tool for aiding birders in making identifications and developing an understanding of morphological characters, it should be used very carefully indeed. Firstly, comparing the DNA of a single vagrant requires an existing database of genetic material from known examples of a given species. Sometimes such a thing may not exist (although this is increasingly not the case) but if it does, it is essential that the data are representative of the taxon as a whole. Following the identification of the two Brown Skuas in the UK mentioned above, the authors embarked on a quest for further Brown Skuas in the north Atlantic, suspecting that, if two could occur within the space of a few months, this species was more common than previously thought. As part of this process, they also analysed the DNA sequences from eleven South Polar Skuas *S. maccormicki* breeding on the Antarctic Peninsula. Once this additional data was included in the analysis, it was concluded that, although the two UK skuas were quite different from Great Skuas, it was not possible to differentiate between Brown and South Polar Skuas and therefore the conclusions of the earlier study were considered unsound (Votier *et al.* 2007). Furthermore, even if an analysis fails to find differences in DNA, this only means there is no difference in the particular genes that have been sequenced. It is not possible to compare all of the genetic material across species (there are around six billion base pairs in the average vertebrate cell) so it is important therefore that the most appropriate sections are compared. The use of genetic evidence is a balancing act between a pragmatic mathematical analysis of the most likely evolutionary scenario and the recognition that, because we cannot actually see birds evolve and speciate, we can never really be sure whether our understanding of their relationships is correct. For example, when the genetic differences between two species are minimal, such as for the southern skuas described above, a very full study of genetic variation within both species is required before any conclusion can be made about the identity of an individual vagrant. When, however, the genetic distance between two taxa is enormous, such as between eastern and western Orphean Warblers, the identity of an individual can be fairly fully resolved even if only small numbers of the two taxa have been sampled.

Similarly, the use of stable isotopes is a balancing act between the conclusions that can justifiably be made on the basis of the data, and the recognition that normally we cannot actually see the birds in question migrating. Ultimately, the skills that make a good birder – keen powers of observation, background knowledge, the ability to evaluate evidence critically, to know one's limitations, and a combination of patience and insane persistence – are the same skills that must be applied to new genetic and chemical 'forensic' technologies. Although technology advances, and will continue to advance in ways we can currently only guess at, this must not hide the fact that good birding technique does not change: forensic technologies complement good birding skills but do not negate the need for them.

References

Bearhop, S., Fiedler, W., Furness, R. W., Votier S. C., Waldron, S., Newton, J., Bowen, G., Berthold, P. & Farnsworth, K. 2005. Assortative mating as a mechanism for a rapid evolutionary divide. *Science* 310: 502-504

Bretagnolle, V., Carruthers, M., Cubitt, M., Bioret, F., and Cuillandre, J-P. 1991. *Six captures of a dark-rumped, fork-tailed storm-petrel in the northern Atlantic.* Ibis 133: 351-356

Chamberlain, C. P., Bensch, S., Feng, X., Åkensson, S. & Andersson, T. 2000. Stable isotopes examined across a migratory divide in Scandinavian willow warblers (*Phylloscopus trochilus trochilus* and *Phylloscopus trochilus acredula*) reflect their African winter quarters. *Proceedings of the Royal Society,* London B. 267: 43-48

Crochet, P., Lebreton, J. D., Bonhomme, F. 2002. Systematics of large white-headed gulls: patterns of mitochondrial DNA variation in Western European taxa. Auk 119: 603-620

Fox, A. D., Christensen T. K., Bearhop S. & Newton J. 2007. Using stable isotope analysis of multiple feather tracts to identify moulting provenance of vagrant birds: a case study of Baikal Teal *Anas formosa* in Denmark. *Ibis* doi: 10.1111/j.1474-919x.2007.00672.x

Hobson, K. A., Bowen, G. J., Wassenaar, L. I., Ferrand, Y. & Lormee, H. 2004. Using stable hydrogen and oxygen isotope measurements of feathers to infer geographical origins of migrating European birds. *Oecologia* 141: 477-488

Leibers, D., de Knijff, P. & Helbig, A. J. 2004. The Herring Gulls complex is not a ring species. *Proceedings of the Royal Society,* London, B 277: 893-901

Maclean, N., Collinson, M. & Newell, R. G. 2005. Taxonomy for birders: a beginner's guide to DNA and species problems. *British Birds* 98: 512-537

Paxinos, E. E., James, H. F., Olson, S. L., Sorensen, M. D., Jackson, J. & Fleischer, R. C. 2002. MtDNA from fossils reveals a radiation of Hawaiian geese recently derived from the Canada Goose (*Branta canadensis*). *Proceedings of the Natural Academy of Sciences,* USA 99: 1399-1404

Votier, S. C., Bearhop, S., Newell, R. G., Orr, K., Furness, R. W. & Kennedy, M. 2004. The first record of Brown Skua *Catharacta antarctica* in Europe. *Ibis* 146: 95-102

Votier, S. C., Kennedy, M., Bearhop, S., Newell, R. G., Griffiths, K., Whitaker, H., Ritz, M. S. & Furness, R. W. 2007. Supplementary DNA evidence fails to confirm presence of Brown Skuas Stercorarius antarctica in Europe: a retraction of Votier *et al.* (2004). Ibis (*Online Early Articles*). doi:10.1111/j.1474-919X.2007.00669.x

Discovering bird sound

How many times have I done it? I mean, been somewhere with other birdwatchers in attendance, and heard an unseen bird, flying over, call out. A tense anxiety creeps over me. The call is somewhat unfamiliar. I want to look up, and speak out the questions in my mind, but potential embarrassment holds me back! For many years I have excused myself from focusing energies on the mastering of bird sound. The truth was, it just seemed so hard. However, a number of factors have conspired to place the knowledge and recording of bird sounds much higher up on the list of skills for the pioneering birder to hone. It's the next big thing! Mark Constantine and the Sound Approach guys have blazed a trail in making the subject both sexier and more accessible to ordinary birdwatchers. The digital revolution has made recording bird sound accessible to all. Innovations such as the bespoke Remembird product can be secured to binoculars while carrying around the facility to play back a library of calls in the field as well as making reasonable recordings. Even mobile phones and MP3 players are viable recorders of bird sound. Already we are beginning to combine these technological advances with the revival in interest of lesser-known forms and subspecies. It is highly likely that, for a number of scarce or rare vagrants, it will become more important to record the sound than the plumage details. Examples include Iberian and Siberian Chiffchaffs, Eastern and Western Bonelli's Warblers, African Chaffinch, Hornemann's (Arctic) Redpoll, Eastern (*albistriata*) and Moltoni's (*moltonii*) Subalpine Warblers, far-flung Yellow Wagtail forms, Laughing Moorhen and first-winter Cretzschmar's Bunting to name a few. Never mind the variety of Crossbills that might next irrupt into Britain or the possibility of having the next Pechora Pipit accepted on fly-over only (as long as you got the sound recorded!).

Dave Farrow is a very likeable and disarmingly danger-embracing guy whose starlight colour illustrations of foreign birds in his notebook used to turn me green with envy many years ago. Now he's left me behind in the realm of bird sounds. His is a familial, heart-warming and inspiring account, and it's already caused me to appreciate my local bird sounds more. *Martin Garner*

Sound Recording: a window into my obsession!

Dave Farrow

'Tyue! Tyue! Tyue!' The flight call of the Greenshank sounded close, and getting closer. 'Tyue! Tyue! Tyue!...Tyue! Tyue! Tyue!' The calling became more insistent. I pictured the unseen migrant dipping its wings as it circled low over the house, dropping its legs as it came down onto the small patch of open ground between the buddleia and the bus stop. It sounded very close now. Either the species had extended its choice of habitat to include suburban front drives, or… Ooh, it's Dad! Again. Same as every day, when he returned home from work, he would announce his presence with a pitch-perfect mimicry of the call of Greenshank. That is the kind of house that I grew up in, full of bird-sound imitation and whistling, my Father playing 'sensei' (teacher or mentor in Japanese culture) in my early development as a birder.

Birding started at a very young age for me; as soon as I discovered diversity, really. That is to say, as soon as I realised that 'bird' wasn't just one species, but could be broken into Starling, Sparrow and Blackbird, etc., I was hooked. My father was instrumental in all of this. He had a good knowledge of birds, and could answer all the questions a five-year-old had on the subject. As I got deeper into the subject, he used to take me out to our local patch, a great place for woodland species, just five minutes' walk from our house. There were two challenges that arose here: the first was that woodland birds usually stay hidden, and the second was that my father's binoculars were so bad that I never even considered the need for a pair until I was ten years old. The talent my father had though was an ear for calls and songs. So, on those early Saturday mornings all those years ago, we would walk through the lush jungles of Hertfordshire, with my Dad telling me what each and every call was. The method of learning was imitation. There was no knowledge of musical construction, octaves or tremolos, it was all mimicked, repeated and worn out by overuse! Akin to learning languages at a young age, I learned quickly and became quite adept at identifying the calls myself, the acquisition of views usually becoming secondary.

Of course in my early years, all my views were with the naked eye, often creeping on my belly until I was as close as possible, such as with my first Dunlin at Benacre Broad while on family holiday in Suffolk. I must have got to within two or three metres of them as they fed along the shallows at the back of the beach, black bellies an' all. In fact, all of our family holidays were great birding opportunities (and were possibly covertly organised as such) usually ending up in Norfolk, Suffolk or Dorset. The range of calls I could recognise expanded.

Fast-forward a few years, and I probably knew all the UK bird sounds. It was time to spread the wings further. Foreign travel commenced at the age of 17 with a visit (appropriately enough) to Faro and the Coto Doñana. At 19, I made my first long-haul trip, to India and Nepal. Knowledge of the calls and songs here became of paramount importance if I was to see much. However, there was no guide to the sounds. You heard something, you went in after it until you found it, identified it, and then came away with that sound (hopefully) lodged in your memory banks. Then you could continue looking for birds, listening out for sounds that were unfamiliar, filtering them out from the ones you already knew, and so on.

The next stage in this evolution was to use a tape recorder. During my early years, my father had experimented with one of the first-generation cassette recorders, one of those desktop boxes with big buttons. I remember him making some recordings of Nightingale and Marsh Warbler songs, but the novelty passed and I never thought about sound recording again until I was much older. It was on a long trip around Asia in the mid-1980s that my travelling companion bought a cheap little Walkman that had a built-in microphone. We put it to use, but the recordings (which still survive today!) were just so terrible, due to the attendant growling motor noise, that it never really caught on. Also, in those days there was an addiction to travelling light, with everything for a long trip packed into a fairly small backpack, so extra electronic items just didn't make it onto the packing list!

A proper microphone was needed, and that addition was made sometime in early 1990s. This marked the beginning of my sound-recording career. In fact the first page of my list of recordings is dedicated to a trip to Thailand and Malaysia in spring 1990, during which I filled one C90 tape from end to end. Of course the microphone wasn't up to much, and nor was the Walkman, so most of the recordings are unusable by my standards today but it marks the start of my current passion.

The next stage was acquiring a proper set of kit, a Sony TCM5000 and a Sennheiser directional microphone, which were issued to me when I joined the tour company BirdQuest in spring 1996. As recording birds is an integral part of tour leading, I began to build up quite a collection of sounds, all recorded onto cassette tape. When I returned home after each trip I would type out a list of the recordings, with the details of the species, locality and date marked by the tape counter numbers. To be effective at finding the birds on a tour, one needed a source of calls and songs of the region, so in addition to instant recording and playback, one had to prepare playback tapes before every trip. This was a laborious process, using a double-deck cassette machine. It involved compiling tapes of all the species roughly in systematic order, then typing up a playlist with tape-counter numbers, which was then printed out and slipped into the case of the tape. Of course, one could use the tapes again and again but, with every trip I made, I acquired more and more recordings so I inevitably had to create new playback tapes before every trip to include new material. It reached the point where I might be carrying six tapes for a tour, and then of course you had to fast-forward and rewind to find the recording that was needed. I became very fast and adept at doing this, but it still seems all so primitive now!

The evolution continued, using sound-editing software to convert tape recordings into digital format to be burned onto CD and played on a CD Walkman in the field. This was followed, and replaced, by an MP3 player that offered instant recall for all the tracks I needed for playback. For recording, having experimented with various devices, I have settled on the Sony HiMD minidisc. Okay, the buttons are a bit fiddly, but the recording volume is more than good enough for the instant record and playback niche that I had been so desperately trying to fill. Not only that, you can record in 'full fat' uncompressed format, and then plug the machine into the PC and upload all of your recordings where they get saved as .wav files. As for microphones, my best one is also the biggest and most cumbersome, a brand called Telinga that comes with a large parabolic dish. I only use this when I can stick it into the boot of my car, otherwise I use the much more compact Sennheiser, but the recordings made with a Telinga are just fantastic!

And so there you have it, from crawling on my belly and looking at birds without bins, pockets empty, I now carry a huge amount of equipment including spares, backup devices, batteries and chargers. Not to mention all the optics, camera, etc.!

Now my addiction to sound is fully fledged. Sitting here at the desk I feel a strong tug to go and do some recording: of anything! Apart from the fact that it is August and raining yet again, I want to be out there, doing it, to immerse myself in the wonderful sounds all around, and record it. On a recent trip to Central Asia, I found myself hotel-bound during a blizzard in the Kazakh Tien Shan. I was so restless to get out and do some birding and recording. I ended up recording the rather vocal resident dogs and their puppies! Like photography, there is always another angle or shot to get, to finally get that perfect recording. And, unlike photography, you never actually need a line of sight on the bird; you can sneak around in cover and record around corners!

Of course, as all birders will know, once you start collecting something, in my case sound recordings, you build up a list of what you have acquired, and then you start to look at the gaps in the collection. I might have great recordings of 14 different species of Wren Babblers, but I still haven't got good recordings of some of the most common birds that live around my house. When I say good recordings, I mean those without background noise, or at least just some very pleasant birdsong or insect noise. No, when I bring the recording up on the computer screen I want that signal spike to be rising out of the oscillogram like a spear, with no noise floor visible! Of course, southeast England isn't the best of places to do sound recording. There is a continual background noise of traffic, aircraft, trains, chavvy families, feral children and those bloody helicopters, but I digress. One species that I still don't have a good recording of is the lowly Collared Dove, and yet they sing on the roof of my house every day. Whenever I go out at a quiet moment, the wind is always blowing and all I can hear is the wind rattling the leaves of the poplar tree in my garden. It is a continual frustration, and a continual challenge. Am I really going to drive miles to a quiet place to record it when they are singing on my house? And so it goes on…

It has become an obsession. I might be sitting on the loo in some wayside café, bed and breakfast or filling station, and through the open window I hear House Martins loudly giving their alarm call, and I'll be thinking "I need that call for my collection. Must rush out and record it". It's a quest for perfection, without end.

Thanks Dad. Now look what you've done!

References

Constantine, M. and the Sound Approach. 2006. *The Sound Approach to Birding. A Guide to Understanding Bird Sound*. The Sound Approach. Dorset.

Farrow, D. 2007. Sound Advice. *Birdwatch* 180: 32-34.

Discovering Vagrancy Theories and Vectors

The art of comprehending bird movement is integral to birding. It's part of the mystery and magic of it. Where do the swallows go in winter? Where do all those geese and thrushes come from in the autumn? How on earth did that Yellow-browed Warbler end up in my Cheshire garden? Are the Siberian vagrants of the 21st century coming from even further away than ever? How can we predict the next big rarity? Keith Vinicombe has done more than any other to champion and make accessible the reverse migration theory. See, for instance, his notes in *Rare Birds in Britain and Ireland: A Photographic Record* (Cottridge and Vinicombe 1996). I quickly bought my requisite globe and piece of string! More recently, alternative theories have challenged the reverse migration theory, or at least some aspects of it, and, to this reader at least, the discussion was getting a little befuddling, if intriguing.

Andy Stoddart is a 'thinking man's birder'! From our visits to Hilbre Island, Cheshire together in the early 1980s I quickly realized he had a penchant for bleak places with seemingly no birds! How he and his fellow sojourners now make the trek out to Blakeney Point so many times each year still confounds me! His love of these little migration hotpots has forged his thinking and here at last is what I think is the most helpful and accessible comment on vagrancy theories so far aired in the current debate. It also seems to open the way for more to be discovered by ordinary birders like you and me.
Martin Garner

Bird Movements and Vagrancy

Andy Stoddart

Twenty-five years ago a brief period of twitching gave me my first significant contact with rare birds in Britain. At the same time I began to venture abroad, seeing for the first time many species which were highly sought-after rarities at home. These twin experiences opened my eyes to the true scale of the avian events that saw their final denouements in Britain. On returning, finally and fully, to old habits of local patch migration-watching I developed a much greater interest in the mechanisms by which birds find their way across the world's still vast expanses. Through time and with increasing knowledge, many of the instances of so-called 'vagrancy' which we began to document during the twentieth century have proven to be regular and in some cases even predictable. Genuinely extreme and baffling acts of vagrancy are now seen for what they are - rare events indeed!

It has become clear that around the edges of birds' normal migration strategies are events and circumstances which can lead individuals, or sometimes large numbers of birds, to appear significant distances away from their normal ranges and migration routes. It is these mechanisms which I have found to be of greatest interest, as an increased understanding of them may lead to an increased ability to predict which birds might appear, when and where they might appear and under what conditions. In refining bird-finding strategies, understanding these broader contexts can be of immense value. Following a long and somewhat bleak period in which migration and 'vagrancy' study had become an unfashionable preoccupation amongst those who search for and chase rarities, there has been a welcome resurgence in interest in these topics during the last couple of years within the pages of the birding press.

Reverse migration and the vagrancy shadow

A variety of theories and counter-theories has now been aired and attracted a variety of responses. Amongst these has been the 'vagrancy shadow' theory. This is not a new theory, for 'reverse migration' was a concept already freely in use in Britain during the 1950s. Then it was used to explain the unexpectedly high occurrence rates of certain central European species (notably Barred Warbler and Red-breasted Flycatcher) which typically migrate in a south-easterly direction in autumn and therefore should be great rarities here. The same concept was also invoked to explain the increasing prominence, from the 1960s onwards, of several Siberian species (notably Richard's Pipit and Yellow-browed Warbler) whose easterly migration track should also preclude their occurrence in western Europe.

With increasing numbers of the sympatric Pallas's, Radde's and Dusky Warblers discovered from the 1980s onwards, this theory seemed ever more persuasive. The modern incarnation of 'reverse migration', the 'vagrancy shadow' theory, has therefore attempted to extrapolate from its model predecessor and seek to explain almost all bird vagrancy in terms of 'mirror image' or 180 degree reversed movement away from the breeding range. Casting the 'vagrancy shadow' back across the planet should, the theory asserts, enable us to both rationalise and predict vagrant occurrences and assist records committees to substantiate their judgements.

Such a theory does indeed appear to fit the occurrence patterns of a number of Palearctic species with a strong east/west component to their migrations. Unfortunately for the theory, as has already been pointed out during the debate, there are many vagrancy events and patterns which cannot be explained by it, or which actually contradict it.

Not reverse migration but Siberian wanderers

A counter-theory has emerged in respect of the very species on whose occurrence patterns the 'vagrancy shadow' model is predicated – the Siberian wanderers. It is proposed that we are not seeing 'accidental reversed migrants' or birds which are 'wildly off course' but instead are witnessing colonisation events in action. That is, attempts by species to establish new (and nearer) wintering grounds, perhaps recovering territory and establishing ancestral migration and wintering patterns obliterated by earlier ice ages. Certainly we now have much evidence of the speed with which bird populations and migration patterns can shift in this way. The new British wintering habits of central European Blackcaps and the explosion into this country of Little Egrets are probably the most obvious examples of this speed of change and of birds' ability to adopt new strategies over only a handful of generations. The inexorable and increasingly well-documented westerly spread of a number of eastern European and western Russian (as well as Siberian) species is further evidence that there is no status quo in bird distributions. Ranges and occurrence patterns for birds have never been static in the past and may be even less so in the future.

This 'wanderer' theory is therefore highly persuasive in terms of certain key species whose appearances are increasingly numerous, in particular the oft-cited Pallas's Warbler and its Siberian taiga companions. Unfortunately, the model is less successful in explaining the appearance of those Siberian species whose numbers remain consistently low in western Europe and is also less than useful for the many other non-Siberian vectors for bird vagrancy.

So what then can we conclude from this? Not, I suggest, that these and other theories are worthless. Each of them is a commendable response to accumulating evidence and each has a useful contribution to make. My conclusion instead is that the very attempt to produce a single 'blanket theory' to explain bird vagrancy is doomed to failure. To attempt to provide simple templates to explain a whole range of bird movements is to deny the very variety and complexity which we should be seeking to celebrate. Rather, let us propose that a great variety of mechanisms is at play and that a whole basket full of models and theories is therefore necessary.

For example, the likelihood of a bird wandering to Britain resulting directly from the act of migration may be influenced by a long list of factors including:

- The location and size of the species' home range
- The length of the species' normal migration
- The direction of the species' normal migration
- The timing of the species' normal migration
- The population size of the species
- The nature and extent of any ecological barriers between the home range and Britain
- The weather conditions at the source area and during the period of the bird's journey
- The species' genetic predisposition to wandering

A simple model is unlikely to be able to evaluate the relative importance of all these variables. Furthermore, we should remember that far-flung bird displacements are not only the result of migration in the conventional sense. Many other mechanisms are at work. For example, a long list of species is prone to irruptive or even nomadic behaviour over truly vast distances, either regularly (Rose-coloured Starling) or very occasionally (Pallas's Sandgrouse), whilst others may be 'altitudinal vagrants' (Wallcreeper) or be 'abducted' and brought here by 'carrier species' (Snow Goose). Others may be long-distance colonists, either across continents (Collared Dove) or even between them (Cattle Egret). Doubtless there are other mechanisms too. With increasing human modification of the planet's habitats and climate we should be alert to all these, and other, possibilities, the first manifestations of which we might temporarily call 'vagrancy'.

We should also be wary of developing theories purely from a British or north-west European perspective. It is surely self-evident that uneven levels of observer coverage across the world currently prevent us from seeing the whole spectrum of bird movements and vagrancy patterns. Note, for example, the recent unexpected discoveries in northeast Asia of western Palearctic species such as Meadow Pipit and European Robin, which no 'vagrancy shadow' or 'colonisation' model could presently explain.

Predisposition to vagrancy potential

In seeking to apply a blanket vagrancy theory we overlook a key reality. Every species of bird is the product of a unique evolutionary history with its own genetic inheritance, its own set of precise ecological requirements and its own unique way of interacting with a familiar or an unfamiliar environment. To see evidence of this, flush a Whinchat, a Willow Warbler and a Sedge Warbler on your favoured migration patch. Faced with an identical environment, each bird will respond in a genetically pre-determined and predictable way. If you are familiar with the local geography you will know in advance that the Whinchat will flee to the distant fence, the Willow Warbler will drop neatly into the willow clump and the Sedge Warbler will bolt for the nettle bed. Birds are not creatures of huge intelligence. Their actions are largely pre-programmed, and if this is true at the 'micro level' (as in this example) it is surely also true at the 'macro level' where broader geographical and meteorological stimuli are responded to in the same way.

These evolutionary, genetic and behavioural influences and the pre-programmed nature of the response give each species its own unique pattern of distribution and occurrence and, as a consequence, its own entirely species-specific predisposition to a pattern of vagrancy. In other words, we must consider each species in its own right and not make the mistake of 'reading across' from one to another. For example, however much their ranges and migration routes might coincide, and however conducive the weather, in the present era, Radde's Warblers in Britain always outnumber Brown Shrikes.

My argument against vagrancy theories is not, however, a counsel of despair. Indeed my argument is for a proliferation of different theories that reflect the diversity of what we see. In avoiding the fashionable conventional wisdom of single over-simplified models we will retain a more open mind about which birds might appear in front of us next and be better prepared to reflect on the new and exciting discoveries which must surely still lie in wait. We will also have at our disposal an increasingly diverse and sophisticated set of rarity-finding tools and strategies based on insights into species dynamics, local and distant geography, climatic trends, transient meteorology and even avian psychology! Above all, we will recognise that the natural world, of which birds form such an important part, is varied and complex in ways we do not yet fully understand. In seeking to rationalise it with a unifying model we deny the sense of wonder which should be our proper response. The keys that help us to understand more about the wonders of bird movement and vagrancy can be observed everywhere, from remote headlands to just outside your front door.

Discovering sites and birds

A model pioneer

When I was 14 years old, I read Rob Hume's paper on 'Variations in Herring Gulls at a Midland Roost'. What I found so inspiring about Rob's approach is that he simply observed and noted down exactly what he saw. Period. Here is a guy, making the most of an unlikely location for pioneering birding: on the edge of a land-locked conurbation in central England. Through his approach to observing birds, in contradiction to the perceived wisdom of the self-appointed elite, he went on to describe the first Yellow-legged Gulls, and the first *argentatus* (Scandinavian) Herring Gulls for Britain. From observations in the Middle East, he described and illustrated Armenian Gulls for the first time. And of course there is Blackpill, where he discovered the first Ring-billed Gull to be seen in the field in the Western Palearctic. What's not to learn from him! He put Dave Quinn and me in touch with each other, a partnership that led to the observation and description of the first Caspian Gulls in the UK, and it was Rob who was the most obvious person to invite to give us confidence over our claims of Caspian Gulls and confirm that we really were seeing something different. I was delighted when he agreed to spell out his long 'discovery' process and kindly reproduce his original illustrations of the West Midlands gulls and the Israeli gulls! Ridicule and disbelief followed by realisation and vindication is a normal path for pioneering birders. Rob Hume has quietly led the way. *Martin Garner*

Discovering Gulls

Rob Hume

It must be admitted from the start that I don't live in a seaside town where the dawn chorus starts at 3 am with the raucous screaming of gulls: perhaps there is too much of a good thing. But, for me, the first and most lasting appeal of gulls is purely an aesthetic one. I just love watching them. There is little to beat a good bit of coast and a little seaside town with its harbour and fishing boats, the smell of seaweed and the sound of squabbling, squealing gulls.

When I was a schoolboy member of the RSPB in the 1960s they sold 45 rpm vinyl records of what was originally a Dutch production by Hans Traber, called *Listen…the birds (Hoor de vogels)*. Each record covered a related range of species or group. I bought just three or four. The seabird disk, short as it was, was excellent.

Why, I was asked, did I buy a record of seabirds when I lived in the west Midlands, as far from the sea as you can get? The answer was given for me: well, he just likes the sounds of gulls and the seaside. That was it: other people have said that the call of the Herring Gull is one of the most powerful, evocative and indeed beautiful of all British bird sounds and I tend to agree.

Some people have been careful about their gulls – and the colour of their feet – for a long time. In the Guardian Country Diary, in July 1934, Arnold W Boyd wrote the following as a short item called 'Wrong-footed':

'The breezy poster 'Llandudno calling', which is to be seen on many railway stations, shows in the foreground a herring gull with a pair of yellow legs. Now the legs of our herring gulls are pinkish in colour; it is the lesser black-backed gull that has yellow legs, and it is necessary to go to the south of Europe or eastern Scandinavia to find a species of herring gull with legs of that colour. The staff of at least one station on the Cheshire lines, with a very proper zeal and a commendable love of accuracy, have used chalk to put matters right, and their herring gull is now standing on its own pink legs. Other stations please copy.'

But for me, in my mid-teens, the idea of a Herring Gull with yellow feet would hardly have arisen, although I did have some reference to this in the Peterson, Mountfort and Hollom *Field Guide* and in Phil Hollom's invaluable, but often overlooked, *Popular Handbook of British Birds*. But these referred to eastern Scandinavian birds, *Larus argentatus omissus*, as well as southern ones, *L. a. michahellis*, and were not so much confusing as inconclusive. In the event, '*omissus*' had anyway since been more or less dismissed as invalid as a race. There was little else to look at as regards yellow-legged gulls.

Nowadays, type 'yellow legged gull' into a Google search of the world-wide web and within a few milliseconds you get references to 708,000 sites. There are innumerable papers and discussions, thousands of published photographs and complicated debates in an information overload, something that has long since passed me by and left me standing. The last serious work I did on these things was some editing of the massive 1997 *British Birds* papers by Martin Garner and David Quinn; a proposed book on gulls, although 90% written, mercifully remained unpublished.

The story of the Yellow-legged Gull in Britain highlights the conflicts between field observation and museum work, although it is easy to paint them too black and white. The field observers could perhaps be illustrated by someone like Keith Vinicombe, who once, at a meeting of the British Ornithologists' Union Records Committee, memorably suggested that, if he could spend some time in the Middle East, India and South-east Asia, he felt he could begin to sort the Herring Gull complex out. When he left the room, he was scornfully derided by some of the 'museum men'. Keith, being so brilliant in the field, could look at birds and work them out by their character, their expressions and impressions, with detailed, accurate and insightful observation of their physical characteristics. The scientists couldn't see, or appreciate, this character – how one group of birds just 'look different' from another – when looking at specimens on a bench. It reached a kind of impasse and birdwatchers, even some bird books, began to refer to the Yellow-legged Gull as a separate species, a done deal, long before the official committees did. It has taken many years for a consensus to emerge.

To be fair, the birdwatchers didn't have to draw a line around the 'species' at the other end of its range, in the east, where things became complicated and obscure: the Mediterranean and north-west European situation was relatively simple. The official list keepers and taxonomists couldn't get away with such sloppy behaviour and had to understand what was going on in northeast Europe, around the Black and Caspian Seas and even far beyond into Siberia.

Few people combine museum skills with field skills in sufficient measure to tackle such problems. Those who saw Lars Jonsson giving his celebrity lecture at the 2004 British Birdwatching Fair will have realised his abilities (not that we didn't all know before then). He showed a field study of a gull's head and bill and said he would be so pleased if someone could identify it, as he had tried hard to capture on paper the distinctive character of the bird, not just 'a gull', nor even 'a herring gull', but a particular individual, of a particular race. It was an American Herring Gull and, somehow, Lars had captured its appearance to perfection, with its own character, which no-one could really define or describe, but which those who knew the bird could recognise. It was a great illustration of Jonsson's fantastic ability as an artist, but he is equally skilful in the museum, and in writing detailed scientific papers on the birds he studies so intently, to such great effect.

When I was learning my birds, I lived in Staffordshire within a long walk or a short bike ride of Chasewater, where there was a gull roost. I was more or less aware of gulls gathering in the gloomy afternoons of winter and also found increasing mention of gulls in the annual West Midland Bird Reports and cyclostyled monthly bulletins. Older and better birdwatchers than me were seeing Glaucous Gulls, a species I had only read about - for example, in the RSPB W H Hudson anthology, *Birds and Green Places*, in which he described the visit of the great Burgomaster, the Glaucous Gull from the frozen north, to a beach in Cornwall. It was one of those birds that no one in the family had even heard of, something a bit mysterious and romantic. But of Yellow-legged Gulls, there was no hint.

Realising new birds and exchanges with elders

For some years in the late 1960s/early 1970s I was a student in Swansea, watching gulls principally at Blackpill and on adjacent fields at high tide. Yellow-legged Gulls are not frequent in South Wales but it was there that I saw my first. What strikes me now as I look back to my notes at the end of my teens is the absence of any mention of gulls at Chasewater and the infrequency of my visits to Blackpill and, again, the lack of reference to its gulls. A few years later it was hard to keep me away from Blackpill where I was studying every gull in sight. Despite gradually increasing my focus on gulls in Staffordshire, I saw both my first Glaucous Gull and Yellow-legged Gull in Swansea, where both were, and still are, much scarcer.

The differences that could be seen in Herring Gulls were more or less dismissed as 'individual variation' and this 'solution' bedevilled the early attempts to make sense of what we were seeing. Now, Herring Gulls aren't the best example of the astonishing consistency of colour shown by most birds. Look, for instance, at a million Black-headed Gulls and you will hardly find one that is darker or paler than the norm, apart from obvious aberrant birds. The point is that, once you get the race of the Herring Gull settled, the colour of the mantle is pretty constant. It is the wingtips that vary, and the degree of streaking on the head, neck and upper breast, and to some extent the bare-part colours. At first, when I was seeing marked differences in the shade of grey on the back and wings, I was falling into the usual 'individual variation' trap, and not seeing the true situation, but it soon began to sort itself out. It was not individual variation but a set of distinct categories.

It was on 7th February 1970, an unusual date, when I found my first Yellow-legged Gull on the playing fields near Blackpill, and I wrote a 'short note' for *British Birds*. My surviving notes are rather brief, but it seems to have been a normal adult *michahellis*. I saw it very well, although also suspected it was of the only race mentioned as a rare vagrant in The Handbook, *heuglini*, 'with six old records'. I received a letter in reply from James Ferguson-Lees, executive editor of *British Birds*, typed in his distinctive bright blue, and dated 11th February 1970. He wrote:

'I am not quite sure what you intend me to do with the Herring Gull [note], however, as this does not really come within the sphere of the Rarities Committee or our ordinary notes. Sub-specific identification in the field is always tricky because individuals of one population will sometimes show some of the characters of another; thus determination of races is really a matter for the museum with specimens in front of one. Herring Gulls are no exception to this and although individuals belonging to other races – notably taimyrensis, michahellis *and perhaps* heuglini *– may occasionally have wandered to Britain and Ireland, there is no definite record of any sub-species other than nominate* argentatus *in this country. In this connection I should perhaps explain that* 'omissus' *which is given as a rare vagrant in The Handbook, is no longer treated as a separate race. There is cline running north-east from* argentatus *to* heuglini *with the populations becoming darker on the mantle as one goes further east. The western part of* 'omissus' *is now sunk in the nominate* argentatus *and the eastern part (with yellow legs) in* heuglini. *The description of your bird seems closest to* heuglini, *but more than that I cannot say.'*

I quoted this letter in my notebook but added that a coincidence of individual variation in mantle colour (in this case very dark, uniform and immaculate), bill colour, head colour and leg colour seemed a bit remarkable and surely indicated one of the foreign races. Furthermore, as no race other than *argentatus* was on the British List, surely this did at least merit publication, somewhere. I concluded that my bird must most likely be *heuglini*, bearing in mind the date, which did not seem to favour a bird coming north from the Mediterranean. This clouded my ideas for years: I later assumed I was looking at birds coming from the northeast, as they were arriving in November.

In late 1972 I was watching gulls intensively at both Blackpill and Chasewater (and finding Mediterranean Gulls at the former and Iceland and Glaucous Gulls at the latter) but have few notes on Herrings. Early 1973 was a great time for gulls and the summer continued that prolific seam. Then on 12 December I made notes on my first suspected Herring × Lesser Black-backed Gull at Blackpill. It introduced another element in the Yellow-legged question and I subsequently corresponded a little with Mike Harris about cross-fostering experiments in Pembrokeshire, but the question of hybrids seemed a bit of a red herring.

Chasewater and Peter Grant

My next encounter with a Yellow-legged Gull was on 2nd November 1974 at Chasewater (a good day, as I also saw a Rough-legged Buzzard, Kittiwake and Great Grey Shrike at the Staffordshire reservoir, while I missed a Hoopoe and a Snow Bunting!). My friend and, in many ways, mentor, Tony (ARM) Blake told me he had seen a similar bird in November of the previous year, and this has generally been accepted as the first Yellow-legged Gull in Staffordshire although I am not now aware of any notes on it.

I had already seen and noted dark-mantled birds roosting at Chasewater in previous years, one or two of them white-headed, but without seeing their leg colour. This one was a superb adult Yellow-legged, and I noted the completed primary moult compared with the still-growing outer primaries of many of the Herring Gulls around at that time. I still felt, especially given this November date, that these birds were of 'one of the eastern races'.

Over several years, I had a long correspondence with Peter (PJ) Grant, regarding Herring Gulls, Mediterranean Gulls and Common and Arctic Tern wing patterns. I didn't meet Peter until March 1973 when we were in search of quite a different gull. I no longer have all his letters (and none of mine to him), but on 13th November 1974, four and a half years after the letter from Ferguson-Lees, Peter wrote, clearly in response to a letter from me regarding this gull:

'I was very interested in your non-L. a. argentatus Herring. I was very surprised to find that no other races had been officially accepted for Britain yet. 'Status of birds in Britain and Ireland' [the BOU official British list of 1971] states 'Herring Gulls belonging to other races – notably L. a. taimyrensis, L. a. michahellis and perhaps L. a. heuglini – may have occasionally wandered to Britain and Ireland, but we are unaware of any record definitely assignable to any subspecies other than L. a. argentatus.' There is a request for information on Herring Gulls with yellow legs 'believed to be of the northern race L. a. omissus' in BTO News no 66 June 1974, I guess you saw that. At least someone is beginning to take an interest in these. A different moult time between subspecies of Herring Gull seems likely – there is a very distinctive wing/tail moult difference between L. f. fuscus and L. f. graellsii probably resulting from the former's migratory range. As for acceptance of race records, the BBRC does consider such: see for example the penultimate paragraph of the editorial, which accompanied the 1973 report (August 1973 BB).'

I watched the gulls much more intently and saw the Yellow-legged Gull several times. I got my eye in and it became very obvious, distinctive in both appearance and behaviour. I had many superb views. Later that month, I obviously wrote of the broader picture at Chasewater and Peter Grant responded once more:

'Thanks for yours of 24th. A very confusing picture, and I can't add anything to clarify the situation. I have noted a variation in mantle shade in Herrings, and of course seen occasional ones with yellow legs (especially last winter) which are darker above and presumably of a different race to argentatus, but I hadn't looked at these very deeply and wasn't aware of other variations such as head colour and size. Clearly the subject is worth investigating and skins of the races would help.
I can't remember any literature on Herring×LBBGulls but will look. In the meantime I'll be looking hard at the local Herrings from now on – I'll let you know of anything of interest.'

Local, to Peter, would have been in Kent. I was surprised at the time at Peter's comment, or throwaway line, 'and of course seen occasional ones with yellow legs'. If so, why had he not taken more notice: were his birds as obvious as my Chasewater one?

Incidentally, in most references there was not even mention of the UK's pale race, *argenteus*. But such pale birds were probably in the minority at the midwinter Chasewater roosts. There was clearly a long-standing dichotomy between 'officialdom' and some of the references I had access to, principally written by Scandinavians.

Barth, Bourne, Dwight and Systematics

In January 1975, obviously following an enquiry from me, I had a letter from the redoubtable WRP (Bill) Bourne from the Department of Zoology in Aberdeen.

> 'A really conspicuously large amount of rubbish has been written about the systematics and appearance of the Herring Gull and its allies in numerous languages, with no obvious permanent conclusion…So far my impression is that they get darker in the mantle north and east from us, and pink-legged birds hybridise with expanding yellow-legged ones east of the Baltic, but I suspect that adequate material of the difficult intermediate populations in that direction and towards Siberia to form an opinion may be very hard to find even when one starts to look for it…
>
> With regard to the birds you describe, streaking of the head is of course merely a variable feature of winter plumage. Large, dark-mantled birds may come from progressively further north-east; Scandinavian ones are known from ringing recoveries to come down our east coast in winter, and could reach Staffs. Yellow-legged birds might come from the east, but you will note Barth says they also occur in Norway and that wing-tips are variable (see also sketches by Dwight in his monumental review of gulls [in 1925]).
>
> These gulls do need more attention, and it might be a good thing if you cared to give it to them, though you are fishing in a bottomless pit. I would be interested to hear how you get on.'

Incidentally, the 1925 review of gulls of the world by Dwight was a fundamental reference work. I was able to get it through an inter-library loan, and photocopy large chunks of it for Peter Grant, which he used in the preparation of his series in *British Birds* on gull identification and subsequent Poyser books.

My observations at Chasewater resulted in a paper in *British Birds* (August 1978) entitled 'Variations in Herring Gulls at a Midland roost'. This was not really welcomed by the editors, but Peter Grant was writing his gull identification papers at the time and I think he persuaded them to accept it. The variations were confusing, but clearly involved *argenteus* Herring, a large number of northern *argentatus* Herrings (underestimated in the paper) with very variable wingtip patterns, and regular but rare Yellow-legged Gulls. Northern *argentatus* raised possibilities of Glaucous × Herring Gull hybrids (said to be abundant in Iceland) as many had so much white, and so little black, in the primaries, but they were generally too dark on the back. Others puzzled me then and still do, being conspicuously dark, sometimes with reduced wingtip black, but remarkably small.

Incidentally, over the years, when I began to see and record the gulls in greater detail and with more precision as I learned more about them, I noted many variations and several individuals that puzzled me, but nothing really like the currently fashionable Caspian Gull *Larus cachinnans*. I think, had they been there, I would not have known what they were, but I would at least have noticed them, as would many of the dedicated gull-watchers who gradually concentrated on the Midland reservoirs. When, many years later, but before they were generally known about, Martin Garner took me to see some of the early Caspian Gulls at a tip near Tilbury in Essex, we found them remarkably obvious. However, at Chasewater it should be noted that I was generally watching many thousands of gulls, far more than are usually present now, albeit frequently and enthusiastically, at an evening roost on a mile-long reservoir. It was always a race against the rapidly fading light, but great fun and a real challenge. The Yellow-legged Gulls were, nevertheless, often around early, and on the shore. Sometimes the gulls would use fields a few miles away and give spectacular close-up views in bright light, but this was better for Glaucous and Iceland Gulls rather than the Yellow-leggeds, which tended somehow to keep aloof.

Simply observing and writing

While I was trying to sort out what I was seeing, I had little real contact with gull-watchers elsewhere. For all I knew, other people had sorted these things long before. I didn't travel south to see birds in Essex or Kent either; it didn't really occur to me. I had some correspondence with a number of other people, more or less useful, but with little real enlightenment. I also had a number of discussions with people such as Keith Vinicombe and various West Midland birdwatchers. But I was naïve throughout this process. It might have seemed arrogant, but it was just that I didn't really know how to undertake a thorough literature search, I didn't know how to go about a museum study of skins, and I lacked the confidence to meet and talk to other people. I tended just to write about what I saw and thought, without much in the way of peer review or detailed correspondence outside my limited handful of contacts.

This is shown, for example, by what happened when I first went to Israel. I saw strange yellow-legged gulls and came back to write up my notes, make a set of drawings, and send in a note to *British Birds*. These were striking (and particularly beautiful) birds, but I had found no obvious reference to them in the 'popular' books so I tried to fill that gap. Hundreds of people must have been well aware of them, but I didn't contact anyone and they hadn't put anything into print. "Call them Armenian Gulls" said Peter Grant, who encouraged the still-hesitant *British Birds* editorial board to publish my notes. Peter encouraged the publication to help fill in "one more piece of the jigsaw". Now, Armenian Gull is nearly universally recognised as a separate species in its own right; my notes did little to help that process, but did at least put the distinctive character of these gulls into a more accessible and more public domain.

Another obvious thing to do was to see Yellow-legged Gulls in their proper place, the Mediterranean. I didn't until the end of the 1970s and then not well; now I have fed them bits of bread from my fingers (standing in the seat next to me in a grandstand at the Monaco Grand Prix) and had plenty of experience. Somehow though, when their identification at home was still a real puzzle, this travelling didn't happen. Nor did I acquire a selection of photographs: only some years later, when I used to give a regular talk to bird clubs about gulls, did I use excellent photographs given to me by Richard Chandler. It seems silly now to think that many of us, not just me, used to struggle along without doing what now seems fairly basic.

My 1978 paper on the Chasewater roost referred to the paler Herring Gulls as *argenteus* and the darker ones as *argentatus*. Yet neither the BOU List of British Birds in 1915, nor the one in 1971, referred to *argenteus*, both referring to British breeding Herring Gulls as *argentatus*. It was only the BOU Records Committee's 12th Report in Ibis, in 1986, that things changed. Finally, following 'increasing evidence' since Barth's recommendation in 1975 and despite admitting a lack of material to make an independent assessment, *argenteus* was split as a race, relegating *argentatus* to a non-breeding winter visitor to Britain.

The 1915 List actually included Yellow-legged Herring-Gull *Larus cachinnans* as a separate species and detailed two records, but the 1971 List made no reference to these. It was the 1986 Records Committee's report that also added *michahellis*, as a race, to the British List, following late-summer and autumn occurrences, including birds ringed in the Mediterranean. So, *michahellis* appeared at last as a race accepted as occurring in Britain (although not, it seemed, in winter) and, when it was eventually elevated to a full species, it was accepted onto the list on the weight of accumulated evidence, without an obvious 'first'.

But *michahellis* was still noted as a race of the Herring Gull. In the regular annual reports of the BOURC, in *Ibis* and on the BOURC website, Yellow-legged Gulls appear rarely. In the 28th report in October 2001, it was said:

'"Yellow-legged" Gull Larus argentatus michahellis/L. a. cachinnans. This lively issue has not yet been resolved. Data concerning the breeding behaviour of michahellis and argenteus in Western Europe are well documented, but much of the published literature regarding the situation in Eastern Europe is anecdotal. Publication of an important peer-reviewed paper in the next few months is anticipated and is keenly awaited.'

The issue does not appear in subsequent reports but was dealt with in a report of the Taxonomic Sub Committee in *Ibis* as late as October 2005:

'Herring Gull Larus argentatus
Yellow-legged Herring Gulls of the Mediterranean and Atlantic populations L. a. michahellis and L. a. atlantis are very similar to each other, and are reported to be diagnosably distinct from eastern Mediterranean and Caspian populations L. a. cachinnans, from Herring Gulls from northwest Europe L. a. argentatus and L. a. argenteus and from Lesser Black-backed Gull L. fuscus, in immature and adult plumages, in coloration of bare parts.'

Present day

The combined evidence of morphology, vocalizations and molecular phylogenetics strongly indicates that *L. a. michahellis* (including *atlantis*), *L. a. armenicus* and *L. a. argentatus* (including *argenteus*) are best treated as separate species. Herring Gull and Yellow-legged Gull are on Category A of the British List. So, in 2005, the issue was finally resolved as far as the British List is concerned.

Meanwhile, Alan Dean has shown that, between 1986 and 2000, the number of Yellow-legged Gulls visiting the West Midlands, including Staffordshire, was probably between 700 and 1,200. By the late 1990s, 70 or more individuals were occurring annually, and up to 16 have been seen at a time at Draycote Water in Warwickshire and up to 11 at Westwood in Worcestershire. It has come a long way from those puzzling but handsome singles at Chasewater in the far-off winters of the late 1970s.

Diagram by Rob Hume

Discovering a new coastal hotspot

The next section has a certain 'read 'em and weep' quality. There is something magical about discovering a new 'hotspot' for birds. I have been fortunate to follow in the footsteps of a few pioneers who have discovered new hotspots for migrant and rare birds and have even dabbled in the process of figuring out my own along the coast. In the armpit of Flamborough Head, East Yorkshire, I currently visit a little hamlet called Speeton. No big rarities yet but many hours of vivid imagining! However Speeton is a long drive from my house and not a local patch. Jimmy Steele is an irrepressible guy with a local patch to die for and he was in on discovering it. The list of rarities that has come out of birding Newbiggin in recent years has been mouth-watering by any standard. Why was the potential of Newbiggin not recognized earlier? Are there any more Newbiggins out there to be found? Will I ever have a local patch like that? Should I give up birding now?! *Martin Garner*

Discovering Newbiggin
Jimmy Steele

It was not me who discovered Newbiggin-by-the-Sea as a birding venue. A bloke called John Hancock got there first. He discovered many things that I never will including Bewick's Swan, which he recognized as a species new to science. Unfortunately he did not discover Bewick's Swan at Newbiggin. That would have been a first for science and a great patch tick, and therefore a memorable double. He did however find Dotterel, Long-tailed Skua (a county first) and Little Stint at Newbiggin (but unfortunately they had already been described to science!). We have recorded all of them since, several times, but he found them without decent optics; indeed, possibly without any optics. I am sure Hancock experimented with Newbiggin in the late 19th century for the same reasons as I did in the late 20th. Being one of the most prominent headlands on the Northumberland coast it should have great potential for seabirds and migrants. Having added Yellow-browed Warbler to the British List by shooting one just down the coast at Whitley Bay, Hancock doubtless saw the potential of the headland clearly visible to the north. Hancock was an outstanding collector and ornithologist and one of the great naturalists of his time. As you would expect from such a scientist, he documented and published his findings, but nobody really noticed that, within those records, Newbiggin-by-the-Sea featured on a number of occasions. Over the next century, Newbiggin suffered significant environmental degradation from heavy industry and all that goes with it, and so, for most of that period, it disappeared off the ornithological map.

But, as they say, adversity drives innovation. In my case the adversity was a new city, a new house, a new baby and a new job. I was never one to drive from Dundee to Devon for a Baird's Sandpiper, so being twenty percent nearer to Devon wasn't seen as an advantage for my birding pursuits. That stuff was all just too time-consuming. I used to wander the Angus or Fife coast trying to find birds, and had been reasonably successful, even if I say so myself. Now, though, I was in north-east England, time was short, opportunities were few and they appeared at unusual times. I started to suffer from withdrawal symptoms and needed to do some proper birding, but I needed to do it close and did not know where to start. What I needed was a patch.

Finding a patch

I can't be doing with hides and ponds. Whilst I flirted with the notion of some of the local reserves in the fine spring of 1989, it didn't last. When I found myself getting up at 5am just to get the first Blackcap of the day before anyone else, I realised I needed more. I dotted around the coast in an increasingly aimless way. I even visited Newbiggin-by-the-Sea during a westerly breeze in April; saw nothing, but noted "potential". By the early autumn I was a desperate and confused soul. Early September brought the first north-easterly of the autumn and I did the unthinkable: I actually crossed the Tyne to seawatch. I was so naïve. The natives at Whitburn were very friendly but seemed to regard me with a sort of benevolent bemusement. You see, unless there is a rarity, you just don't cross the Tyne for birds. Why would you when there is such untapped potential on your own side of the river (whichever side that is)? I got the message, and redoubled my efforts by going back to the north again and focusing there.

I had another crack at Newbiggin one Sunday morning in early October. I confess the decision was not completely spontaneous as some local birders had reported good seawatching earlier in the autumn (when I was misguidedly south of the river). There had also been a few other interesting birds during recent years, though nothing you would turn off the main road for. But, that day, the moon, the stars and the planets all aligned with the weather and within half an hour a whole new vista had begun to open up. It was a breathy shout that did it. I was enjoying a promising seawatch when suddenly I heard "Little Bunting". I hadn't found the Little Bunting, but I had possibly found my patch. The Little Bunting had been dug out by another birder who I think was (amazingly) seeking the same sort of revelation as myself on the same early October morning. He also turned into a Newbiggin regular.

Since that first Little Bunting nearly 18 years ago I have birded this site regularly, making nearly 1500 visits and seeing 238 species of bird. In that very first October, despite the bunting, I was still not totally convinced it would deliver. That was until I experienced the site on a proper wet easterly blow. Suddenly there really were birds, lots of birds, real migrants. Bramblings wheezed overhead as hordes of Goldcrests flicked through. I kicked Woodcock and Water Rail out of the big ditch and, soon afterwards, located a brown *Phyllosc* that went "tac" and eventually turned into a Dusky Warbler. I was well and truly hooked. By the end of the year I had added Hume's Warbler, Little Auk and a few other odds and ends. Species number 100 (a Swallow) followed by the end of April and the spring even produced a few goodies too. The autumn was better again and by the end of my second October, Rustic Bunting, Olive-backed Pipit and many others had been added and the list of species exceeded 150. By now there were a few of us birding Newbiggin. In February 1996 I hit 200 species with a Slavonian Grebe (a little delayed). It has been predictably slower since then, but every new bird that gets added now is a good one.

A BIRDER'S MAP OF NEWBIGGIN

Diagram by Jimmy Steele

The anatomy of a coastal hotspot

Newbiggin in the late 20th century was (and still is) an odd place. A three-way hybrid – part fishing village, part seaside resort and part mining community – it is probably unique. There is no conventional birding habitat, or wasn't until some mining subsidence produced a couple of ponds a decade ago (Green-winged Teal, Hooded Merganser, Franklin's and Bonaparte's Gulls). Until the ponds were created, the birding was done along a golden sand beach (delicately dusted with coal), on the fringes of a golf course (also delicately dusted with coal) or around the houses in the village (with coal dust). Or on "the mound", a wooded patch on the old pit head, which is delicately dusted with a variety of former household appliances. Lobster and heroin are both available, if you know the right people, though I suspect the latter may be easier to procure and is more widely used. Above all, the sense of simmering lawlessness gives everything an edge that you either love or hate, or both. Let's face it, when there are no birds (which is about 90% of the time on a patch, on any patch, including Fair Isle) a police helicopter chasing a hoodie-clad youth on a trail bike is fantastic entertainment. It flushes the plover flock but so what? You don't get that on the Out Skerries AND we've had both rare Goldies.

I have included a sketch map. Admittedly this looks a bit like something from Treasure Island, but you'll get the gist. I wanted to write "here lies danger" somewhere to make it more authentic, but then I realised that everywhere lies danger and the place is full of pirates. What makes it good for birds though? And is it any better than any other coastal headland?

The attraction for birds lies in it being a coastal headland of course, but I am not sure it is as simple as that. I am also not sure that it really is any better than many other similar sites. For one thing, you learn a patch. As every year goes by I would contest that the obsessive patch person becomes finely tuned to the subtleties of wind, light, shelter, date and a whole lot of indefinable things which, after years of persistence, help to put you in the right place at the right time. It seems like luck, but isn't, not completely. The quality of the birds that I and the few other stoic supporters found over the first decade or so of watching gradually improved, and have culminated in Fea's Petrel (1996 and 1998), Black-faced Bunting (1999), Pallas's Grasshopper Warbler (2001) and even a 1st-winter Hooded Merganser (2002). To establish whether a likely spot measures up cannot be judged on the basis of a couple of visits, it requires real persistence and faith during times of bird famine.

There are some subtle aspects of geography that might be important though. I raise these really because there are probably a few more undiscovered Newbiggins around the coasts of the British Isles and these subtle factors might help to find them.

Any bit of land that sticks out from a relatively flat stretch of coast is advantageous for watching seabirds, but at Newbiggen the very tip of the headland (Church Point) sticks out quite suddenly at the north end of a wide sweeping bay. Furthermore the headland is low, only a couple of metres above sea level, which, although causing a problem for spotting small petrels in a high tide and big sea, has its advantages. As every serious east-coast seawatcher knows, most good seabirds fly north, and this is equally true at Newbiggen. Birds follow the wide sweep of the bay or cut across the outer bay, but because of the low altitude of the point itself they sometimes find themselves almost over the rocks before they know it, particularly in high seas or poor visibility. Skuas and Little Auks sometimes come over the grass of the point itself whilst almost all of our Great Shearwaters have flapped through the "Eider zone" just beyond the tidal rocks. Newbiggin is really not significantly better than any other suitable sites to the north or south, but I think we get better views of the best birds.

There are also some important aspects of geography when it comes to little migrants. When I first started birding at Newbiggin, I spent a lot of time on "the mound". There were fewer household appliances then and probably a bit less surrounding cover. The mound had isolation, and isolation is everything. It also had just the right amount of cover. A large area of dense cover is not good. It attracts birds but they become difficult to find. Conversely, one bush works on an island but not on the mainland where migrants don't hang around without cover and melt away. The mound was great, being small enough to be workable but with enough cover and food to hold birds. It effectively acted like an island and I have seen many a migrant from high drop almost vertically into the trees, including a Golden Oriole on one memorable May morning.

The final element in my analysis of the effect of geography is a diversity of habitats of a large enough scale including, for example, a rough field big enough for a rare lark and a bit of water big enough for a duck to hang around. Mind you, you can (and I do) spend far too much time wandering over empty rough fields or scanning empty water, but at least there is the chance of variety.

Discovery...of all kinds

So I did not discover Newbiggin as a birding site. But perhaps I helped to rediscover Newbiggin. I am quite proud of my role in that, but there were and are others, including at least one resident, who deserve equal credit. I think we also discovered the potential, perhaps almost the full potential, for a site like Newbiggin.

I discovered some things that are also fairly personal. I discovered that I could genuinely like a place that most regard as awful, and that my patch, to me, is almost as much about the people who live there and an entire culture as it is about the birds. The average Newbiggin dog walker has a better knowledge of birds than most dog walkers in the land (and better than a few birders come to that). I have discovered that, if the place you spend your time in can be more than a list, then life becomes more interesting. I discovered that good birding is more than just good birds. I punched the air when I saw my first Newbiggin Pheasant some three years after I started birding there. I would still be excited about Nuthatch because I have only seen one and that was on a seawatch. I discovered that you can still push boundaries even in pretty mundane places. I have seen birds at Newbiggin that I would never have thought possible when I started. I think that patch birding, despite the hours of relative boredom without even a helicopter chase for entertainment, stopped me from getting bored with birding.

The world is full of birding places, some loitering in unexpected places. Maybe to discover them you need to bird outside the comfort zone.

Discovering visible migration

"Can anything good come out of Sheffield?" I thought upon moving to this land-locked city in 2001. Well "yes" is the obvious answer, but for birding? Then I remembered experiences I had in the Luton area (Bedfordshire) in the early 1990s where I began to flirt with observing visible migration. "Vis-migging" as it is known hadn't even been in my ornithological vocabulary before then. I had been intrigued by Ian Wallace's account of his experiences, which included visible migration at Regent's Park in London. He describes his time there as "likely to remain the core of my whole ornithological experience" (Wallace 1979).

The Luton experience, at a patch dubbed 'Little Norfolk' and watched sporadically by Stuart Winter and I, was a step towards my conversion. The Wryneck that visited his nearby garden demonstrated at least what was possible. However until you meet a hardened vis-migger in the field, perhaps you don't know what you are missing. Sheffield proved to be the place where I met two such birders, Messrs Clarkson and Hill, and since encountering them, I have succumbed. I have found my own little hilltop and relish each opportunity to discover a whole new realm of birding. As birds migrate on a fairly broad front across the country, there must be many potential visible migration watchpoints as yet undiscovered and untapped. Read Keith Clarkson's passionate journey of discovery and find somewhere to pioneer vis-migging for yourself! *Martin Garner*

Visible migration through the Southern Pennines
Keith Clarkson

It's the 1970s, Roxy Music, David Bowie and mullets are all 'in' and instead of watching the great Sheffield Wednesday or wooing Penny Collis, then the love of my life, I'm sat on a dam wall overlooking the boulder-strewn shores and blackened peat-stained waters of Redmires Reservoir. I stare eastwards, scanning along a Pennine ridge that falls into the very heart of the City of Sheffield. Here, 70 miles inland, on the moorland fringe, 1500 feet above sea level, I wait.

With youthful naïvety I wait for migrant birds, inspired by the prospect of seeing Garganey, Velvet Scoter and the plethora of migrant waders that had been reported in the 1941 Yorkshire Naturalist's Union Annual Report, a copy of which I had chanced upon at a meeting of the Sorby Natural History Society. Such birds were something of a rarity in Sheffield and usually warranted trips further afield to Spurn, Blacktoft, Cley, and of course Wath Ings, now RSPB Old Moor.

Reality and discovery

Of course I hadn't realised that for every 'record' in the report that there would be a dozen days when nothing appeared to happen. It was on those quiet autumn days when the stillness would only be disturbed by the resident flock of 30-40 Meadow Pipits that my perception of migration changed. Indeed, it soon became apparent that this flock was anything other than 'resident'. Close observation revealed that there was a constant turnover of birds with new birds arriving from the north and east replacing others that departed to the south and west. To my surprise, dawn and dusk observations made at the local, typically dispersed, pipit roost on the local moorland confirmed that birds tended to follow the same pattern of behaviour. It occurred to me that these were not local birds following a circular feeding route; rather, they were migrating through the Pennines, calling off to feed and roost before continuing their journey south. The challenge was to demonstrate that this was in fact the case.

And so it was, armed with a single-shelf mist net and with the help of the late John Atter, whose cheerfulness will be sadly missed, we started to catch the Meadow Pipits. We trapped over 350 birds and never caught a retrap or saw a ringed bird in the flock again. There could be little doubt these were real diurnal migrants. This small piece of detective work, together with an increasing awareness that other species always tended to fly south in the mornings and not return in the evenings, triggered a growing realisation that I was witnessing one of the great spectacles in the birding calendar. It gradually became clear that Redmires was playing host to the visible migration of hundreds of thousands of migrant birds.

It's easy to see how this phenomenon had largely gone unrecorded across much of the country. During the autumn months, the attentions of more mobile birders are focused on searching out the unusual, whereas the migrants I refer to are commonplace – the pipits, wagtails, thrushes, finches, and even pigeons, that often travel incognito, in small or dispersed flocks in the first few hours of daylight. Their true intention is only revealed to the patch-worker, through the regular observation and recording of numbers, times and direction of flight.

The learning experience

In the mid-1980s, my circumstances changed. A job with the Peak District National Park Authority introduced me to the joys of working flexi-time and an opportunity to carry out systematic, daily, two-hour watches at nearby Rod Moor. With the support of Clare, my remarkably understanding wife, I turned out from September through November in all weather during the first two hours of daylight before work. With all the rigour and obsessiveness of a would-be scientific researcher, I recorded the birds, the weather, and the direction of movement, the flock size and any behaviour that caught my attention. I was also able to compare sightings with those at Redmires Reservoir where Richard Hill had picked up the gauntlet. Seven years later, having counted over a million migrant birds during these watches, my understanding of both the scale and pattern of diurnal visible migration was transformed.

Firstly, the scale and diversity of movement was beyond my dreams. Who could have predicted that the most abundant visible migrant would be the Wood Pigeon, a bird that in the words of the migration guru, Chris Mead, now also sadly departed, was not a migrant? And yet, in a typical year over 100,000 Wood Pigeons will move south through Rod Moor, in a three-week period, with the largest movements involving over 40,000 birds. Furthermore, spectacular movements of over 30,000 Redwings, 20,000 Fieldfare and over 10,000 Meadow Pipits have also been seen in a morning. Equally interesting is the frequency of rarer migrants with Richard's Pipit, Lapland and Snow Buntings probably being annual visitors.

The seasonal pattern of visible migration is also striking and fairly consistent from year to year. Each species has its own specific preferred period of passage. Moreover, it is possible to predict within a few days when the peak movements of most species will occur. For example, Meadow Pipits typically peak on 21st September and Wood Pigeons on 1st November.

The diurnal pattern reveals that movement is concentrated in the first two or three hours of daylight with a much less obvious peak in the late afternoon. Movement appears in waves, presumably as birds dispersing from different roosts pass overhead. Here in the southern Pennines there is often a second phase of movement, a couple of hours after dawn, as continental migrants surge through the area. These are often associated with clear skies and migrant-less days on the east coast as the birds fly over at height undetected by observers on the ground. Perhaps they are only seen as the land rises towards the Pennine hills. On 'big' days, passage will continue through the day, easing off around mid-day. A few species, including Swift, Skylark and the hirundines, often buck this trend and only start moving once the sun has risen.

The scale and direction of movement is of course greatly influenced by weather. In the case of both British migrants and continental immigrants moving north or south through the country, migration is most evident in a light headwind, usually associated with cyclonic weather ahead of, or just behind, a frontal system. So, in the autumn when birds are heading southwards, it's a case of checking for light south-westerlies and southerlies. The exceptions are the Wood Pigeon and Pink-footed Goose, both of which seem to prefer a light tailwind. In anticyclonic conditions, birds appear more likely to feed up and, if they do move, do so in widely dispersed small flocks on a broad front.

It also became clear that topography and habitat have a major effect on the routes that migrant birds follow. Valleys and ridges will channel birds, especially in windier conditions, whereas hilltops will attract migrants in calmer weather. The presence of rush-covered fields will draw passing Reed Buntings away from woodland stands where Chaffinch and thrushes concentrate. Linnets and Skylarks channel themselves along the farmland edge, as do the Wood Pigeons that skirt round the open moorland except on the clearest of days. Whilst food availability and access to shelter are obvious reasons for these behaviours there is also a need to avoid predation. The open moorland of the Pennines creates the equivalent of a second coastline; to cross it carries huge risks and many migrants fall prey to Peregrines, Merlins and Goshawks, which often gather at the heads of the valleys.

Anticipating the big movements of continental migrants becomes a feature of most autumns. Anticyclonic conditions, or a north-easterly wind, over Scandinavia will first raise the expectations of any student of migration. If these conditions coincide with a low-pressure system passing over southern Britain, then the adrenalin really starts pumping! As the depression moves over, the winds are dragged round from the east from Scandinavia across central England, bringing an almost inevitable influx and passage of continental Redwing, Fieldfare, Brambling or Chaffinch, depending upon the time of year. The first time I witnessed such a movement was during 28–30th October 1986. A huge movement of Brambling and Chaffinch was underway over southern Scandinavia and diverted eastwards by the strong winds and frontal systems that lay to the south. Channelled along a narrow front at the northern edge of the rain mass, the migrants poured into Yorkshire. Concentrating in the upper reaches of the east–west-running Pennine valleys, thousands of birds passed through at head height as heavy cloud on the hills pushed the birds down below the cloud base. It was an unforgettable experience, being surrounded by several thousand Bramblings and Chaffinches. I remember spinning like a top, the hairs standing up on the back of my neck and tears in my eyes as I witnessed this wonderful spectacle.

A new understanding

Over the next ten years, visible migration in the Sheffield Peak District became the driving purpose of my birdwatching. I became inspired by the work of David Lack, made most accessible in his wonderful book *Enjoying Ornithology* (1965) and more recently by Thomas Alerstam, whose *Bird Migration* (1997) has become a constant companion, as has the monumental *Atlas of Bird Migration* edited by Chris Wernham, and published by the BTO (2002). From reading, it became clear that the observation of visible migration was not a new phenomenon but one that had fallen from grace and become distinctly less fashionable. In the 1950s David Lack had used radar to track bird migration. Flocks of migrating birds were recorded on the radar screen as small echoes or 'angels'. Using these tracks, Lack was able to record the scale, height and direction of migration. The results were spectacular. Migration was occurring on a vast scale, at heights unseen to the naked eye and often in the opposite direction to those reported by observers on the ground. Was the value and credibility of visible migration in tatters?

I could understand that birds migrating over large inhospitable areas such as the North Sea or English Channel would want to gain as much height as possible and use light tailwinds to help reduce the energy demand, but surely this wasn't the case 70 miles inland? Here, for example, British migrants are able to follow routes over suitable habitat and avoid unfavourable places. They are able to stop for shelter and feed up for journeys ahead that may require greater energy demands and risks. What benefit could there be, in such a situation, in gaining great height and flying with a tail wind and therefore risk being blown off course? The challenge was how could I prove it.

The answer came in the shape of a hot air balloon. In the autumn of 1987, thanks to the support of the Nationwide Anglia Building Society, I was able to use their hot air balloon to record the volume and height of bird migration over Sheffield during a five-day period. Working with Kevin Gould and birders from the Sheffield Bird Study Group, we were able to compare sightings from the balloon with sightings from across the Sheffield area. It was a stunning experience watching Goldcrests in the tree-tops, Hen Harriers quartering Ringinglow Bog and our first-ever Turtle Doves moving over the Hope Valley. But more than anything else it confirmed that the migration of British diurnal migrants, in anticyclonic weather conditions, was largely restricted to the first 1000 feet above ground level with fewer birds flying at higher altitude. It appeared that visible migration, for British migrants at least, is indeed giving us a reasonable picture of what is really happening.

Now, thirty years on, visible migration appears to be undergoing a resurgence. Thanks to the fantastic efforts of Dave Barker and the Bradford Ornithological Group a new Migration Internet forum has been established – vismig@yahoogroups.com – which enables migration watchers, from across the UK, to co-ordinate their observations. Supplement this with the information on BirdTrack www.birdtrack.co.uk and the UK section of the Trektellen website www.trektellen.nl, co-ordinated by the indefatigable Clive MacKay, and together they create a marvellous new opportunity for us to make more sense of the bird migration that occurs wherever we live. Go and try it, but be warned: it's addictive.

References

Alerstam, T. 1997. *Bird Migration*. Cambridge University Press.

Lack, D. 1965. *Enjoying Ornithology*. Methuen.

Wernham, C. *et al.* 2002. *The Migration Atlas.* T & AD Poyser, London.

Wallace, I. 2004. *Beguiled by Birds*. Christopher Helm, London.

Wallace, I. 1979. *Discover Birds*. Whizzard Press, London.

Discovering new rare bird islands

It's hard to think of a better example of the pioneering spirit than that of the Barra boys who, in the shortest space of time, have stepped out of the box of conventional autumn rarity-hunting and reaped great rewards. I stayed with Stuart Rivers on the Isles of Scilly in 1984 which, back then, seemed like pioneer birding (or at least represented some wise coat-tail hanging of our pioneering forebears). Stuart and his friends have researched, planned and implemented a strategy for finding "good birds" and the rewards have confounded the expectations of even the most optimistic. I reckon any account that includes "the best birding day in Britain any of us had ever had" is worth reading. You may have heard or read of some of their adventures on Barra. Here Stuart gives a full overview of their strategic thinking and the results of the first five years. It makes you reach for the map to look again at the likes of the Monachs, Papa Stour, and Vatersay. Where is rare-bird gold still waiting to be struck? *Martin Garner*

Autumn migrants and vagrants in Scotland-The Barra Experience

Stuart Rivers

From 1982 to 1994 I spent each autumn on the Isles of Scilly, most of them in the company of other Scottish (based) birders, among them the five 'lads' who would later form the core crew of our Barra trips: Keith Gillon, Stuart Green, Tony O'Connor, Mark Oksien and Calum Scott. However, in 1995 Mark and I changed our focus and spent our autumn holiday on Shetland, driven by a desire to catch up with various "Sibes" and eastern vagrants, and I was now increasingly aware of my 'Scottish Lists'. We switched to Fair Isle in 1996, the first of five consecutive autumns on Shetland where Calum and Keith also joined us during the latter trips.

We saw plenty of good birds, typically in "crowds" of ten or fewer birders, while the ratio of rarities to common migrants was remarkable compared to our experiences on the east coast of Scotland or even Scilly. I was very fortunate, and managed to get great views of several individuals of each of my main target birds. Lanceolated, Pallas's Grasshopper and Paddyfield Warblers, Yellow-breasted Bunting and Great Snipe were all seen in my first four autumns on Fair Isle. In addition, during the six years, we saw a whole array of other top-class vagrants such as Little Bustard, Isabelline and Black-eared Wheatears, White-throated Sparrow and Bobolink, and even had birds such as Pacific Golden Plover as 'garden' ticks!

After these first few glut years on Fair Isle my next autumn yielded only Dusky Warbler as a Scottish tick, and it seemed likely that to continue on Fair Isle would give a diminishing return of new species, and I started to think about what to do next. We had discussed the merits of Scilly and Fair Isle at various times, but the attraction of going back to Scilly was no longer as strong and our attitudes were now very much towards finding our own good birds. Our focus was still very firmly on Scotland, with a strong desire to explore somewhere under-watched, and where our efforts might be the main, or even only, source of records for our chosen site.

Catalytic conversion

I had started to consider a number of options, and looked at parts of Shetland, Orkney, and the north and west mainland of Scotland, but was increasingly drawn to the Outer Hebrides. This idea became even stronger when I read an article in *British Birds* by Ian Wallace, Anthony McGeehan and Dave Allen (Wallace *et al.* 2001) about their exploits at Rocky Point in County Donegal. The main question now was where to go? Then it was just a matter of convincing others that it would be worthwhile, and to get enough of them to commit to giving it a try.

Eventually I picked Barra, an island about eight miles by five at its widest points. There seemed two obvious points in its favour. Firstly, the spatial distribution of habitat, especially cover for migrants, and their ease of access. The islands to the north (Lewis, Harris and the Uists) all have decent areas of vegetation, but the main patches of cover are spread over wide areas, too far apart to cover all the sites regularly. Although Barra and Vatersay (attached by a permanent causeway) comprise a relatively large area (about 30 square miles), the central portion of Barra is mostly moorland. The more promising birding areas are largely confined to the outer edges and close to the main circular road or its northward extension to Eoligarry/Scurrival or the southern extension to Vatersay. Secondly, Barra sits at the southern end of the Outer Hebrides, and should benefit in autumn from a funnelling effect of the migrants filtering southwards from Lewis, Harris and the Uists. These birds may not have even made their first Scottish landfall on the Outer Hebrides, but could in turn have originated from the Northern Isles or the north mainland of Scotland.

A bit of research into published records showed that a number of good birds had been found before on Barra but that it was vastly under-watched in comparison to the main islands to the north. Little information from Barra appeared in the earlier Outer Hebrides Bird Reports, though the situation was improving as a result of more recent day trips to Barra under suitable conditions in autumn by Outer Hebrides resident birders such as former and current recorders Andrew Stevenson and Brian Rabbitts, and several other individuals.

These had produced scarce migrants such as Barred and Yellow-browed Warblers, Firecrest, Red-breasted Flycatcher and Common Rosefinch, suggesting that prolonged coverage could prove rewarding (Rabbitts 2001). A concentrated effort from a team staying on the island seemed likely to stand a chance of finding more of the same, and possibly something rarer, and would at least be contributing more records to the bird report. At worst we would have a new destination to explore and some resident species to look through and count. The regularity and cost of the ferry service from Oban to Barra meant that it would actually be easier and cheaper for us to get to Barra than to travel to Shetland.

Most people I contacted about forming a crew to go to Barra thought the idea was interesting, and the consensus of opinion was that we might get some good seawatching, possibly a scarce migrant, or an American wader or gull if we were lucky, but I knew many thought we would probably see nothing of note. This was borne out by the fact that, apart from the core team named earlier, only two others showed sufficient belief to make the trip – Brendan Doe and Alistair Shuttleworth, who joined us in the second week.

2002 – the start of the five-year plan

When we set off from Oban on 19th September 2002 we all had high hopes. We had talked about our prospects for over a year with anyone who would care to listen. While our more optimistic thoughts ventured towards an American passerine, we knew many reckoned we would see nothing of real note. Fortunately for us they were to be proved wrong, though the reality was a little beyond even our predictions.

Within thirty minutes on the first morning, Stuart Green discovered a Lesser Whitethroat, an uncommon migrant back on the east coast of Scotland. This was the first of several we were to see over the fortnight and perhaps proof of the funnelling effect of the Outer Hebrides on migrants. He did even better an hour or so later when he picked out a first-year Rose-coloured Starling behind the school near the north end of Traigh Mhor, the beach used as the island airfield. The elation in the group far exceeded that which the plumage state of this starling would normally elicit! The prospect of failure had been banished, and less than two hours after we had been in the field! Subsequent attempts to photograph the bird proved amusing after Calum discovered he had to walk back up the road away from the bird to focus his video recorder on it, while the rest of us were trying to sneak ever closer. Even if we found nothing else we could go home with our heads held up though, as it turned out, we need not have worried.

A couple of days later we were enjoying the sunshine and checking gardens on the east side of Castlebay, following a shopping trip, when Stuart discovered an Arctic Warbler, a first for the Western Isles. The attempts to see this bird resulted in Keith finding a Common Rosefinch in the same garden. The following day Keith also found a Blyth's Reed Warbler just a short distance from the Arctic Warbler, but sadly it bounced out of the net during the initial attempts to trap it. We spent a further two days trying to trap the bird, but to no avail; though during our attempts to document the record Calum did manage to obtain some video images of bits of the bird among the vegetation. It was all very frustrating, and in the end Keith decided not to submit the sighting.

Throughout the first week there was a small trickle of common migrants, plus a Yellow-browed Warbler which did cooperate with Mark's attempt to ring it, but the second week proved quieter and we spent more time seawatching and checking through waders and gulls. The main highlight of the second week was an immature Surf Scoter. This was our only "Yank" of the trip and a good bird to see but with some irony we noted that it was a species more usually seen by us in flocks back in the Firth of Forth!

2003 – raining rarities and the icing on the cake

With the success of our first autumn regularly recalled in conversations for months beforehand, we set sail to Barra for our second year. The five-hour trip was wet and dull and our spirits were soon dampened. As we arrived at Castlebay, with about an hour until dark, the overcast, rainy conditions did little to lift the gloom. Keith, in typically pessimistic fashion, summed it up when he said "What are we doing?" as the prospect of two weeks being battered by the elements loomed large.

We had trimmed our transport for Barra from three cars to two at Oban so, on arrival at Castlebay, with both cars now filled to the roof with bags and food supplies, there was no room for Stuart Green. So Mark and I headed for the cottage to offload and come back to pick him up, while a half-hour in the pub seemed a good idea to Stuart. As we were ferrying boxes and bags into the cottage, the phone rang. Much to his credit Stuart had foregone the comforts of the pub and had instead checked out the gardens at Gleann on the east side of Castlebay, where he had duly found a Red-breasted Flycatcher. A speedy ride back to get him was interrupted only by a shout to the other lads about the flycatcher as we passed them at Creachan 'Community Woodland', an open stand of tall birches and pines with dense scrub. Having found Stuart and seen the flycatcher we headed back north, where the others were still at the wood, having had very brief views of a pale '*Acro*-like' warbler. Sadly darkness fell before it could be pinned down, but it meant we knew exactly where to start in the morning.

A wander around Creachan for thirty minutes or so had shown no trace of the previous night's bird, but then a dull *Acrocephalus* warbler popped up onto the back fence of the cottage next to the woodland. As the realisation sunk in that it was a Blyth's Reed Warbler our minds turned back to the previous year. While Keith was making his characteristic despondent comments, a second bird flitted up to perch on the fence beside the other. Both looked identical. This really was too much to take in. After close scrutiny through bins and scopes, and re-affirming the suspected identifications, Mark was encouraged to set up his nets to settle the matter one way or other. Fortunately it was not another three-day event! Indeed, within thirty minutes one bird was gently shepherded into the net where Keith rapidly moved in to ensure it did not get away. The other individual was not seen again, but much to everyone's great relief the in-hand examination of the trapped bird confirmed what we desperately wanted. A potentially morale-sapping encounter and nightmare start to the trip had been turned into a triumph and everyone was overjoyed and amazed at how quickly the previous year's ghost had been laid to rest.

We eventually gave up on the second bird (and never submitted it to the BBRC) and headed down to Castlebay. Stuart set off for his adopted patch at the trees by the football pitch, while the rest of us covered the gardens on the east side of town, where the Red-breasted Flycatcher was still performing. A short while later my amusement at seeing Stuart running along the road in his wellies rapidly turned to joy and concern as he shouted up the hill that he had found a Citrine Wagtail! The other lads were alerted and soon we were all gathered at the football pitch to watch and admire our second BBRC species of the day. Eventually we dispersed, heading up the east side of the island, totally keyed-up and buzzing, if somewhat incredulous, about earlier events.

"The best birding day in Britain any of us had ever had"

Stuart, Mark and I were due to sort out the cooking that evening, and I was having a shower before embarking on that when the door of the cottage was flung open and Tony shouted through that Keith and Calum had just found a Paddyfield Warbler down the road from the cottage. I was mindful of a 'wind-up' carried out by some Scottish birders some years earlier, on a friend who was having a shower while staying on Scilly. A shout of "Tengmalm's Owl" elicited the desired response, and a partly naked, desperate birder rushed out of a cottage holding his bins, only to be greeted by a round of applause and much laughter. However, the present ominous silence as I shouted to find out more details meant that I was in a fumbled rush to grab clothes and binoculars. My headlong sprint down the road ended almost as soon as it began as, literally 50 yards from the cottage, the lads were all lined up beside a ditch filled with irises and with a derelict fence running along it. Working its way back and forth along the ditch was indeed a Paddyfield Warbler!

We gave up watching the bird as it got dark, having noted, photographed and videoed every detail, but mostly we just enjoyed the moment as we took in the fact that this was our third BBRC species of the day and a first for the Outer Hebrides! As we gathered by the dining table afterwards, Stuart produced a bottle of champagne he had purchased at lunchtime to celebrate our earlier successes. We were stunned by the events of the day and expletives flowed. It was the best day birding in Britain any of us had ever had. The five-year plan went out the window and we all pledged that every autumn from now on would be spent on Barra.

The rest of the trip was barely less eventful, as it included the re-identification of a female *Aythya* duck as Scotland's first Redhead (Scott *et al.* 2004), an unsuccessful twitch to North Uist for a Snowy Owl, and the discovery of a Woodchat Shrike by Jim Dickson, an Argyll-based birder who also spends time on Barra in autumn. Add to this a Rustic Bunting flushed from a roadside ditch near our local pub by Calum and Keith (further reward of their policy of walking back from Northbay at the end of the birding day), plus a regular stream of new birds passing through including a Melodious Warbler, another Hebrides rarity. Another interesting find was a Little Auk found by Stuart at Cleatt beach as he was looking for somewhere out of sight for a quick pee. Sadly Mark and I dipped the auk.

One evening during this purple patch, my phone rang, a rarity in itself given the extremely poor mobile coverage on the island. It was Ian Wallace and Anthony McGeehan phoning from Rocky Point to offer their congratulations on our success, a fantastic gesture and the ultimate accolade!

A fitting finale to an amazing trip was provided when Stuart, Tony, Keith and I decided to try again for the Snowy Owl, with hindsight a strange decision given the number of birds turning up on Barra, but hopefully you learn from your experiences. We reached Vallay Strand with no sign of any birders or the owl, but after a downhearted series of telescope scans Stuart finally picked out a white speck among the furthest dunes. A successful approach gave us some stunning views of this fine bird and we set off back to Barra, elated and ready to tell Mark and Calum, who decided not to repeat the journey since they had actually seen the bird in the summer. Of course, such ideas are prone to backfire, and so it proved. As we were heading south through South Uist for Eriskay my phone rang, it was Mark and he duly imparted the good and bad news. He had found a Red-eyed Vireo at Aird Mhor Plantation back on Barra and we were on the wrong island.

We had all hoped to find an American passerine during our trips and, now that moment had come, our decision to twitch off the island looked to be a disastrous one. In my panicked state I told him we were close to the ferry and famously said "don't flush it". This was a somewhat ludicrous suggestion given the number of trees, bushes and brambles wedged into the cut which formed the plantation and, in characteristic fashion, Keith articulated the dawning realisation that seeing the bird could prove a bit tricky to say the least!

An hour or so later we arrived at Aird Mhor, the ferry terminal on Barra, thankfully very close to where we needed to be. Previous worries were compounded for, on arrival, Mark's car was gone and there was no-one to be seen. I have seldom been so pleased to hear, and then see, Calum as he appeared at the entrance stile to say he had last seen the bird just a few minutes earlier. While this news helped dispelled many fears, the anxiety and nervous tension was enormous. We duly followed him back up the track and he stopped after only thirty yards where the bird had been keeping to a set of Alders beside the small burn running down the cut. Mark arrived soon after, having been away trying to contact Jim (Aird Mhor sits in one of the many mobile phone black spots), and the tense, nervous wait continued. However, within five minutes the lumbering shape of the vireo was picked out at the far end of the Alders and the bird obligingly worked its way towards us. The relief was audible and then so was the celebration. The icing had been applied to what was already quite a remarkable cake as our hoped-for Yankee passerine was there in front of us, and what could have been a very awkward division at the dinner table that evening was avoided. As more champagne flowed that evening, claims of being the only four birders in Britain to have seen Snowy Owl and Red-eyed Vireo on the same day were a somewhat transparent mask of near-disaster, but our spirits were yet again riding high.

The final curtain did not fall on the trip until we were almost at the ferry to come home. Jim had found a Little Bunting at Gleann and Stuart and Mark just managed to get views of it on telegraph wires before it dived down back into cover and we had to rush to join the ferry queue with only a minute or two to spare.

2004 – hard work gets its reward

Given the amazing run of birds we had encountered during our second autumn trip, we entertained ambitious thoughts as we arrived for year three. A week of strong winds, rain and very few migrants soon put paid to all that, and we were now resigned to the increasing possibility that the pendulum had swung fully the other way. It looked like this would be our first blank year for a rarity. We knew that we would get one at some stage, and possibly several lay ahead of us in the near future, but it all seemed rather cruelly emphasised by the contrast with the highlights of the year before.

The Saturday morning of our middle weekend saw me sitting in the cottage adding up the species trip total for the first week in the hope of generating something positive to say. The tally of 94 was pretty good and included a Turtle Dove, new for our cumulative list, which was found on a cultivated field on Vatersay, but sadly only seen by three of the crew before it headed off over a hill never to be seen again. By the time Mark and I left the cottage it was late morning, and the others had all gone. We headed south towards Castlebay, passing several places we had stopped at the previous day, before Mark turned off at Breibhig.

A check of the gardens at the end of the road revealed nothing new, and I headed to the gardens along the approach road in the hope of seeing the Reed Bunting that had been present a few days earlier which would at least be a Barra year tick for me. With no luck on that quest after twenty minutes, I turned round to head back to the car and glanced into the gardens again on the way. In the last garden before the burn I saw a movement deep within a hedge and was surprised to see a small black eye with a yellow feather surround staring back at me. The bird was largely obscured, but thoughts briefly turned to Yellowhammer, a rare bird now on the Outer Hebrides and one we had never seen. Fortunately, rather than disappearing back into the bush the bird moved up to the edge of the hedge and the reality proved far more welcome. It was a Yellow Warbler!

I gestured to Mark, and he managed very brief views before the bird flew off towards the end gardens, looking amazingly bright in flight. My previous lack of expletives was cured quite spectacularly in the next few moments as I followed it in my bins. We saw where it landed but could not find it again but, convinced that it was still present, Mark headed off to get the others. Within ten minutes, he and the Edinburgh lads had returned, but I had still not relocated the bird. I was beginning to wonder whether I had seen enough to exclude Wilson's and Hooded Warblers and whether or not it would vanish before the others saw it to provide proper confirmation. Fortunately all these worries evaporated when Calum relocated the bird back in the original garden, and soon we all had excellent views. I also had a good look at the undertail to satisfy myself the initial identification was correct.

Calum left shortly after, to go and find Stuart who had intimated he would be down at Castlebay. When Calum arrived by the library, Stuart was just coming out the door having just spent much of the morning e-mailing his large network of contacts about how rubbish (not his actual words) Barra was proving this year. After convincing him that he was not being wound up (possibly a common paranoia in Scottish birders) there was a sudden and rapid exit as Stuart made it to Breibhig in record time. He too was soon enjoying excellent views of our second Nearctic waif in consecutive years, and the news was duly phoned out.

Birders from the Uists managed to arrive the same day, and the first of the mainland visitors managed to get to Barra (via Benbecula) next day (Rivers 2004). Over the following days, the Yellow Warbler performed well and brightened up our daily searches, but we found nothing new. In total, around 70 birders managed to twitch the bird before its departure on the Thursday night, some six days after its discovery and during the first break in the weather. This heralded an influx of birds, which had presumably been queuing up on the Northern Isles held back, until now, by the strong south-westerly winds and rain. On the Thursday, a Common Rosefinch was found at Sgallaraidh, and on Friday Keith and Calum found another at Northbay and then yet another elusive Blyth's Reed Warbler, this time at Nasg, which also hosted a Yellow-browed Warbler. The Blyth's Reed was still present on the Saturday morning, and Mark obtained permission to erect a net in a garden to try to get in-hand confirmation. Experience gained from the previous two years obviously paid off as there was no three-day vigil without reward or thirty-minute wait this time. Within a couple of minutes of the net going up the bird was being examined in the hand and another one was nailed beyond any doubt. The efficiency of the capture was much admired by the assembled crowd, including many who had dipped the Yellow Warbler but at least they got a good consolation prize. In addition, yet another Rosefinch was discovered heading south through the gardens at Nasg as we waited for the Blyth's to perform. It was a nice flurry to end another successful trip.

2005 – two weeks of toil for a Yankee hat-trick

If we thought 2004 had been hard work then we had not reckoned on what happened to us the following year. Strong winds, rain and a lack of birds moving through the Northern Isles meant that the daily round of our usual sites was consistently very hard work and usually fruitless. The weather forecasts indicated there was little prospect of improvement until the second week. Despite all this, or probably because of it, our resolve to find something was still high and we did manage to add several new species to our cumulative trips total: a live Corncrake seen by Stuart, a Black-tailed Godwit seen by Keith, Calum, Ewen and Tony but which eluded the rest of us, and a short-staying Yellow Wagtail on the Castlebay football pitch which Mark and I missed. I was despondent at missing the latter two which would have been 'new' birds for my Barra list, but three others – Siskin, Tree Sparrow and Dipper – all thankfully hung around long enough for us all to connect with them. The Dipper, which Keith found at Brebhig, was of the 'Irish' race *Cinclus c. hibernicus* which is the form which breeds scarcely on South Uist and uncommonly on Lewis/Harris, but it transpired that this was the first record of the species on Barra for over 100 years (Rivers 2005). Given the weather at the time it seemed just as likely that it could have come from Ireland!

The break in the weather promised in the earlier forecasts was being delayed on a daily basis, and it seemed our two weeks would end before it finally arrived. So, as we set off on the last full day, it was with a certain resignation that this was likely to be our first SBRC/BBRC rarity-free year and that things were almost certainly going to change and birds would be flooding down the islands as we departed the island on the Sunday morning.

By lunchtime, Mark and I were at Breibhig, scene of triumph the previous year, but this was now beyond clutching at straws or of lightning striking twice. We needed a miracle. Viewing back down to the village from the hillside, I saw the arrival of the Edinburgh lads' car. This would at least provide a conversation to pass some time so I began to amble back down the path. I then noticed there was only Tony in the car and, as he got out, it all changed – he was waving his arms and shouted to Mark who immediately turned towards me, waved, and shouted. I heard nothing but was already running. Tony, or, as it transpired, Keith, had provided our miracle.

Half an hour later we were assembled at Aird Mhor Plantation all tensely poised trying to get views of a Rose-breasted Grosbeak in the trees and thick cover. After a few brief sightings, the bird finally obliged by sitting in the top of a tree for several minutes where it was duly captured on chip for posterity (Gillon 2005). Tension eased, relaxed banter followed and the moment was all the more glorious because we were aware that this was only the second Scottish record of this chunky American waif and it completed our own hat-trick of Nearctic passerines in consecutive years on Barra.

Had Walt Disney written the script? Well possibly, because less than two hours after the bird's discovery a couple of friends from Central arrived. I was totally stunned by their appearance and speechless (very unusual apparently!). When conversation resumed we discovered that they had been on Benbecula unsuccessfully searching for the Upland Sandpiper at Liniclate when the news of the Grosbeak reached them (we had twitched the sandpiper a few days earlier to help bolster our flagging morale). A frantic dash for the Eriskay/Barra ferry culminated in the proverbial 'snatch of victory from the jaws of defeat' for them which was made all the more dramatic given that the Grosbeak disappeared only an hour or so later and was never relocated. As luck, and Keith's persistence, would have it, our last night was turned into one of celebration in our local, the Heathbank Hotel, and the journey home the following morning was not the funereal wake it had once seemed destined to be. It was, however, now tinged with some regret as to what might turn up in the next few days.

2006 – more hard work but a handle on migration timing and routes

After the dramatic events of 2005 we were enthusiastic about our return, the countdown starting in January! Our usual discussions beforehand saw the customary flights of fancy as we now entertained all manner of possibilities, but we knew that it was the vagaries of the weather that would dictate whether or not we were in for another roller-coaster trip of highs and lows or another long haul, especially as Mark and I had both managed to lengthen our stay to three weeks.

Our first full day on the island, Sunday 24th September, produced a number of the commoner migrants; in fact the range was already greater than in our last few trips. We took this to be a good omen, particularly when the Edinburgh lads found a Black-tailed Godwit amongst the Bar-tailed Godwits and Curlews on the Borve machair, and a sore personal miss from the previous year was quickly reversed. The first of a remarkable tally of Yellow-browed Warblers was found at Northbay on the Tuesday, a Redstart at Creachan was the first since our 2002 trip, and Common Whitethroat was finally added to the cumulative autumn trips total, with at least three eventually seen during our trip. By the end of the week our initial excitement was diminishing as we started to feel that things were getting very static with many birds having moved on but nothing new arrived in replacement.

This air of slight despondency was blown away on Saturday. During the late morning Keith found an Isabelline Shrike at Breibhig, and Tony was again the welcome herald of the news for Mark and I as we had been checking the dense cover of the wooded garden at Ardveenish. When the news was phoned out, we discovered that an Isabelline Shrike had previously been present for about a week on the Isle of Lewis and represented the first record for the Outer Hebrides. Plumage details indicated that this bird was of the form *Lanius isabellinus phoenicuroides* which is given full species status by some authorities and referred to as 'Turkestan Shrike' (Scott 2006). Our bird was undoubtedly the same individual, last seen on Lewis on the Friday evening. It had travelled to Breibhig overnight, a distance of just over 100 miles as the Hooded Crow flies, but it would almost certainly have taken an easier less direct route largely following the coast, a distance closer to 115 miles.

The second week of our 2006 trip saw a further trickle of commoner migrants and a continued arrival of Yellow-browed Warblers, but the general lack of other vagrants passing through the Northern Isles and the southerly track of all the transatlantic weather systems meant we had little prospect of anything more. The third week was even less inspiring with south-west and then south-east winds blocking any prospect of mass arrival of birds filtering down the island chain. Even so, the final total of at least 11 Yellow-browed Warblers was exceptional compared to previous years. Interestingly for us, the relocation of the shrike and the staggered arrival times of Yellow-browed Warblers on Barra, compared with the north end of the Outer Hebrides (Long Island) and the Northern Isles, provide our best information so far, in the absence of actual ringing recoveries, on the distances travelled and the times taken for migrants and vagrants passing through Barra.

Other trips

Stuart Green and I spent a few days on Barra in June 2005, and Calum and I spent New Year 2006/07 back on the island, a notably wet and windy way to spend a week. In both cases we found birds we had not seen on our autumn trips, though Common Whitethroat and Swift seen on the June trip both subsequently featured in our total for autumn 2006. A notable feature was that we saw several Common Shelducks on both trips but have never yet encountered this species in autumn as presumably they go elsewhere at this season, perhaps to moult at traditional sites. Another striking observation was the near-total absence of Stonechats (just four birds seen) on the winter visit. These were present in good numbers on the summer trip and are one of the commonest passerines seen in autumn, so their apparent exodus for the winter raises questions as to their possible destination.

Looking back – the story so far

In five autumn trips we have spent a total of 77 full days and ten part-days on Barra. During this time we have managed to fulfil our initial aim of generating bird report material for a previously under-recorded and under-covered area, and amassed a cumulative total of 157 species in the process (Table 1). Little did we think when we started that this would include four "firsts" for the Outer Hebrides (including a first for Scotland) plus the relocation of another, three second-records and three third-records, and a fourth and fifth as well (Table 2).

Perhaps the biggest surprise is that, while we have enjoyed a good showing of rarities and scarce migrants (Tables 2 and 3), there have been comparatively small numbers of what are generally regarded as 'common' migrants to accompany them (Table 3). Our trips may be just too late in the season to encounter the main passage of these birds, but it seems just as likely that their numbers are usually on the low side since these birds typically use migration routes further east in Scotland and are seldom displaced to the west coast or can readily re-orientate when they are. If the latter explanations are true, then the factors leading to rare and scarce Palearctic birds reaching the Outer Hebrides, and perhaps western Scotland as a whole, are notably different to those delivering birds to the east coast.

Looking forward

We intend to vary our visit times across the autumn period to get a better idea of the range and numbers of migrants moving through Barra. There are many questions to be considered which relate to the differences in both species and numbers encountered on Barra compared to those present during the autumn passage on the east coast of Scotland. While it is becoming clearer to us where many of the birds that pass through Barra are coming from, it is still uncertain where they head once they reach the south end of the Hebridean island chain. This remains the biggest question still to be answered but will hopefully be resolved by Mark's ringing efforts in the coming years.

Acknowledgements

I am particularly indebted to the other five 'lads' who have formed our team on Barra in the last five autumns - Keith Gillon, Stuart R. Green, Tony O'Connor, Mark Oksien and Calum Scott. Without them, the trips would never have been so successful, both in terms of bird finding and the social aspects after. In addition we have been joined at one time or other by: Ian Dillon (2004), Brendan Doe (2002), Ewen Forbes (2005), Brian Orr (2004) and Alastair Shuttleworth (2002). Jim Dickson, though not part of our group, found the Woodchat Shrike and Little Bunting during our stay in 2003.

References

Gillon, K. 2005. The second Scottish record of Rose-breasted Grosbeak, Barra, 8th October 2005. *Birding Scotland* 8: 151-153

Green, S. R. 2002. Barra, Autumn 2002 - a Barra-load of birds! *Birding Scotland* 5: 172-177

Oksien, M. 2003. The Red-eyed Vireo on Barra, 5th-7th October 2003. *Birding Scotland* 6: 184-187

Rabbitts, B. 2001. Birding…the Western Isles part two: Berneray to Barra & Vatersay. *Birding Scotland* 4 (3) 111-120

Rivers, S. L. 2003. Barra – the one to watch. *Birdwatch* 135: 20-21

Rivers, S. L. 2004. Yellow Warbler on Barra - the third Scottish record. *Birding Scotland* 7: 195-198

Rivers, S. L. 2005. White-throated Dipper *Cinclus c. hibernicus*. *Birding Scotland* 8: back cover

Scott, C., Gillon, K. & Rivers, S. L. 2004. The female Redhead on Barra, September 2003 to April 2004 - the first Scottish record. *Birding Scotland* 7: 130-135

Scott, M. 2006. The Turkestan Shrike on the Outer Hebrides. *Birding World* 19: 393-394

Shaw, K. D. 2003. North by north-west. *Birdwatch* 135: 18-19

Wallace, D. I. M., McGeehan, A. & Allen, D. 2001. Autumn migration in westernmost Donegal. *British Birds* 94: 103-120

Wallace, D. I. M. & Rivers, S. L. 2002. Pioneering Spirit. *Birding Scotland* 5: 167-171

Table 1

Seen every year

Mute Swan	Pink-footed Goose	Brent Goose	Eurasian Wigeon
Eurasian Teal	Mallard	Tufted Duck	Common Eider
Red-breasted Merganser	Red-throated Diver	Great Northern Diver	Little Grebe
Fulmar	Manx Shearwater	Northern Gannet	Great Cormorant
European Shag	Grey Heron	Common Buzzard	Golden Eagle
Common Kestrel	Merlin	Peregrine	Oystercatcher
Great Ringed Plover	European Golden Plover	Northern Lapwing	Sanderling
Dunlin	Common Snipe	Bar-tailed Godwit	Eurasian Curlew
Common Redshank	Ruddy Turnstone	Great Skua	Black-headed Gull
Common Gull	Herring Gull	Great Black-backed Gull	Kittiwake
Common Guillemot	Razorbill	Black Guillemot	Rock Dove
Collared Dove	Skylark	Barn Swallow	Meadow Pipit
Rock Pipit	Grey Wagtail	Pied Wagtail	Winter Wren
Dunnock	European Robin	Common Stonechat	Northern Wheatear
Blackbird	Song Thrush	Blackcap	Yellow-browed Warbler
Common Chiffchaff	Willow Warbler	Goldcrest	Hooded Crow
Common Starling	House Sparrow	Chaffinch	Common Linnet
Twite	Lesser Redpoll	Common Reed Bunting	Corn Bunting

Seen in 4 years	Seen in 3 years	Seen in 2 years	Seen in only 1 year
Whooper Swan	Barnacle Goose	Slavonian Grebe	Northern Pintail (2004)
Greylag Goose	Common Scoter	Leach's Petrel	**Redhead** (2003)
Long-tailed Duck	Sooty Shearwater	Corncrake	Greater Scaup (2006)
Black-throated Diver	European Storm Petrel	Black-tailed Godwit	Surf Scoter (2002)
Hen Harrier	White-tailed Eagle	Eurasian Whimbrel	**Balearic Shearwater** (2005)
Eurasian Sparrow-hawk	Common Moorhen	Common Tern	Water Rail (2003)
Red Knot	Grey Plover	Little Auk	Curlew Sandpiper (2002)
Purple Sandpiper	Ruff	Common Wood Pigeon	Eurasian Woodcock (2006)
Jack Snipe	Atlantic Puffin	European Turtle Dove	Grey Phalarope (2004)
Common Green-shank	Whinchat	Short-eared Owl	Glaucous Gull (2004)
Arctic Skua	**Eurasian Reed Warbler**	Common Redstart	Long-eared Owl (2004)
Lesser Black-backed Gull	European Gold-finch	Fieldfare	Common Swift (2006)
Arctic Tern	**Common Rose-finch**	Sedge Warbler	Tree Pipit (2003)
Redwing		**Blyth's Reed Warbler**	**Citrine Wagtail** (2003)
Lesser Whitethroat		**Barred Warbler**	Yellow Wagtail (2005)
Garden Warbler		**Red-breasted Fly-catcher**	White-throated Dipper (2005)
Spotted Flycatcher		**Rosy Starling**	**Paddyfield Warbler** (2003)
Pied Flycatcher		Brambling	**Melodious Warbler** (2003)
European Green-finch		Eurasian Siskin	Common Whitethroat (2006)

Seen in 4 years	Seen in 3 years	Seen in 2 years	Seen in only 1 year
Common Redpoll		Lapland Bunting	**Arctic Warbler**(2002)
		Snow Bunting	Common Treecreeper (2002)
			Isabelline Shrike (2006)
			Woodchat Shrike (2003)
			Eurasian Tree Sparrow (2005)
			Red-eyed Vireo (2003)
			Yellow Warbler (2004)
			Common Crossbill (2002)
			Rustic Bunting (2003)
			Little Bunting (2003)
156 species			**Rose-breasted**

BBRC, SBRC or Outer Hebrides RC description species denoted in bold

Table 2.
Significant records during our autumn trips to Barra 2002-06

Rarities   (fewer than 20 records on Outer Hebrides)

Redhead	1st Scottish record
Citrine Wagtail	2nd OH
Paddyfield Warbler	1st OH
Blyth's Reed Warbler	2nd & 3rd OH
Melodious Warbler	5th OH
Arctic Warbler	1st OH
Woodchat Shrike	3rd OH ★★
Red-eyed Vireo	3rd OH (7th Scottish)
Yellow Warbler	1st OH (3rd Scottish)

Rustic Bunting	11th OH ★
Little Bunting	4th OH ★★ (5th bird)
Isabelline Shrike	relocation of 1st OH
Rose-breasted Grosbeak	2nd OH (2nd Scottish)

Scarcities (fewer than 60 records on Outer Hebrides)

Surf Scoter	Yellow-browed Warbler ★★★
Balearic Shearwater	Red-breasted Flycatcher
European Reed Warbler ★	Rosy Starling
Barred Warbler	Common Rosefinch

★ 4th records away from St Kilda
★★ these bird found by Jim Dickson
★★★ Outer Hebrides total passed 60 during the period

Table 3.
Autumn trip totals of 'common' & 'scarce' migrants Barra 2002-06

	2002	2003	2004	2005	2006
European Turtle Dove	0	0	1	0	1
Whinchat	2	1	0	1	2
Northern Wheatear	13+	3+	2+	10+	23+
Common Redstart	0	3	0	0	1
Sedge Warbler	3	0	0	0	1
Garden Warbler	1	1	1	1	7+
Blackcap	7+	1	4+	0	12+
Lesser Whitethroat	2	3	1	1	0
Common Whitethroat	0	0	0	0	3+
Common Chiffchaff	0	3	3	1	c10
Willow Warbler	13+	9+	5	8	4+
Spotted Flycatcher	2	1	0	1	1+
Pied Flycatcher	3	1	0	0	1
European Reed Warbler	0	1	0	1	1

Barred Warbler	0	1	0	0	2+
Yellow-browed Warbler	1	1	1	1	11+
Red-breasted Flycatcher	0	1(2)	0	0	1
Common Rosefinch	1	0	4	0	1

Scarce migrants (latter group of five species) are defined as those requiring a description to be assessed by Outer Hebrides Records Committee for acceptance of record.

Discovering hidden vagrants

The handful of Barrow's Goldeneye, Canvasback, Bufflehead and Redhead that have been accepted onto the British List could all have been escapes. These four species all occur commonly in captivity and apparent escapes have been seen at large in Britain. So why are they on the British List when other species, such as Baikal Teal and Falcated Duck, are not?

After all, Baikal Teal and Falcated Duck have both occurred in an apparently wild state in Britain on several occasions. The evidence is compelling. There is a pattern of both species arriving in the Western Palearctic with 'carrier species' such as Eurasian Wigeon and Common Teal and Gadwall from Siberian breeding grounds in the late autumn. There is even the significant evidence for long-distance vagrancy in both species from the analysis of stable isotope composition in feathers. A Baikal Teal found shot in Denmark apparently came from Siberia and (using a less complete isotope analysis – based on one feather) a Falcated Duck shot in Orkney was shown to have come from further away than Western Europe (Eastern Europe at least if not from further east).

Okay, so I am being provocative, but hopefully the point is clear. That some potentially vagrant wildfowl are on the British List and some are not seems to be based on an arbitrary and largely inconsistent process. A similar situation exists with some passerines. Why is Chestnut-eared Bunting 'on the list' but not Mugimaki Flycatcher? Both occur in the cage-bird trade, though ironically Mugimaki Flycatcher is *less* common in the bird trade than Chestnut-eared Bunting. Both have occurred at times that coincide with their migration in the Far East (Harrop 2007); both have been recorded only once in Western Europe; both were young birds in their first autumn. Again it is somewhat ironic that the breeding range of Mugimaki Flycatcher actually extends further north and west than Chestnut-eared Bunting and its migration takes it further south over a greater distance to its wintering grounds. They should, by all logic, be treated the same. However the less likely vagrant is on the list, and the more likely one is off and given 'only' Category D status (*Species that would otherwise appear in Category A except that there is reasonable doubt that they have ever occurred in a natural state.*) Frustratingly, there have been times in the past when members of the British Ornithologists Union Records Committee (who maintain the national list) have demonstrated surprising levels of ignorance or indifference about the subject matter upon which they are adjudicating, indicating the level of prejudice with which the assessment of Category D species can sometimes be approached. Greater public accountability and transparency of the work of the BOURC would not go amiss, given the privileged position of those involved.

Clearly not *all* Category D birds should be categorised the same. Some do have more complex issues surrounding their status. I think all three raptors listed below have 'shades of grey' about the records and it is self-evident, after a bit of research, that the records of Chestnut Buntings in Britain do not accord with the migration dates, patterns and age class of the vast majority of other Siberian passerine vagrants. Greater Flamingos, White Pelicans and Yellow-headed Blackbirds all have their own complicating factors in assessment, though they could still could occur or may have already occurred as vagrants. Certainly all such birds should be seriously reported to relevant local and national committees so that patterns of occurrence can be collated and periodically reviewed. Other species not even given Category D status in Britain are potential vagrants and have been accepted as such elsewhere on the near-continent of Europe. Examples include Demoiselle Crane and Dalmatian Pelican, and the occurrence of every example of these species in Britain should be carefully recorded.

Here then is Keith Vinicombe, the undisputed champion of certain Category D species, and a former BOURC member, who (together with a couple of interjectors) brings his comprehensively studied perspective to the debate. *Martin Garner*

Category D vagrants
Keith Vinicombe

One of the commonest subjects of discussion amongst birders relates to a small group of species that has been seen in Britain, apparently in a wild state, but which the British Ornithologists' Union Records Committee, in their role of maintaining the 'official' British List, have refused to accept onto it. Instead, these birds are placed in a state of limbo in 'Category D', a kind of holding pen for species that might have had a captive origin. The important point to make, however, is that if a record is placed in Category D it doesn't mean that the bird was definitely an escape; it just means that this was a possibility. To put it simply, it's D for 'Don't Know' and not D for 'Duff'!

Birders argue incessantly about the pros and cons of counting Category D birds on their lists. Many refuse to count them, maintaining only a pure 'untarnished' list of wild Category A species combined with self-sustaining introduced or escaped species that reside in Category C. But many *do* count those Category D species for which a wild origin is arguably likely. For example, apparently all Shetland 'listers' count Category D species as fully 'tickable' on their Shetland List (Mike Pennington in lit.).

The one group of birds that most frequently ends up in Category D is of course wildfowl. Ducks, geese and swans are commonly kept and they frequently escape. Understandably, this simple fact is used by the BOURC as a reason for exercising caution and for relegating many potential vagrants to Category D. The problem though is that *patterns* of occurrence and changes in the population profiles of a number of these species clearly suggest that some of them probably had a wild origin. The Committee's unenviable role is to try to decide which individuals are wild and which are escapes; in other words, to sort out the wheat from the chaff. As this is difficult, the Committee errs on the side of caution and tends to reject any wildfowl, particularly Palearctic species, for which a captive origin is a possibility. But by closing its mind to these species, it is often accused of abrogating its responsibility by failing to perform the very function for which it exists.

There are of course no certainties, but the following is a list of species for which I believe an argument can be made for wild vagrancy. Most of these have at some point been written about at greater length in *British Birds* and/or *Birdwatch* and the relevant references are given at the end of each species account.

Wildfowl

Ross's Goose

This species breeds mainly on the western side of Hudson Bay in north-eastern Canada and is a long-distance migrant which heads south-west in autumn to wintering grounds in south-western USA and Mexico. The species is common in captivity and does escape, as is the case with most other vagrant geese on the British List (i.e. Lesser White-fronted Goose, Snow Goose, Arctic/Cackling and Canada Geese and Red-breasted Goose). In the early 1960s a pair of Ross's Geese escaped from captivity. Being ringed, they could be tracked as they joined a group of wild Greylag Geese, summering with them in Iceland and wintering in central Scotland. They even attempted to breed in Iceland in 1963, with the last individual being found dead at Loch Leven in January 1972. This example is often used to pour scorn on possible wild examples of the species in Britain.

Historically, Ross's Goose has had a relatively small world population, numbered at only 2,000 birds in 1950. In recent times, however, its population has increased enormously: reaching 650,000 by 2001, and it has become one of the world's most successfully recovered species. Of particular relevance to British vagrancy: its breeding range has increased with colonies spreading east to within 500 miles of Greenland (van den Berg 2004). Over the years there have been a number of Ross's Geese seen in Britain amongst flocks of Pink-footed Geese, which breed in Iceland and eastern Greenland. The theory is that these could have been related to wild birds that became lost in the Arctic and then tagged on to flocks of Pink-footed Geese, 'abmigrating' with them to Britain; Snow Geese, wild Canada and Arctic/Cackling Geese arrive here by precisely the same method. In November 2001, a first-winter Ross's Goose was discovered in north Norfolk amongst the huge flocks of wintering Pink-footed Geese. It returned in the subsequent winter and was also seen on its migrations through northern England and Scotland. It behaved throughout like a wild bird and its appearance followed the huge increase in its native North American population. This bird was widely counted by those who saw it. See *Birdwatch* (2002) 115: 8. In winter 2007-2008 no fewer than four adult Ross's Geese of arguably wild origin accompanied Pink-footed Geese wintering in Britain.

Ruddy Shelduck

A major influx of at least 59 Ruddy Shelducks into Britain and Ireland occurred in 1892, with others at that time reaching as far west as Greenland. This influx has always been considered to relate to wild birds and the species resides on Category B of the British List (species seen in an apparently wild state only before 1950). The numerous records since then are treated by the BOURC as relating to escapes. While many undoubtedly are, there is a strong pattern of late-summer occurrences (mainly July-August) and many, if not most, of those records relate to small flocks, a classic characteristic of an irruptive vagrant. In 1994, there was a major irruption into north-western Europe, involving as many as 351 birds, including about 262 into Fenno-Scandia. This is thought to have involved birds that moved out of south-east Europe and/or south-western Asia in response to drought. There were about 55 seen in Britain that year, including flocks of up to twelve. Despite this, the BOURC refused to admit Ruddy Shelduck into Category A, one of the reasons being the existence of a feral population based on the Askania-Nova steppe reserve in Ukraine, a site that is however very close to the species' natural range.

Since then, small flocks of Ruddy Shelducks have continued to occur in late summer, but there have been further important developments. One is the establishment of another feral population based on Moscow Zoo, which reached 294 in January 2004, and another feral population based on lakes and reservoirs in northern Switzerland, which reached 280 in August 2003. Most significant is the establishment of a moult migration to Eemmer, Utrecht, in the Netherlands, which reached 430 in July 2006. There is a widespread belief that these birds come from a large feral population in Germany, but there is a snag to this theory: there is no large feral population in Germany! Contemporaneous counts confirm that they do not come from Switzerland. The Dutch do not know where these birds come from but the prevailing view is that they are wild. Intriguingly, there has recently been some evidence of a regular passage through northern Italy, thought to involve birds travelling to and from Switzerland and perhaps originating in the Balkans.

Interestingly, it is now known from ringing recoveries that the feral population in Ukraine is mixing with wild birds in southern Russia, the population of which has increased significantly in recent years. This is supported by the fact that only 80-90 pairs nest at Askania-Nova whereas up to 2,000 may be present in winter.

Bearing in mind that (1) there are now over 700 Ruddy Shelducks moulting in Western Europe every summer and (2) the barriers between wild and feral birds in the natural range are breaking down, there is no reason why Ruddy Shelduck should not be added to the British List. Even if, for the sake of argument, the birds that reach these shores are feral, then they are clearly countable as Category C vagrants. See *British Birds* (1999) 92: 225-255 and an update in *Birdwatch* (2004) 141: 42-44.

Wood Duck

This North American species has occurred in both the Azores (including a bird ringed from North Carolina) and Iceland, where records are treated as being of wild origin. There have been many records in Britain, but they are always considered to relate to escapes; it is, after all, common in captivity. Like Ross's Goose, however, its status in North America has changed most dramatically over the last century. In the early 20th century its numbers were so low through over-hunting that extinction had become a real possibility. As a result of one of the greatest recovery programmes in North America, the species has increased rapidly in numbers since the 1960s, so much so that it vies with Mallard for the title of the commonest species of wildfowl in eastern areas. Most northern breeders are migrants and it is clearly a potential, and indeed highly likely, vagrant. All the evidence clearly suggests that some records in Britain should be taken far more seriously. It would probably take an immature in a remote westerly location to provoke greater interest in this species so a better understanding of its ageing characters would be beneficial; juvenile males quickly moult to an adult-type plumage, thus first-winter males could easily be assumed to be adults.

Examples of likely vagrants include two from Shetland: a male shot at Sae Water, near Voe on 30th October 1977 and another male shot near Quoy, Fair Isle on 27th November 1979. The stomach contents of the latter were sent to the Scottish Museum for seed analysis (in the days before isotope analysis) but they were then lost in the Esso Bernicia samples. In the light of such records it is surely an oversight that this species isn't even in Category D.

Falcated Duck

This Eastern Palearctic duck escapes from time to time but there is also a long tradition of it turning up in winter amongst flocks of Eurasian Wigeon and occasionally with Gadwall (particularly in the Netherlands). Since ringing recoveries indicate that some Eurasian Wigeon *breed within the breeding range* of Falcated Duck, it is highly plausible that some Falcated Duck reach Western Europe by tagging onto westward-bound wintering Wigeon flocks. It would also not be that surprising to find some Wigeon alternating between wintering grounds in southeast Asia (and thus regularly wintering with large numbers of Falcated Duck) and western Europe. This has already been demonstrated for Common Pochard: one ringed individual wintered in alternate years at Slimbridge WWT and the Sea of Japan! The fact that vagrant Falcated Ducks sometimes reach the west coast of North America in the company of Eurasian Wigeon (which only occur there in very small numbers!) by the same abmigration process is surely significant. See *Birdwatch* (2001) 111: 24.

An adult male shot on Shapinsay, Orkney on 24th November 2000 arrived at the same time as a large influx of Teal and Wigeon. One breast feather of this bird has undergone some stable isotope analysis, which shows that the bird clearly did not originate in Western Europe. The analysis was incomplete but the bird's origin lies somewhere well to the east of Britain. Falcated Duck is already on the Dutch List and an analysis of records in the Western Palearctic was recently published (Berlijn 2007).

Baikal Teal

This Eastern Palearctic species is thought likely to reach western Europe by the same mechanism as Falcated Duck. One reason for not accepting the species onto the British List was that, in the 20th century, it suffered a catastrophic population decline in its native range. But, in the 1990s, a huge wintering population was discovered in South Korea, reaching over 400,000 by 2001; it is now South Korea's commonest wintering duck. Firm evidence that wild vagrants can reach Europe came from a first-winter female that was shot in Denmark (mistakenly thought to be a Teal) in November 2005. Isotope analysis revealed that its juvenile feathers had been grown in Siberia, thereby confirming a wild origin. An apparent first-winter discovered at Minsmere, Suffolk, in November-December 2001, was considered a very good candidate for a wild bird, as was a male at Dix Pit, Oxfordshire in December 2002 and a male at Belfast Lough, Co. Down, Northern Ireland, in January-February 2006. At the time of writing the BOURC is considering whether to once again add the species to Category A of the British List. See *Birdwatch* (2002) 115: 4.

Marbled Duck

This species breeds in southern Spain and north-west Africa and east into the Middle East and Central Asia. It has declined markedly in recent years but concentrations of up to 4,250 were discovered in northern Tunisia in October 1999. The important point to make about Marbled Duck is that it is a nomadic species, moving in response to the erratic droughts that characterise its breeding range. There is a long history of vagrancy to northern Spain and to the Camargue in southern France, where it has bred. What is interesting is that the distance from its regular breeding sites in southern Spain *north-east* to the Camargue is not hugely different from the distance *north* to Britain (southern Spain to the Camargue is c.700 miles, southern Spain to southern England is c.900 miles). In France, where the species is infrequent in captivity, it is treated as an irruptive vagrant with most records in late summer (August-September) when drought conditions further south are most severe. There is a secondary peak in April. Interestingly, the British records conform to this pattern. One criterion used by the BOURC to count against Marbled Duck is that there are no old British records, which is surprising given that the species was formerly more numerous and wildfowling much commoner. However such a criterion is inherently flawed as it does not account for changes of behaviour that bird populations often show over time. For example, Lesser Scaup shows no historical record and the status of Little and Great White Egrets has changed massively in recent years. It is perhaps conceivable that the recent upsurge in records of Marbled Duck could be related to increases in drought conditions in its breeding range, brought about by global warming. See *Birdwatch* (2001) 109: 26-29. Following an analysis of occurrence patterns, the species has recently been added to the Dutch List (Winters 2007).

Hooded Merganser

There can be little doubt that some records of this colourful and ornate duck relate to escapes from captivity. However, it also has to be considered a likely vagrant, particularly since every other duck from eastern North America is already on the British List, with the exception of Wood Duck (see above). Records from Iceland, the Azores and the Canaries, including juvenile/first-winter birds, further confirm its vagrancy potential. The problem is sifting out the potentially good records from the bad. There are two particularly good candidates for vagrancy to the UK. The first, a bird seen on North Uist, Outer Hebrides, in October-November 2000, not only occurred at a perfect time of year and location, but also involved a juvenile male (Vinicombe, in prep.). The second candidate is a first-winter female at Newbiggin, Northumberland, in March 2002. This bird occurred within days of two further juvenile/first-winters on Flores, Azores and in Iceland, and in the same winter as other juvenile/first-winters in Iceland and on Tenerife, Canaries. It is also worth noting that, apart from the records listed here, there are virtually no records of Hooded Merganser, specifically in confirmed juvenile/first-winter plumage, from anywhere else in Europe. The coincidence of the 2002 records is surely best explained by genuine vagrancy. See *Birdwatch* (2002) 119: 16-17.

White-headed Duck

This is a species that has declined across much of its European range although, in recent years, the Spanish population has increased significantly, reaching its current level of about 2,000 birds. It has a long history of winter vagrancy across Europe, with records from as far west as Germany, the Netherlands, Belgium and France. In recent years, the pattern of occurrence has changed, with most French records now occurring in early autumn, mostly September. Their arrival is thought to relate to post-breeding dispersal from Spain, probably provoked by occasional drought conditions. Up to 15 were recorded in the autumn of 2000 which included 12 at Lac de Grand Lieu, Loire-Atlantique, a site which is only 250 miles from the coast of southern England. In 2003, there was a significant influx into southern England, involving a minimum of four and a maximum of nine, with a 'best guess' of five (one adult male and four juveniles). This corresponded with ten extra-limital continental records between August 2003 and February 2004 from France (at least three), Belgium, the Netherlands, Germany, Hungary and north-east Spain. See *Birdwatch* (2004) 145: 24-27.

Greater Flamingo

There are numerous British records of this species, including a flock of 12 seen off both Weybourne and Sheringham, Norfolk, in July 1980, and a juvenile on the Isle of Man on 31st August 1996. This is a species that has increased significantly at its Mediterranean breeding sites but it is, of course, also common in captivity. The BOURC refuses to admit the species onto the British List for two main reasons: Firstly, despite the fact that many thousands have been ringed in France and Spain, none has ever been recovered in north-western Europe. However, northward dispersal from the Camargue has been confirmed in recent years by regular occurrences in Switzerland, including ringed birds. Secondly, there is a feral colony of about 40 birds on the Dutch/German border which could be a potential source of British 'vagrants'. This view is in fact incorrect as the colony, which was established in 1983, relates to Chilean Flamingoes and there have only been occasional appearances of Greater Flamingoes in this colony. Meanwhile up to ten Greater Flamingoes present on Dutch wetlands in recent years are considered most likely to have originated from the Camargue colony and, given their longevity, some are continuing their stay for many years (as with, for example, some Glossy Ibis in Britain). See *Birdwatch* (2001) 111: 23.

Raptors

Black Vulture

The sole British record relates to an adult that was seen at various localities in mid-Wales from November 1977 to February 1978. It was heavily twitched and it behaved throughout like a wild bird; in fact many people found it to be astonishingly timid. Despite publicity in the national media, there was never any indication that the bird had a captive origin with no reports of escaped individuals. Investigations confirmed that Black Vultures have a long history of erratic northward vagrancy in Europe, including a record from the Netherlands in October 1948 that was accepted onto the Dutch List. In the Far East, winter vagrants have reached small islands off the southern tip of Japan. Most European vagrancy, however, had traditionally been in summer, including groups of up to 60 in the 19th century in the former Czechoslovakia. In recent years, the species has once again been recorded in the Netherlands, along with large numbers of Griffon Vultures and even the occasional Lammergeier, but, again, these records have been in summer. See *British Birds* (1994) 87: 613-622.

Booted Eagle

Perhaps the most controversial Category D record concerns the Booted Eagle seen in 1999 and 2000. It was first seen on 5th March 1999 near Dublin, where it was aged as a juvenile (i.e. hatched in 1998). Its Irish 'arrival date' was used by the BOURC as a reason for rejecting it: they considered it too early for a genuine vagrant. What the BOURC failed to grasp is that a bird's arrival date and the date of its first sighting are not necessarily the same. For example, nobody assumed that the Golden-winged Warbler in Kent in 1989 actually arrived in Britain on 7th February, when it was first seen. In seems far more likely that the Booted Eagle arrived in southern Ireland the previous autumn and remained undetected for several months until its discovery. A similar scenario could well have unfolded with the Short-toed Eagle on the Isles of Scilly in October 1999 if that bird had missed that archipelago and continued north until reaching Ireland.

During the summer of 1999, the Booted Eagle travelled all the way to Northern Ireland before disappearing off the radar. It was next seen in October-November 1999 in west

Cornwall, where it was heavily twitched. It then disappeared for three months before being rediscovered in Somerset in February 2000. This long period between the Cornish and Somerset sightings added weight to the theory that it had remained undetected in Ireland prior to its initial discovery. It seems likely that the eagle then left Britain, although subsequent unrelated sightings in Kent (April 2000) and Orkney (June 2000) were assumed by the BOURC to relate to the same bird, as was an earlier record from Kent in September 1999, despite there being no evidence whatsoever to back this up. Observers of the Kent individual are adamant that it showed significant plumage differences compared to the wide-ranging individual in the West Country and Ireland.

Another reason used by the BOURC to reject the record was that the amounts of wear and damage to its primaries and secondaries indicated a captive origin. They chose to ignore the fact that (1) large raptors regularly become tatty and worn, (2) in Somerset, the eagle was seen to stoop into tall vegetation to kill a Coot, the likely effect of such an action on its plumage being obvious, and (3) photographs seem to indicate that some of the damage to its feathers occurred between the initial sightings in Ireland and the sightings in Somerset. The BOURC also pointed out that few Booted Eagles winter north of the Sahara (now known to be untrue) and that Booted Eagles are not known to cross large expanses of sea (despite a record from Iceland!). The final reason for rejection was that the species was known to have been held in captivity in Britain. This was perhaps the most astonishing reason of all. There were in fact only two Booted Eagles known to be in captivity at the time, both of which remained there. More to the point, the bird had first been seen in Ireland, where captive Booted Eagles are apparently unknown!

Saker

Saker breeds in eastern Europe, eastwards into Asia, and it is a fairly long-distance migrant, moving south to winter in the Mediterranean, the Middle East, north-east Africa and southern Asia. They are of course also kept by falconers and some of them escape. There have been a few records with reasonable credentials for true vagrancy, such as those in Shetland in October 1976, May 1978 and October-December 1986, two of which were immature birds. The problem of certain identification is always a real challenge; of those accepted, at least two were initially misidentified as Gyr Falcons. Furthermore some escaped falconer's birds can include scary lookalike hybrids. See *Birdwatch* (2001) 111: 24.

Passerines

Brown Flycatcher

The only British record of this species was of a first-summer individual trapped on Fair Isle on 1st-2nd July 1992. The date is, on first sight, puzzling but its appearance can be explained by long-range spring overshooting across Siberia and Fenno-Scandia and down across the North Sea. The distance travelled explains its late date of occurrence. Interestingly, there have been several similar early-July records of both Arctic Warbler and Yellow-breasted Bunting. The BOURC placed the bird in Category D despite the fact that it has never been recorded in captivity. See *Birdwatch* (2001) 111: 24. The uncertain status of Brown Flycatcher in respect of the British List was finally ended with the discovery of a first-winter bird at Flamborough Head, Yorkshire in October 2007. It would be indeed remarkable if the species were not now added to the British List.

Mugimaki Flycatcher

The sole British record concerned a first-winter male at Stone Creek, East Yorkshire, on 16th-17th November 1991. The BOURC placed this record in Category D as there was evidence that the species had occurred in captivity. Yet the age of the bird, its date of arrival and the east-coast location all suggested wild vagrancy. It is arguably a more likely vagrant than Chestnut-eared Bunting, which was recently added to Category A of the British List. See *Birdwatch* (2001) 111: 24-25.

Daurian Starling

There have been three British records of this species: Fair Isle (7th-28th May 1985), Northumberland (26th August-5th September 1997) and Highland, Scotland (24th-27th September 1998). The date of the Northumberland bird does not accord as well with potential wild vagrancy, while the main problem with Daurian Starling is that it is apparently common in the cage-bird trade. It has been argued that the Fair Isle bird could have been on its way back east, having wintered in Western Europe. The Highland individual is arguably the best candidate for wild vagrancy since, like a first-winter bird seen in Norway on 29th September 1985, it occurred on dates which coincide with normal movements in southeast Asia (Harrop 2007). It has a breeding range somewhat similar to Chestnut-eared Bunting, though the wintering range extends further south, making it a longer-distance migrant. A bird at Vlieland, Netherlands on 11th-12th October 2005 with 3000 Starlings and two Rose-coloured Starlings was recently accepted as the first national record and added to the Dutch 'A' List. See also *Birdwatch* (2001) 111: 25.

Red-headed Bunting

There are some 276 British records of this species but most occurred in the 1950s, 1960s and 1970s when the species was very common in the caged-bird trade. Numbers decreased after 1982 when India imposed a ban on the export of wild birds. They continued to occur at a reduced level until the mid 1990s. Since 1998, there have been only three British records, all in May-June. In addition, there were two apparent records from October of first-winters from the Isles of Scilly in 1994 and 1997, which are likely to have related to wild birds, given that the species is rarely bred in captivity. Current rates of vagrancy across Europe are now compatible with wild vagrancy, which has always been likely given the species' migration routes between Central Asia and India. In January 2007 it was announced that the European Union was to ban the trade in wild birds, so it will be interesting to see how the picture continues to unfold. See *British Birds* (2007) 100: 540-551.

Chestnut Bunting

There have been several British records of this species. Given its breeding and wintering ranges, it is certainly a possible vagrant, arguably more likely than Chestnut-eared Bunting and, on face value, of similar likelihood as Black-faced and Yellow-browed Buntings. The problem is that none of the records has related to a first-winter at a classic time of year or place. For example, there have been records of a first-summer male on Fair Isle (June 1986), an adult female on the Out Skerries, Shetland (September 1994), and an adult male at Salthouse, Norfolk (30th May to 1st June 1998). Accepted records of mainly first-winter Chestnut Buntings with the more normal credentials of Eastern Palearctic vagrants have occurred in the Netherlands, Norway, former Yugoslavia and Malta in October and November, so the first credible British record may be only a matter of time.

Yellow-headed Blackbird

There have been several records of this species in Britain, including a first-winter male on Yell, Shetland (May 1987) and a first-summer male on Fair Isle (April 1990), which are arguably the best candidates for true vagrancy. Both could of course have been escapes, perhaps having migrated north to Shetland after escaping in the Low Countries, which is a core region of the cage-bird trade in Europe. On the other hand, the species does have a long record of vagrancy to the north-eastern states and provinces of the USA and Canada. Interestingly, it is regular in Newfoundland with several records in May-June. There are also records from Norway (May 1979) and Iceland (July 1983). See *Birdwatch* (2001) 111: 25. This species has recently been added to the Dutch 'A' list on the basis of an adult male seen on Terschelling on 2nd-3rd July 1982 (*Dutch Birding* 29:3).

Conclusion

So what do we count? Many birders count only those species accepted by the BOURC onto Categories A and C of the British List. Many others count the larger number of species advocated by Lee Evans and his UK 400 Club. Others follow the recent *Birds of Britain - The Complete Checklist* that is published by the magazine *Birdwatch*. This attempts to follow a sensible middle road between the other two lists. The important point to make about the BOURC is that it is a scientific organisation that publishes its 'official' British List for scientific and legislative purposes. The Committee has never made any secret of the fact it is not concerned with the 'sport' of listing. But, by taking this stance, it is distancing itself from the only people who passionately care about what it does. Frustratingly this whole controversy would evaporate if the BOURC made a clear and unambiguous announcement that, for listing purposes only, Category D species are countable. By doing this it would, at a stroke, satisfy the only people really interested in its adjudications *and* deflect the relentless criticism that is levelled against it. Surely it's time for some kind of a compromise?

Acknowledgments

Arnoud van den Berg and Martin Garner provided additional information and comments which further enhanced the text.

References

Berlijn, M. 2007. Falcated Ducks in the Netherlands and the Western Palearctic. *Dutch Birding* 29: 139-146.

Harrop, A. H. J. 2007. Eastern Promise: the arrival of far-eastern passerine vagrants in autumn. *British Birds* 100: 105-111.

van den Berg, A. 2004. Population Growth and Vagrancy potential of Ross's Goose. *Dutch Birding* 26: 107-111.

Winters, R. 2007. Marbled Duck near Doornenburg and Pannerden in August 2004. *Dutch Birding* 29: 147-152.

Species identification accounts

Grebes to Geese

Pacific Diver

Martin Garner

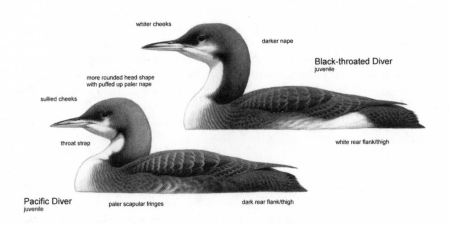

The beginning of 2007 brought a paradigm shift in the thinking of British birders with regard to Pacific Divers. Unless the events of January and February of that year amount to some kind of freak event, Pacific Diver might actually prove to be a regular visitor to our shores. Indeed, remarkably, two of the individuals reappeared in Cornwall and South Wales the following winter. This meant that even in 2007 with the plethora of books, DVDs, websites and world-savvy birders there are real rare birds that, in all probability, are still going unnoticed. Will there be more Pacific Divers? I'm sure of it. Personally I was amazed to discover how near to us the species may actually breed. Given the number of seabirds that arrive in the winter from the Greenland/northeast Canada region, you might be forgiven for wondering why Pacific Diver isn't an annual visitor in small numbers. Pioneering birders who want to add a new species to their country or county avifauna may well be hoping it is.

Geographical range

Pacific Diver *Gavia pacifica* is essentially a Nearctic species, breeding from Hudson Bay eastwards to Alaska and northeastern Siberia where it overlaps with the green-throated *viridigularis* form of Black throated Diver, *Gavia arctica*. It winters primarily around the Pacific Ocean south to eastern China and along the western seaboard of North America south to Baja California. It occurs occasionally in the interior of western North America as well as on the Atlantic coast (most frequently from Maine to New York). It has occurred in western Greenland, and may even breed there (Russell 2002). In recent years it has become apparent that it occurs on the eastern seaboard of North America rather more commonly than had been previously thought. It could even be described as regular off Massachusetts in March/April, though its exact status is obscured by poor documentation of records and in part confusion caused by some distinctly contrasting plumages of Red-throated Diver *Gavia stellata*.

Vagrancy potential

With a breeding range that reaches to Baffin Island in the Canadian Arctic, and possibly even western Greenland, the vagrancy likelihood of Pacific Diver is actually very high. However, while Pacific Diver is reckoned to be the most numerous diver species in North America, in winter it is also clearly the most pelagic. Off British Columbia, it is possible to see congregations numbering over 1000 at the entrance to the Straits of Georgia (pers. obs.), viewable by boat, but the species becomes much scarcer along the mainland coastline. One could easily imagine odd birds regularly reaching the continental shelf off the western approaches of Britain and Ireland, but such occurrences are likely to remain unrecorded. However, the unprecedented occurrence of two juveniles and an adult in Britain during early 2007 coincided with a widespread influx of Great Northern Divers *Gavia immer* (most likely originating from a northwest vector) and clearly demonstrates the vagrancy potential of this species.

IDENTIFICATION

The key criteria for identifying Pacific Diver have only recently been elucidated. As recently as 1990, in comparing Black-throated and Pacific Diver, Ken Kaufman, stated that "...the field identification of these two species in winter should be considered an unresolved challenge that all of us have to look forward to". Ensuing papers by Reinking & Howell (1993) and Birch & Lee (1995 and 1997) opened up the identification criteria that were further tested and developed in Britain in 2007 (Taylor, Garner & McLoughlin 2007; Astins & Brown 2007; Ahmad 2007). The identification of a vagrant Pacific Diver could appear particularly challenging. It is important to be aware of the variety of appearance shown by Black-throated Divers, with which potential vagrants will always be compared. However, there are a number of subtle characters in all plumages of Pacific Diver which, while not always individually diagnostic, can produce, in combination, a distinctive appearance that, should render the identification of most well-seen individuals relatively straightforward. No doubt there is still more to be discovered about the extent of variation to be found in both species.

Features common to all plumages

Overall body size and shape
Pacific Divers are approximately 10% smaller than Black-throated Divers. This considerable size difference can be effectively illustrated by comparing field experiences between different continents. In a Western Palearctic context, the normal challenge in winter is the separation of Black-throated from Great Northern Diver (due in part to their similar size, bulk and, to some extent, head shape and 'weight' of bill), while the identification of Red-throated Divers is usually less problematic. However, in eastern North America, Pacific Divers are

frequently confused with Red-throated Divers that show particularly contrasting plumage tones or are juveniles with darker 'faces'. The two juveniles in Britain in January/February 2007 both appeared close in body length to nearby Great Crested Grebes!

Perhaps even more important than size assessment is an understanding of the subtle structural character of Pacific Diver. In all plumages, individuals can conjure up the impression of a rather compact, lightweight bird, more reminiscent in bulk of a Red-throated than Black-throated Diver. The body appears shorter and more compact than Black-throated Diver, with a slightly more hump-backed appearance.

Head shape
Obviously the head shape can vary with posture and behaviour. The head shape of Pacific Diver is, however, less angular, less prone to 'lumpiness' on the forehead and less flat-topped than often shown by Black-throated Diver. The nape can appear puffed-up or loose and 'fluffy' and at times curiously 'ballooned' creating a rather distinctive appearance quite different to typical Black-throated Diver.

Bill shape and size
The bill of Pacific Diver clearly averages shorter (Russell 2002) and thinner than that of Black-throated Diver, which in contrast has quite a hefty bill that at times can approach the 'weight' of Great Northern Diver. Some Pacific Divers have particularly small-looking bills with the rather broad base evenly thinning to a very fine tip, giving an overall effect which can even be a little suggestive of Red-throated Diver. However, other birds have slightly weightier and longer bills that approach some Black-throated Divers, but nevertheless appear at the slim end of the scale for the latter species. Observers of summer-plumaged birds in Alaska have noted that, in direct comparison, Black-throated Divers (of the form *viridigularis*) tend to hold their bill slightly more up-tilted than Pacific Divers, which usually hold their bill on a more level plane (Birch & Lee 1995, Julian Hough pers. coms). However, this is not so applicable to Black-throated Divers of the nominate form *arctica*, which usually hold their bill straighter.

Rear flank/thigh patch
The most important field character in all plumages of Pacific Diver is the dark rear thigh patch. More specifically this is the dark feathering at the front of the bird's 'thigh' or tibia. This tibia feathering is white (contrasting with dark posterior tibia feathering) in all plumages of Black-throated Diver. On relaxed Black-throated Divers this normally shows as an obvious upwards-flared white patch in the rear flank zone which, depending on posture, runs into a white line along the full length of the flanks and is clearly visible just above the water line (at least in calm conditions). This white patch can temporarily 'disappear' on birds which are low slung in the water. The same area is entirely dark on Pacific Diver. Similarly, the flanks of Pacific Diver are also mostly dark with, at best, only a narrow white line visible above the water line. Crucially though, the flared white patch at the rear of the flanks as shown on Black-throated Diver is entirely absent on Pacific Diver.

Summary of key features (all plumages)

- Body size and shape: lightweight version of Black-throated Diver with a shorter a more compact body
- Head shape: typically less angular, more rounded and with puffed-up nape

- Bill shape and size: variable but usually shorter, thinner and less weighty than Black-throated Diver
- Rear thigh patch: the most important field character. Diagnostic dark anterior tibia feathering produces a dark rear flank zone. The same feathering is white on Black-throated Diver and produces a white rear flank patch usually visible in all conditions except when birds are slung low in water

Juvenile and adult winter plumage

A potential Pacific Diver in non-breeding plumage will attract attention by the generic characters listed above. In addition, to varying degrees and partly dependent on the age of the individual, the following features can be useful in confirming the identification.

Throat strap
Although sometimes called a 'chin-strap', this field mark is technically not on the chin but at the top of the neck, thus 'throat-strap' or 'bridle' are perhaps better descriptions. A conspicuous and solid dark line joining the dark lower cheeks by looping under the throat is, when present, highly indicative (but not diagnostic) of Pacific Diver. Birch and Lee (1995) describe the throat strap as varying from 'dark and conspicuous to extremely pale and faint'. Furthermore, Reinking & Howell (1993) found that after an examination of 150 specimens of Pacific Divers some 91% of adult winters and 54% of juveniles had a dark throat strap. This implies that nearly half of all juvenile Pacific Divers only show a faint throat strap or none at all. Somewhat confusingly, Black-throated Divers do occasionally show an ill-defined dusky throat strap (see *Birding World* 9: 321).

Facial pattern
There is a line of demarcation which runs along the side of the face, separating the dark crown and hind-neck from the white face and fore-neck and this can be a useful feature in separating Pacific from Black-throated Diver. The tendency is for Black-throated Diver to exhibit a horizontal line of demarcation running though the bottom of the eye and back to the rear cheeks before heading more vertically down the neck sides. Conversely, on Pacific Diver, the demarcation is more diffuse and the line runs approximately at a 45° angle from the rear of the eye towards the top of the neck. Thus there is a larger area of dark below and behind the eye on Pacific Diver. Juvenile Black-throated Divers can have more dark in this facial region than adults and some Pacific Divers can have a face pattern more like Black-throated, so caution should always be exercised.

Nape tone on juveniles
It is well known that, in adult breeding plumage, the base of the nape feathers is white in Pacific Diver and grey in Black-throated Diver, and it would appear that a similar difference exists in juvenile plumage. On the two juveniles which appeared in Britain in early 2007, the hind-neck appeared conspicuously pale, contrasting with a dark vertical line on the neck sides. When the hind-neck was more extended and exposed (e.g. when preening) it appeared almost whitish. The combination of rounded 'puffy' head shape and striking paleness of the hind-neck was distinctly different from the normal appearance of Black-throated Diver. Its usefulness as a feature in adult winter birds is less clear.

Upperpart feather fringes on juveniles

The appearance of any vagrant bird inevitably invites further exploration towards the boundaries of identification. In the case of the first two British records, the pale scapular fringes were particularly striking, being apparently both broader and perhaps paler than typical juvenile Black-throated Diver. Pale fringing on the dark flank and rump feathers also seemed more conspicuous. The whole effect was of noticeably paler and scalier birds. This particularly pale-scaled appearance of juvenile Pacific Diver versus Black-throated Diver was reminiscent of the paler-fringed upperparts of juvenile White-billed Diver compared with Great Northern Diver.

Vent strap

A dark bar running through the vent was originally described by Walsh (1998) as present in all plumages of Pacific Diver, but faint or absent in Black-throated Diver. This was further researched by Reinking & Howell (1993), who found that 93.5% of juvenile Pacific Divers examined had a complete brown vent strap. Only 69.5% of adults in both summer and winter plumages showed a complete vent strap, while five out of six Black-throated Divers examined had only a partial vent strap at best. However this perhaps only relates to Black-throated Divers of the form *viridigularis*, as limited research of the nominate form in Western Europe (pers. obs., Astins and Brown 2007) indicates that a complete dark vent strap is not unusual (at least in some plumages) and perhaps should no longer be considered a key feature of Pacific Diver. More research should establish any useful parameters of this feature.

Summary of key features of Pacific Diver (specific to juvenile and non-breeding plumages)

- Throat strap: a highly indicative feature present on about half of juveniles and
- most non-breeding adults
- Face pattern: a variable feature but well-marked birds have obviously sullied cheeks, lacking the cleaner-cut look of many Black-throated Divers
- Nape tone: obviously paler (even whitish-looking at times) on some juveniles
- Feather fringes: paler and wider on the upperparts of juveniles producing a scalier appearance than on typical Black-throated Diver

Adult summer plumage

A potential breeding-plumage Pacific Diver is likely to attract attention first by its pale silvery/whitish-looking nape contrasting strongly with a darker grey 'face'. This is because, in adult breeding plumage, the base of the nape feathers is white. In summer-plumaged Black-throated Diver these feather bases are grey with the nape normally appearing lead-grey and more uniform with the rest of the head, though it can flash paler when light catches it in bright sunshine. As in other Pacific Diver plumages, there should be an absence of white on the rear flank area due to dark anterior tibia feathering. Careful recording of these two features is critical for establishing identification. A potential Pacific Diver should also show a set of general structural characters such as a smaller, more compact, body than Black-throated Diver, a less angular, more rounded, head shape with 'puffed-up' nape, and weaker bill.

The pattern of vertical black and white stripes on the neck sides has been cited as useful (Birch & Lee 1995), with the suggestion that Pacific Diver tend to have broader black stripes and narrower (and sometimes fewer) white stripes but there seems much variation and overlap in this character. It may be useful in extreme examples (obviously broad white in some Black-throated and very thin, fewer white stripes in some Pacific Divers) but should be seen as generally incidental compared to other characters. The dark vent strap sometimes quoted as a feature of Pacific Diver (see above) is also found in Black-throated Divers of the nominate form in summer plumage.

Summary of key features of Pacific Diver (specific to adults in summer plumage)

- Smaller, more compact diver, rounder head, puffy nape and weaker bill than Black-throated Diver
- Striking silvery-white nape which contrasts with darker grey foreface
- Dark rear flank, lacking white upflared patch
- On extreme examples, obviously thinner and fewer white vertical neck stripes

References

Ahmed, M. 2007. The Pacific Diver in Cornwall - the third for the Western Palearctic. *Birding World* 20: 62-63.

American Ornithologists' Union. 1985. Thirty-fifth supplement to the American Ornithologists' Union check-list of North American birds. *Auk* 102: 680-686.

American Ornithologists' Union. 1998. *Check-list of North American birds*. 7th ed. American Ornithologists' Union, Washington, D.C.

Astins, D. & Brown, J. 2007. The Pacific Diver in Pembrokeshire - the second for the Western Palearctic. *Birding World* 20: 57-61.

Birch, A., Lee, C. T. 1995. Identification of Pacific Diver - a potential vagrant to Europe. *Birding World* 8: 458–466.

Birch, A., Lee, C. T. 1997. Arctic and Pacific Loons: field identification. *Birding* 29: 106–115.

Hunter, E. N., Dennis, R. H.. 1972. Hybrid Great Northern Diver × Black-throated Diver in Wester Ross. *Scottish Birds* 7: 89–91.

Kaufmann, K. 1990. *Advanced birding*. Houghton Mifflin, Boston.

Reinking, D. L., S. N. G. Howell. 1993. An Arctic Loon in California. *West. Birds* 24: 189–196.   www.suttoncenter.org/1993_Reinking_and_Howell_Arctic_Loon.pdf

Robertson, I., M. Fraker. 1974. Apparent hybridization between a Common Loon and an Arctic Loon. *Canadian Field-Naturalist*. 88: 367

Russell, R. W. 2002. Pacific Loon (*Gavia pacifica*) and Arctic Loon (*Gavia arctica*). In *The Birds of North America*, No. 657 (A. Poole and F. Gill, eds.). The Birds of North America, Inc., Philadelphia, PA.

Taylor, G., Garner, M. & McLoughlin, J. 2007. The Pacific Diver in North Yorkshire - a new Western Palearctic bird. *Birding World* 20 (1); 20-25

Walsh, T. 1988. Identifying Pacific Loons: some old and new problems. *Birding* 20: 12–28

Pacific Fulmar
Martin Garner

Fulmars tend to be relegated to the status of also-rans in most seawatches, save for the occasional Blue Fulmar being detected. However, several years ago during a monster session off Kilcummin Head, County Mayo in north-westerly gales, a number of us clocked up some 65 Sabine's Gulls, over 1000 Leach's Petrels, 800 Great Skuas and a record-breaking 3,700 Sooty Shearwaters. In the stream of expected celebrity seabirds, some of us also noted the occasional 'extra pale' Fulmar. The following winter brought an adult Thayer's Gull to Killybegs Harbour in County Donegal. Nearby, but almost overlooked, was a dark Fulmar; so dark that it was described as almost blackish by some. The photos of this bird were poor quality distance-shots that prove nothing but nevertheless I am left with the nagging feeling that Pacific Fulmar might have already occurred in the Western Palearctic. So I hope that by flagging its vagrancy potential and key features, we might really nail one!

Geographical range

Pacific Fulmar *Fulmaris glacialis rodgersii* is reported to breed along the coasts of eastern Siberia and Alaska and on many of the islands in the Bering Sea region including the Kurile Islands, north of Japan, Sakhalin, the Commander Islands, the Pribilofs, Wrangle, St. Lawrence and the Aleutians. They migrate long distances, wintering as far south as Japan and off southern Baja California. This is considerably further south than the normal wintering range of Atlantic Fulmar *Fulmaris glacialis glacialis*.

Vagrancy potential

Pacific Fulmar has yet to be recorded in the Western Palearctic. They are known to occur within 600 to 700 miles of Atlantic Fulmars in the western Canadian Arctic. Atlantic Fulmars from this area are known to have occurred around British waters during the wintertime, while young birds are known to disperse widely and travel great distances (Cramp and Simmons 1977). It therefore seems highly feasible for a young Pacific Fulmar to abmigrate into the North Atlantic, and it is perhaps most likely to do so during the winter months.

Dark-morph birds are estimated to constitute 80% of all Pacific Fulmars, but the light-morph birds are the most northerly breeders (the reverse is true in the Atlantic (Palmer 1962)) so it could be argued that any vagrants that reach the Western Palearctic are just as likely to be light-morph, if not more so.

Atlantic and Pacific Fulmars do not overlap in the breeding season and show subtle structural differences as well as normally obvious plumage differences, so they may be good candidates for a taxonomic split.

IDENTIFICATION

Pacific Fulmar shows significant differences in plumage from Atlantic Fulmar as well as subtle differences in bill structure and colouring.

Plumage

The key to Pacific Fulmar identification is to understand that they have more extremes of plumage in both light and dark morphs compared to Atlantic Fulmars. If we take the white-bodied/white-headed Fulmars normally seem around Britain, then pale-morph Pacific Fulmars are even paler (we'll call these birds 'triple lights' or LLL). As well as the head and body being white, there is much patchy, bright white in the mantle, scapulars and upperwing, making a mottled pattern of contrasting white and dark areas. Dark-morph Pacific Fulmars are, on average, darker ('triple darks' or DDD) than dark-morph "Blue" Atlantic Fulmars and often show a subtly browner tone to the dark grey plumage, which becomes most obvious when the plumage is worn.

The single most important plumage feature when attempting to identify a vagrant Pacific Fulmar is the tail. On Atlantic Fulmars the tail is typically rather pale grey and very similar to, or almost concolourous with, the rump. It can be slightly darker but is only marginally so. The whole of the upperparts, rump and tail is usually of the same uniform grey tone, or on some birds the rump and tail can even be slightly paler. However, on Pacific Fulmar the tail is typically the darkest part of the plumage. On some striking-looking pale-morph birds this can amount to an obvious dark tail band contrasting with a white tail base and white rump, whereas on some dark-morph birds the darker tail can be more difficult to discern.

The one caution is the existence of very pale Atlantic Fulmars, which I call Atlantic triple lights. I have seen a number of these birds now, which mimic the palest of the Pacific Fulmars by having large areas of bright white in the upper wing, and an overall more pallid appearance. One such bird was well seen and photographed by Ashley Fisher off the Isles of Scilly. Typically, however, these birds have the same tail and bill colour as other Atlantic Fulmars.

Bill

The bill of an Atlantic Fulmer is typically thick, blunt-ended and varying in colour from olive-green to blue-grey, with an obvious yellow tip. The tubes tend to be darker than the rest of the bill, ranging in tone from yellow-brown to grey-black. In comparison, Pacific Fulmars have a slightly more slender bill, which often looks almost wholly yellow or even orangey-yellow. The tubes are usually more concolourous with the rest of the bill.

Identification summary (features of Pacific Fulmar)

- Plumage extremes greater than Atlantic Fulmars, with whiter and more mottled
- pale morph (triple lights) and darker dark morph (triple darks)
- The main plumage feature is the tail, which is darker than the rest of the upperpart plumage in both light and dark morphs
- Bill is slightly slimmer and of a brighter, more uniform yellow or orange/yellow colour
- Beware of occasional very pale Atlantic Fulmars (Atlantic triple lights)

Finally, and perhaps of no particular use in identification, is a difference in their preferred food. Atlantic Fulmars have a varied diet (although the smaller-billed Atlantic Fulmars of the Canadian Arctic are seemingly more specialised plankton feeders), but Pacific Fulmars have a particular penchant for jellyfish (Palmer 1963)!

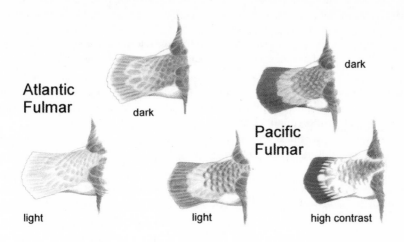

Tail sections and patterns of Atlantic and Pacific Fulmars. There is not much difference in the tails section between paler and darker Atlantic Fulmars and the rump and tail are usually concolourous. There is however considerable variation in the rump and tail pattern of Pacific Fulmar, and the tail (or tail band) is always the darkest part of the plumage, often strikingly so.

References

Cramp, S. & Simmons K. E. L. (eds.) 1977. *The Birds of the Western Palearctic.* Vol. 1. Oxford.
Palmer, R. S. (ED.) *Handbook of North American birds. Volume 1: Loons through flamingos.* New Haven, RI, London. Yale University Press (1962).

Cape Gannet
Martin Garner

The Cape Gannet has flirted with the British List for decades. A specimen said to have been taken on the Bass Rock, Lothian in May 1831 was recently rejected by the BOURC. While the identification of the bird in question is not in doubt, the possibility of the bird having been imported from abroad could not be ruled out. More recently the awareness that some Northern Gannets could, in sub-adult plumage, appear very similar to adult Cape Gannet resulted in a complete cessation of claims.

Unfortunately the identification discussion did not focus on the underwing pattern, which is much more reliable in distinguishing sub-adult Northern Gannets from adult Cape Gannets. This wanderer from the southern oceans surely remains a highly likely vagrant, and in the light of the more recent occurrences of Yellow-nosed Albatross and Masked Booby in Britain, the Cape Gannet deserves to be back on the radar of keen sea watchers throughout northwest Europe.

Geographical range

Cape Gannet *Morus capensis* breeds on six islands on the west and south coasts of South Africa and coastal Namibia between 25° and 35° S. There is also a very small population on St Paul Island, in the Indian Ocean where Australian Gannets *Morus serrator* also occur. The normal winter range extends up the west coast of Africa north to the Gulf of Guinea and, on the east coast, regularly north to Mozambique.

Vagrancy potential

While its normal range is south of the equator, the Cape Gannet is a true oceanic wanderer. It has been recorded on several occasions from Australia, New Zealand, the Indian Ocean, Argentina, Brazil and, more recently, an amazing record of a bird photographed in July 1999 off Northern Peru (Garcia-Godos 2002) and another from Oman in March 2004 (Eriksen 2004). The species is firmly on the Western Palearctic list on the basis of a ringing recovery of a first-year bird at sea off Western Sahara in 1966 at 21° 40' N, which is not far south of the Canaries! There have also been a number of claims from Spain, although only one, a record from the Mediterranean, 30 km east of Tarragona in January 1985, is currently accepted as indeterminate Australian/Cape Gannet (deJuana *et al.* 2001). When you add together the ringing recovery, the far-flung vagrancy patterns of Cape Gannet and the likely mixing of Cape and Northern Gannets off Western Africa, it's worth considering as a very likely vagrant.

IDENTIFICATION

Based on plumage alone it is only possible to attempt identification of adult Cape Gannets which, compared to Northern Gannet, have virtually all black secondaries and all black tail. Both of these feather tracts are white in adult Northern Gannet. However, even an adult Cape Gannet needs to be seen well to rule out a sub-adult Northern Gannet with retained black secondaries and tail feathers. For this it is crucial to see the underwing coverts and check for the presence of dark feathers. A bird showing a full suite of black secondaries and tail and pure white underwing coverts should prove to be an adult Cape Gannet.

For all ages and plumages there are other features which facilitate positive identification. The most important of these is the length of the gular stripe – the strip of bare black skin running through the chin and throat. On Cape Gannet this is three to four times longer than in Northern Gannet. Amazingly close views would be required to see this feature on dark-headed immatures, although in second or third calendar year birds, when the head becomes whiter, the gular stripe should be visible and thus, in the right conditions, some sub-adult plumages of Cape Gannet could be identifiable in the field. Note that whereas Northern Gannets take 4-5 years to reach definitive adult plumage, Cape Gannets take 3-4 years.

A potentially useful feature to help identify Cape Gannet is their (on average) slightly smaller size which is likely to result in them having a slightly 'flappier' flight action or at least a different flap/glide sequence to any accompanying Northern Gannets. A critical examination of flight action should also reveal that, in direct travelling flight, gannets have the habit in most weather conditions of tilting their body first one way and then the other. This means that the birds regularly bank in such a way that the underside of the far wing is visible and could crucially indicate the presence of a fly past adult Cape Gannet. Practice in watching gannets in direct flight and assessing the potential of seeing the patterning in the underwing coverts may prove fruitful.

Juveniles and 1st-2nd calendar year birds

First calendar year birds are the most likely to occur as vagrants as this is the age at which birds disperse most widely (Snow & Perrins 1998). The ringing recovery off Western Sahara was a first-year bird. Currently, birds of this age can only be identified by observation of the length of the gular stripe and with biometrics. Dead or dying immature Gannets are always worthy of careful scrutiny!

Sub-adults

Once the head becomes whiter in the second and third calendar years the diagnostic longer black gular stripe becomes visible. Thus any older immature Gannet, which may have at least attracted initial attention by its smaller size or more flapping flight, should be scrutinised for this feature. To confirm the identification would require very close views to see the gular stripe.

Adults

Again, the diagnostic feature is the longer black gular stripe. This probably needs to be seen to establish a confirmed site record. However an individual adult Cape Gannet could well attract attention long before the black gular stripe is seen.

Compared to Northern Gannets adult Cape Gannets have black secondaries (apart from the innermost, which are white) and, usually, an all-black tail. According to Marchant and Higgins (1990), 89% have an all-black tail, and 11% show one or more white outer tail feathers. The confusion in the North Atlantic is caused by near-adult Northern Gannets which have retained black secondaries and some black tail feathers and therefore superficially resemble adult Cape Gannets. However, immature Northern Gannets, even those very close to full adult plumage, retain the presence of some dark feathering in the underwing coverts even when all of the upperwing coverts appear essentially white.

Differences in the timing of moult between the two species may assist with identification of adults. Northern Gannets complete primary moult from July–September (February) whereas Cape Gannet moult from January to June/July (Snow and Perrins, 1998). Given that the biological clock of a vagrant Cape Gannet in the North Atlantic is likely to be in sync with the austral summer, its state of moult, notably primary moult and body moult affecting colouring on the head, may contrast with accompanying Northern Gannets.

As with birds of other ages, the potentially useful feature of smaller size and more flapping flight of Cape Gannet may also help to positively identify an adult.

Cape and Australasian Gannets have hybridised and the identification of the two species as well as appearance of hybrids is well covered in Robertson and Stephenson (2005).

Identification summary

- Cape Gannets can be identified at all ages, but the youngest birds only at very close range
- All ages may draw attention by their slightly smaller size and more flapping flight
- Sub–adults with pale heads can be identified at close range by their longer gular stripe
- Adults can be identified by all-black primaries and secondaries (apart from innermost) combined with all white underwing coverts and all-black tail
  They may have a different intensity of the yellow on the head compared with accompanying Northern Gannets. The long black gular stripe is diagnostic.

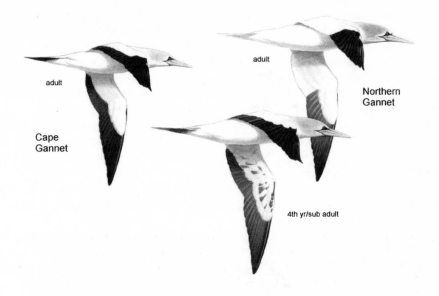

adult

adult

Northern
Gannet

Cape
Gannet

4th yr/sub adult

Adult Cape Gannet flying with adult and near-adult Northern Gannet showing slightly smaller size and unique combination of black primaries, secondaries and tail with all white underwing coverts. Near-adult Northern Gannet also shows black secondaries, some black in tail but always shows some dark marks of immaturity in underwing coverts. As Gannets are observed in travelling flight it is usually easy to see the pattern of the underwing coverts on the far wing as the bird rhythmically tilts its body.

References

deJuana, E, *et al*. 2001. *Ardeola* 49: 141–171.

Eriksen, H. 2004. The first Cape Gannet in Oman and the Middle East. *Sandgrouse* 26: 146-148.

García-Godos, I. 2002. First record of the Cape Gannet *Morus capensis* for Peru and the Pacific Ocean. *Marine Ornithology* 30: 50.

Marchant, S. & Higgins, P. J. (eds). 1990. *Handbook of Australian, New Zealand and Antarctic Birds. Vol. 1. Ratites to Ducks*. Melbourne: Oxford University Press.

Robertson, C. J. R & Stephenson, B. M. 2005. Cape Gannet (*Sula capensis*) breeding at Cape Kidnappers, New Zealand. *Notornis* 52: 238-242.

Paterson, A. M. & Riddiford, N. J. 1990. Does the Cape Gannet enter European waters? *British Birds* 83: 519.

Snow, D. W. & Perrins, C. M. 1998. *The birds of the Western Palearctic: concise edition. Vols. 1-2*. Oxford University Press, Oxford, UK.

Yelkouan Shearwater
Martin Garner

A trip to Corsica in 1983 included the ferry journey from Marseille in southern France. It was a delight to get amazing views of Cory's Shearwater, but more perplexing were the large numbers of apparent 'Manx Shearwaters' here in the Mediterranean! Of course, what I was watching were Yelkouans, seabirds whose true appearance and taxonomic status has been the subject of genuine revelation only in very recent years. The potential of their occurrence and the notion that vagrants might be successfully identifiable is one of the greatest challenges facing observers of seabirds in northwest European waters. With an increasing number of Balearic Shearwaters occurring each summer, the pessimist might argue that Yelkouans are simply not showing up, but the optimist declares: "be prepared, any day now!"

Geographical range

Yelkouan Shearwater *Puffinus yelkouan* is numerically the commonest shearwater in the Mediterranean region, breeding on islands and sea cliffs from Menorca (Balearics) and the Gulf of Marseille eastwards, with largest numbers occurring in the Adriatic, Aegean and Black Seas and off the Levant coast. It winters mostly at sea.

Vagrancy potential

Of the three species of shearwater most commonly occurring in the Mediterranean, two are recorded annually in the North Atlantic. Scopoli's Shearwater *Calonectris diomedia diomedia* (the Cory's of the Mediterranean) regularly leaves the Mediterranean and has occurred off eastern North America, with credible claims off the Isles of Scilly and the west coast of Ireland as well as in the North Sea and the Baltic. Balearic Shearwaters *Puffinus mauretanicus* occur every summer as part of their post-breeding dispersal, normally from late June around Britain and Ireland but some also occur in winter. Since the mid 1990s, there appears to have been a northward shift of the post-breeding population with increasing numbers occurring in northwest European waters (Wynn and Yesou 2007).

However the third 'Mediterranean' shearwater species, the Yelkouan, is not normally known to occur outside of the Mediterranean Sea, though the issue is dogged by the difficulty of its separation from both Manx Shearwater *Puffinus puffinus* and pale examples of Balearic Shearwater. Mixed flocks of Balearic and Yelkouan Shearwaters are the norm in the Western Mediterranean. The species has been recorded regularly off Gibraltar and, more recently, claimed in the North Atlantic off northwest Spain (Gutierrez 2004). This would suggest at least the possibility of occasional occurrence of Yelkouan Shearwaters further north in the Atlantic.

IDENTIFICATION

Identifying a Yelkouan Shearwater in British and Irish waters will realistically require excellent views, forearmed with relevant information and experience of Manx Shearwater. For a claim to be accepted by a national records committee, a photograph is likely to be a prerequisite. Despite considerable concern about their identification in the past,

Yelkouan Shearwaters do have a subtle but distinctive combination of structural, plumage and behavioural characters, which should enable vagrants to be identified away from the Mediterranean. However, until one is recorded alongside Manx Shearwater, the value of some features remains inevitably hypothetical.

It is essential to have a constantly updated knowledge of and familiarity with Manx Shearwater as the "bread and butter" small shearwater to be seen in northwest European waters. This can be facilitated by going beyond simply recording how many Manx are seen on a particular seawatch, to making personal observations loaded with such questions as: What do you notice about flight style? How often do they flap/glide? What does the underwing pattern look like at close range and at greater distance? How do different weather conditions affect flight? Do they behave differently alone or in groups? How does different lighting affect the appearance? These are skills in observation that need to be learnt or honed depending on your present level of seawatching experience. In essence a common bird must be seen with new eyes that are searching for greater knowledge of the common species so the observer is fully trained for that moment when the rarer species really appears.

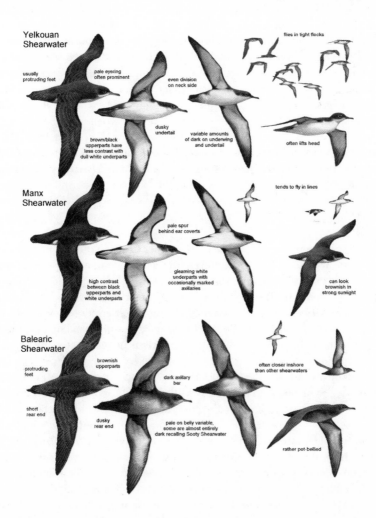

Size and structure

Yelkouan Shearwaters have slightly shorter wings especially the outer 'wing-hand' and shorter tail than Manx and the skull is also shorter with a steeper forehead (Peter Hayman pers. comm., Gutierrez 2004). Although overall biometrics indicate they are very close in size to Manx Shearwater, by themselves Yelkouan have the 'feel' of a three-quarter-sized Manx. On a simple scale of perceived size where Little Shearwater is small and Manx is large, then Yelkouan can feel like a medium–sized small shearwater. This, combined with more prominent pale eye-rings than Manx, can even bring Audubon's Shearwater to mind. Field experience indicates that whereas Manx appear to have longer, thinner and more rakish-looking wings, the wings on Yelkouan look slightly shorter, especially the wing-hand (outer section), and less pointed and more rounded at the tip. Having watched hundreds of Manx and then hundreds of Yelkouans on consecutive days, the impression I have gained is that Yelkouan is clearly a different-looking, overall more compact, bird. Such subtle structural differences have already proved helpful in the Cory's versus Scopoli's identification challenge, in that two apparent examples of Scopoli's seen off the Isles of Scilly and Ireland immediately 'looked different' to the observers using their experience of Cory's. But you have to know Manx well in order to be prepared to notice this kind of difference.

Another structural difference between typical Yelkouan and Manx Shearwaters, that of the longer projection of toes beyond the tail of Yelkouans, is perhaps not a particularly useful feature in most seawatching conditions! When viewed from above, the toes of Yelkouan Shearwater can appear as an obvious peg-like projection but bear in mind that Manx can often show toes projecting somewhat beyond the tail such as when stalling or taking off and, especially, in loafing flight when rafting in numbers. Good views in relaxed travelling flight, at close range such as from a boat, would be needed to establish that the toes on a Yelkouan genuinely extended well beyond the tail (further than on Manx) partly as a function of the shorter tail of that species.

Behaviour

There are some behaviour clues that could make it easier to pick out out a potential Yelkouan Shearwater. Firstly, Yelkouans, in the Mediterranean at least, are much flappier in flight than Manx, apparently in all weather conditions. To put it simply, Yelkouan flap much more than they glide, so the impression is of a shearwater that prefers to flap continually with short glides providing a brief respite in the flapping rhythm. Conversely Manx prefers to glide, seeming to flap only in order to get the bird to the next period of gliding or shearing. Very approximately, Manx glides at least 50% of the time whereas Yelkouan seems to glide only about 30% of the time.

Secondly Yelkouans love to raise their head up and down in travelling flight, a habitual character that can also be observed in flying Red-throated Divers and (more comparatively!) Little and Balearic Shearwaters. It is not a regular habit of Manx which, at most, can be seen to do a little head jerk but you have to look hard and be concentrating to see it. Yelkouans lift their head up and down frequently, most often at either end of a flapping sequence. Yelkouans also have a tendency to turn the head sideways as if looking up to the sky (or down to the sea), which causes the whole face to 'flash' extensive white, again recalling Little Shearwater. Sometimes they raise the head and look upwards at the same time.

The last behavioural feature is probably not much use in UK waters since it applies to the structure of flocks of the two species. Flocks of Yelkouans look like packs of Starlings, bunched close together, with a random shape often rather flat over the water's surface. Manx usually fly in more strung-out lines and, even in flocks, look less 'together' than Yelkouans.

Plumage

Yelkouan versus Manx Shearwater
This is a tricky, subtle and untested identification challenge. Really good views will be needed, preferably alongside Manx Shearwater.

Yelkouan Shearwaters are typically 'pied' looking, appearing from almost blackish to dark grey-brown above and white below. The overall impression is of a shearwater with a clear divide between the dark upperparts and white underparts, which forms a neater, straighter line than on Manx particularly at the head. Most Manx have an obvious white spur which divides the dark ear coverts from the large dark 'half collar' and which intrudes into the neck and breast sides. Manx also tend to have a more obvious white oval on the rear flanks. Thus the dark/white divide on Manx is much more 'interrupted' than on Yelkouan especially over the head, neck and breast area. There is however overlap in these features and some Yelkouan can have more obvious white on the rear flanks. However the difference in face pattern is potentially a very useful feature if seen sufficiently well. To put it simply, the dark/light plumage divide on Yelkouan is a fairly straight line but is more broken on Manx, which has a big patch of white at the rear of the wings and a large block of dark in front of the wings.

The upperpart tone is not generally much help in itself as this is affected not just by lighting and atmospheric conditions but also distance. So both Yelkouans and Manx can look to have either blackish or grey-brown upperparts, the latter frequently the case with more distant Manx seen against the light. Yelkouans do, however, on average, look rather dark greyish-brown at close range and never as contrastingly 'pied' as Manx seen under ideal lighting.

On the underwing, Yelkouans often appear to have a wholly pale underwing (with some diffuse wash) framed in a thin dark fringe all the way around. The underside of the primaries often looks barely darker than the rest of the underwing. In contrast at close range Manx shows gleaming white underwing (contiguous with the white underbody) with blackish rim and more contrasting and extensive sooty-black underside to the primaries. Close views are needed, as the contrast on Manx is less obvious at greater distance. A dark diagonal line on the underwing coverts is a feature found in both species and perhaps only useful in identification of those Yelkouans that have the dark bar particularly well developed. A more useful diagnostic difference is found in the undertail coverts. Many Yelkouans (approximately 70% - pers. obs.) have dark undertail coverts whereas on Manx the undertail coverts are always white.

Other more minor features include the tendency for Yelkouans to have a more prominent pale eye-ring, recalling Audubon's Shearwater. Together with the neater divide between the dark upperparts and pale underparts this can create a rather distinctive facial appearance of the species.

Yelkouan versus Balearic Shearwater
In direct comparison, Balearics are usually a clearly bigger-bodied, more 'pot-bellied', longer-winged seabird with a more powerful energetic flight than Yelkouans. In the same flight path, Balearics normally seem to overtake Yelkouans. The same features of Balearics are noticeable when alongside Manx. Establishing size and comparative flight style could be

an important first step in eliminating a pale-bodied Balearic Shearwater. Furthermore even the palest Balearics still tend to show more diffuse dark patterning around the head and neck, smoky dark feathering in the axillaries and a dirtier 'rear end' than most Yelkouans.

Although most Yelkouan Shearwaters appear to be typically cleanly 'pied'-looking, and therefore unlike most Balearics, there is some variation away from this standard type. Personal observations (in early June) have revealed that some (20-30%) appear slightly less clear-cut having just a slightly darker wash to the underwing and flanks with a more conspicuous dark bar on the underwing coverts. Two individuals have been seen which were disconcertingly indistinguishable on plumage from pale Balearic Shearwater, but were of the same size, structure and flight style as other Yelkouans alongside (pers. obs., Ian Lewington pers comm.). The reasons for these variations are unknown. Some may be age-related. Recent studies have documented the occurrence of birds from Menorca with Yelkouan-like plumage but with biometrics and genetics intermediate between Balearic and Yelkouan Shearwaters (c.f. Wynn and Yesou 2007). Clearly there is much to be discovered!

Key features of Yelkouan Shearwater

- Although approximately the same size, they look like a three-quarter-sized Manx with shorter looking wing-hand and more rounded wing tip
- Flight style more 'flappy' with less gliding (versus Manx which flap less and glide more)
- Head regularly raised in flight (not seen in Manx)
- Approximately 70% have at least some dark in undertail coverts (all-white in Manx)
- Neater line dividing dark and light plumage areas produces different 'face' pattern and straighter line of contrast, lacking Manx's white spur and dark breast sides which create an interrupted pattern
- Diffuse grey/white underwing with thin dark rim (versus Manx bright white underwing and contrast with darker underside of primaries)
- Longer peg-like projection of toes than Manx but needs close views
- Structurally slightly smaller and slighter than Balearic with slower flight
- Cleaner line dividing the dark and light plumage areas around the head and neck usually lacking the more diffuse patterning in this area shown on Balearic
- Usually less dark on axillaries compared to most Balearics

References

Garner, M. 2005. Identifying Yelkouan Shearwaters. www.birdguides.com

Gutierrez, R. 2004. Identification of Yelkouan, Balearic and Manx Shearwaters. *Birding World* 17: 111-122.

Wynn, R. B. & Yesou, P. 2007. The Changing Status of the Balearic Shearwater in northwest European waters. *British Birds* 100: 392-406.

Cormorant races
Martin Garner

Dynamic changes are happening to the two forms (or species) of Cormorant that occur in north-west Europe, and they are happening right now! If the breeding range expansion of continental Cormorants in NW Europe continues apace, the North Atlantic Cormorant could become extinct or at least restricted to Iceland and North America. Aware of the incoming tide of colonising Continental Cormorants I set myself the task in 1998 of finding the first Continental Cormorants (ssp. *sinensis*) to be seen in Ireland. A bit of prudent research meant it was a bit of a 'no-brainer'. There was already a single record of an individual from Lough Neagh (presumably found dead) whose ring declared it was a *sinensis* all the way from Denmark. Well if you can get a ringed bird...how many are going unnoticed? (The same supposition had already proved its worth in helping to find the first Caspian Gulls for the UK.) It was no surprise that, upon visiting a large roost of Cormorants inland from the south Down coast, up to five *sinensis* birds were found. Following the usual incredulity and suspicion that surrounds such claims, *sinensis* Cormorants are now regularly observed in Ireland.

I am convinced there is still much to be learnt about the locally changing dynamics at county and even local patch level of the two Cormorants. Therefore I endeavour to record the specific identify of each Cormorant that I encounter in the Sheffield area. If at some stage they are split into two species there will, of course, be a surge of interest from those unaware of historical local patterns, and it will be pioneer observers who provide the data. Of course, those who look at Cormorants more carefully are all the more likely to be those who locate Britain's next Double-crested Cormorant (and be familiar enough with the *sinensis* lookalikes not to be fooled!).

The following is written with special thanks to Richard Millington who really blazed a trail with these birds and helped me over repeated phone calls to understand the differences properly and find the Irish birds. He is directly or indirectly responsible for most of the material here.

Geographical range

The North Atlantic Cormorant *Phalacrocorax carbo carbo* is essentially coastal and cliff-nesting, breeding around the North Atlantic coasts of northern France, Britain, Ireland, Iceland, Norway, and the Kola Peninsula in north-west Russia and across to Greenland and eastern North America. Away from these areas it is a rare bird.

The previously documented breeding range of Continental Cormorant *Phalacrocorax carbo sinensis* is from Belgium in the west right through the Black and Caspian Sea regions, to Central Asia and China, and south to Indonesia. In Western Europe it ranges north to the Baltic region and south to the Mediterranean.

Continental Cormorants have undergone a massive range expansion since 1965 following a reduction in persecution. The first effects of this expansion in Britain began at Abberton Reservoir, Essex in 1981 when a tree-nesting colony of Continental Cormorants was formed. By 2002 no fewer than 17 inland colonies had been established in Britain, with, to date, an estimated breeding population of 1,400 birds. Most of these birds are considered to be Continental Cormorants. In Norfolk there are now 50-100 pairs of *sinensis* breeding annually but with no real evidence of interbreeding despite *carbo* appearing in the main colony at Holkham (Millington pers. comm.).

To casual observers, in many inland counties, the Cormorant has gone from being a scarce, or even rare, bird to one which is much more frequently recorded. Continental Cormorants are highly dispersive migrants, so the possibility of one reaching Iceland and even North America, should be borne in mind!

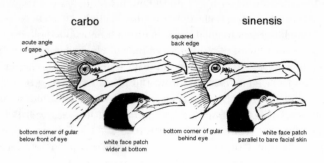

Diagram by Richard Millingtom

IDENTIFICATION

The notion that these two Cormorants could represent two different species has good credentials already. They have been shown to have similar genetic divergence to that found between Hooded and Carrion Crows (Goostrey *et al.* 1998), which have been recognized as two separate species for some time (Knox *et al.* 2002). They have a number of differences in structure and plumage. There are degrees of variation in these characters, which means that any one of them (apart from the gular angle) can only be seen as a 'soft' feature, i.e. one that is somewhat supportive or indicative of identification. The only singly reliable structural feature for identification, when correctly assessed, is the gular angle. However, the subtle differences created by the 'soft' features combine to produce an appearance in individuals of each type of Cormorant, which, with practice, helps to render many birds readily identifiable. Use of the illustrations while reading the text on gular angle and facial features should hopefully bring light to an otherwise complex subject

Gular angle

Learning to assess the gular angle is essential when learning to identify these Cormorants. While the descriptions of the angles and precise measurements may seem complicated and convoluted, in reality the 'reading' (assessment) of the gular angle is normally quite easy once understood and quickly identifies many individuals almost immediately.

In the hand and on specimens, a gular pouch angle of 65° or less (when measured between the gape and the rear edge of the bare skin) indicates *carbo*, whereas a gular pouch angle of 73° or more indicates *sinensis*. Although the gular feature was first introduced by Per Alström over twenty years ago, it has only recently been quantified. Scientific analysis has arrived at the conclusion that the gular angle (when formulated in combination with bill structure) can correctly identify over 98% of birds of known sex (see Newson *et al.* 2005).

When observing birds in the field it is helpful to develop a mental image of the typical gular shapes of both forms. Various words can be used to describe the mental image of the gular shapes – 'squared' for *sinensis* and more 'acute' for *carbo* being examples. A good rule of thumb is that the rear edge of bare skin below the gape angles sharply forward on *carbo* and is nearly perpendicular (vertical) on *sinensis*. An additionally very helpful feature is the alignment of the bottom 'rear corner point' (Albione 2005) of the gular pouch in relation to the eye. When a bird's head is in profile (with the bill held roughly horizontally) this point is directly below the eye in *carbo* and clearly set further back than the eye in *sinensis*.

The reason for the differences in gular shape between *carbo* and *sinensis* may be down to a simple, practical function. One of the functions of the gular pouch may be to dissipate heat, particularly when the birds are panting. It would make sense for birds in hotter countries to have more gular skin to facilitate the rapid loss of heat and less gular skin in cold climates where heat needs to be retained more. This view appears to be validated by Newson *et al.* (2005), who found that "male *carbo* from England and Wales had a mean gular pouch angle of 61.3°: in Scotland it was 59°, whilst in Iceland it was 52.1°." Icelandic birds apparently have the smallest area of bare skin. Conversely in *sinensis* the gular pouch angle (and presumably the overall area of bare skin) increased eastwards towards hotter climes: "…male *sinensis* from the Netherlands and Denmark had a mean gular pouch angle of 87°; in Iraq it was 103°, whilst in Vietnam it was 127°."

Other facial features
The shape of the white face patch, which covers the area of cheeks and throat, is also indicative and contributes to the overall distinctive differences between the two Cormorants. In *carbo* the white face patch is narrower at the top (behind the eye) and clearly broadens towards the bottom (at the throat sides) which produces a shape rather incongruent when compared with the bare skin around the face. In *sinensis* the white face patch is of similar width from top to bottom and runs essentially parallel with the bare skin around the face.

There are also general differences in the colour of the gular skin and the extension of this around the eye. There is a tendency for the gular skin of *carbo* to be a rather insipid yellow, versus the brighter, more vivid 'egg-yolk' yellow in many *sinensis*. Incidentally, some *sinensis* also show more bare skin in front of and around the eye than in *carbo*, giving the impression that the bird is wearing colourful plastic goggles.

Size and structure

On average *carbo* is larger than *sinensis* but, in both forms, males average larger and females smaller. Such sexual dimorphism produces much overlap in size between small female *carbo* and large male *sinensis* and renders size assessment alone only useful as a feature at the ends of the scale. However there are also subtle structural differences that become more apparent with practice and can then be applied to many individuals.

Large male *carbo* tend to show most clearly the *carbo* 'character' of a large flat-topped (ironed out) head with an angular rear crown set on a thick muscular neck. The bill of such a bird will be long and thick (particularly at the base) and robust-looking. Combined with a bulky body and proportionately short tail the overall character is complete. In comparison, a small female *sinensis* will showcase the *sinensis* 'character' of a rather more rounded head with a slimmer, shorter bill (with a concave sweep to the profile of the culmen in some). It will have a rather slim neck and body, which together with bill and head shape can cause some birds to appear remarkably Shag-like. It will also have a proportionally slightly longer tail.

Moult

Juvenile *sinensis* tend to have a browner wash to the underparts compared with *carbo* in Western Europe. It has also been reported (Millington 2005) that the moult strategies between *sinensis* and *carbo* are "very different". In essence it seems *sinensis* may moult more rapidly. More work is needed to find out if this factor would provide useful clues for identification in the field.

Plumage

Gloss colour

This is perhaps more important than moult. The shiny gloss to the body plumage is variable in colour in both forms of Cormorant. The colour is most evident in the spring when some *carbo* can show a particularly bluish-purple gloss colour which, seen alongside the equally vivid bottle-green glossed *sinensis* would seem to be quite obvious. However there is overlap and, especially outside the spring, the character is of little value in separating the two.

White-headedness

A long-held myth was that fully white-headed birds were *sinensis*. In fact, many male *carbo* have a full 'bonnet' of white filoplumes. These are probably older birds which tend to breed earlier than younger males. Nevertheless, the character has some value. The white filoplumes appear just prior to the onset of egg-laying. As the tree-nesting *sinensis* start to breed over one month earlier than *carbo*, any Cormorant in December to January with a full white head is likely to prove to be *sinensis* when other features are checked.

Identification summary (*sinensis* versus *carbo*)

- Gular pouch more extensive with an angle that looks more squared in *sinensis* compared with the smaller and acutely angled gular pouch of *carbo*
- Bottom rear corner of the gular pouch is clearly set further back than the eye in *sinensis* whereas in *carbo* it is directly below the eye
- White face patch in *sinensis* is of similar width from top to bottom and parallel with the bare facial skin, whereas in *carbo* it is obviously wider at the bottom and not parallel with bare facial skin
- The 'character' of smaller *sinensis* is obvious with rounded head, slimmer, shorter bill, slimmer neck and body, and longer tail. The 'character' of larger male *carbo* is equally obvious with flat-topped angular head, thick neck, longer and thicker bill, bulky body and slightly shorter tail
- Gular skin tends to be brighter yellow and with more bare skin around eyes on *sinensis*
- In extreme spring plumages *carbo* can be glossed very blue-purple and *sinensis* has bottle-green gloss, but much overlap
- Birds with full white 'bonnet' in December to January probably *sinensis*, otherwise feature not useful outside this period
- Juvenile *sinensis* tend to have a browner wash to the underparts than *carbo* in Western Europe and also moult more rapidly.

References

Albione, M. 2005. Cormorant Identification: a different angle. *Birding World* 18 262.

Goostrey, A., Carss, D. N., Noble, L. R. & Piertney, S. B. 1998. Population introgression and differentiation in the Great Cormorant *Phalacrocorax carbo* in Europe. *Molecular Ecology* 7: 329-338.

Knox, A. G., Collinson, M., Helbig, A. J., Parkin, D. P. & Sangster, G. 2002. Taxonomic recommendations for British birds. *Ibis* 144: 707-710.

Millington, R. 2005. Identification of North Atlantic and Continental Cormorants. *Birding World* 18: 112-123.

Newson, S. E., Ekins, G. R., Russell, I. C. & Sellers, R. M. 2005. Separation of North Atlantic and Continental Cormorants. *Birding World* 18 107-111.

American (Laughing) Moorhen
Martin Garner

A hunch is how it usually starts. I think the guys I was with in southern Ontario, Canada, in spring 1986 must have thought I was daft to be harping on about how the Moorhens seemed to look different from our British birds, when nearby there were up to seven colourful *Dendroica* warblers as well as Yellow-headed Blackbirds to look at. I eventually came to the conclusion that they were a bit leggier and more gallinule-like, with more 'square-topped' frontal shields than our British birds. However with some variation in the shield character in both the Old and New World forms I wondered if it would ever be possible to identify a vagrant '*cachinnans*' Moorhen (or Common Gallinule, as it used to be called) in Western Europe. I sort of gave up until the British Birdwatching Fair in 2006. There I met Mark Constantine launching one of the most pioneering birding books of recent times. He and the 'Sound Approach' guys introduced me to a fresh perspective on the American Moorhens… they called differently! So, with vagrancy potential perhaps somewhere between American Coot and American Purple Gallinule and a suite of structural, plumage and vocal characters to work with, the only question remaining is where and when will the first one be found?

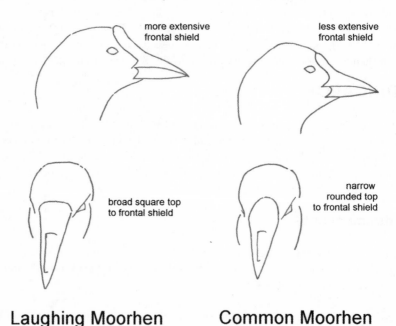

more extensive frontal shield

less extensive frontal shield

broad square top to frontal shield

narrow rounded top to frontal shield

Laughing Moorhen   **Common Moorhen**

Diagram by Mick Cunningham

Geographical range

Laughing Moorhen *Gallinula chloropus cachinnans* has a wide-ranging, scattered breeding distribution. It is essentially resident across the southern and western USA into Mexico and

Central America, Bermuda and the West Indies. However, it is largely a summer migrant across much of the central and eastern USA and eastern Canada, reaching the extreme south of Quebec, eastern New Brunswick and western Nova Scotia to the north and the Atlantic coast states to Florida and the Gulf region to the south where birds are again resident. Central and eastern populations migrate to winter in coastal areas from North Carolina to Texas, with some reaching Panama, the West Indies and South America (Bannor *et al.* 2002). It is a casual visitor to eastern Quebec, Newfoundland and Prince Edward Island in the summer.

Vagrancy potential

To some extent the vagrancy potential of Laughing Moorhen can be measured by comparing it with its two sibling North American species which have already crossed the Atlantic on several occasions, the American Coot and American Purple Gallinule. American Coot *Fulica americana* is a medium- to long-distance migrant, which is being increasingly detected in recent years with about seven records in Britain as well as having reached the Azores (20 records), Spain, Ireland, Iceland and the Faeroes. American Purple Gallinule *Porphyrio martinica* is a short-distance migrant that has nevertheless reached the Azores (6 records), Iceland (2) and Britain, Switzerland, Norway and Spain (1 each).

In comparison, the Laughing Moorhen is a medium-distance migrant in the eastern part of the range, but a proportion of the population may be long-distance migrants if, as suggested, some reach South America. On range alone it seems a considerably more likely vagrant than American Purple Gallinule. It has already reached Greenland as a vagrant (Bannor *et al.* 2002), but a complete lack of awareness has meant that very few birders will have it on their 'radar' for a bird to look out for in the Western Palearctic.

IDENTIFICATION

The subject of the field separation of Eurasian and Laughing Moorhen is still in its infancy. The following ideas will need to be tested and developed. Direct comparison of a potential vagrant Laughing Moorhen alongside Eurasian Moorhen would seem to be an essential starting point. A vagrant is most likely to attract attention by its size and structure but might, by the extra-astute observer, be located by its call.

Importance of calls

The significant difference in calls between Eurasian and Laughing Moorhens was first highlighted by Constantine *et al.* (2006). Their commentary on discovering the differences in call is worth quoting in full:

"Birders can play a part in 'uncovering new biodiversity', not least because their increased mobility is now taking them abroad more often. The observation that 'this species sounds totally different back home' might just be the first of many steps towards realising that this is not the same species, even if its plumage appears totally indistinguishable. The separation of Nearctic from Palearctic taxa has also been and probably will continue to be the most productive areas of opportunity for budding taxonomists. So, it is hardly surprising that another side effect of allowing Old World participants to take part in the World Series of Birding in New Jersey, was the realisation that in the spring the North American Common Moorhen Gallinula chloropus cachinnans *sounded nothing like its European counterpart.* G. c. chloropus.

In New Jersey, Common Moorhens are migrant opportunists, waiting for Beavers to create new ponds, which they quickly populate. An uncommon species, its habitat preference seems to encourage a need to attract a mate or defend territory in a different way. In crepuscular, nocturnal and marsh-dwelling birds like petrels, owls and rails, including Moorhen, sound is of more importance for pair formation than appearance. Consequently differences in sounds can indicate that speciation has taken place sooner than any other feature.

Whoever named the North American subspecies of moorhen cachinnans must have suspected that it was something quite different. As explained with the gulls (Caspian Gull), cachinnans means 'laughing' and this American has a laugh, louder and somehow more brash, never heard from moorhens in the Western Palearctic. The Laughing Moorhen sounds far more rail-like."

Size and structure

In direct comparison to Eurasian Moorhen, a Laughing Moorhen will clearly appear to be a larger bird with an obviously longer bill, a more extensive, square-topped frontal shield (especially in adult plumage) and, most notably, longer tarsus and toes, producing a leggy, more gallinule-like gait.

Shape of bill and frontal shield

It is worth detailing the exact differences in the shape of the bill and frontal shield. The frontal shield of adult Laughing Moorhen is larger and more extensive with a subtly different shape compared with Eurasian Moorhen. It reaches higher up the forehead, being broadest at the top, with a straight top edge and squared-off corners. In comparison, the frontal shield of Eurasian birds is typically less extensive and narrows to a rounded top. The larger frontal shield is also accompanied by a slightly lumpier forehead, which peaks at the front in Laughing Moorhen, being more gently rounded in Eurasian birds. The difference is subtle and may not always be apparent, but, when it is, the forehead shape can be somewhat reminiscent to that shown by a Crested Coot *Fulica cristata*. The difference in shield shape is also discernible in some specimens of first winter birds even when the shield is not fully grown. This may be a useful distinction in the field for younger birds but needs further testing.

Plumage

There are no really obvious differences in the plumages between Eurasian and Laughing Moorhens of any age. Adult Laughing Moorhens do have a slightly warmer, browner (less olive or oily) tone to the upperparts which may be detectable in the field. From specimens it appears that some young birds are slightly paler above and below compared with their old world counterparts.

Key features of Laughing Moorhen

- Larger bodied with obviously longer tarsus and toes
- Frontal shield more extensive with wider, squared-off top end (usually obvious in adults but may also be useful in some first winters)
- Bill longer

- Plumage of adults is warmer and browner above
- Certain calls clearly different; a continuous series of connected notes sounding like brash, nasal 'laughter'

There may be other structural and plumage features indicative of Laughing Moorhen, to varying degrees, but there needs to be further research into their variation within both forms to establish their usefulness.

References

Bannor, B. K. & Kiviat, E. 2002. Common Moorhen (*Gallinula chloropus*). In *The Birds of North America, No. 685* (A. Poole & F. Gill, eds.). The Birds of North America, Inc., Philadelphia, PA.

Constantine, M. and the Sound Approach. 2006. *The Sound Approach to Birding. A Guide to Understanding Bird Sound.* The Sound Approach. Dorset.

White-fronted Geese of four kinds
Richard Millington

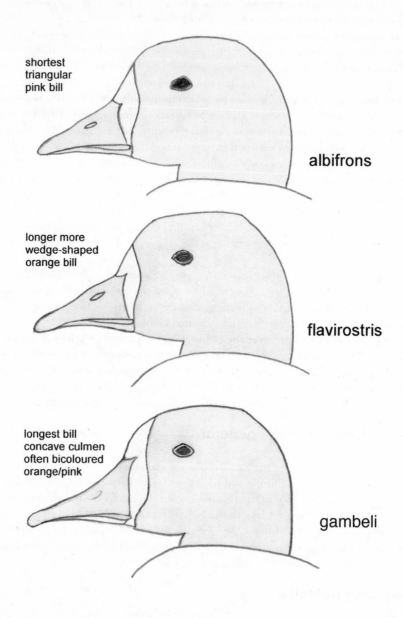

shortest
triangular
pink bill

albifrons

longer more
wedge-shaped
orange bill

flavirostris

longest bill
concave culmen
often bicoloured
orange/pink

gambeli

Diagram by Martin Garner

Sometimes I'm asked "What are you looking into at the moment?" Well presently the White-fronted Geese are right near the top of my list. I think there are vagrant forms occurring, possibly even annually, in the Western Palearctic, despite the fact that none has yet made it onto any national list. Those wanting to be 'in on the action' could do considerably worse than make purposeful searches of the flocks of Greenland White-fronted Geese in Ireland or Islay for *gambeli*, or the wintering flocks of European White-fronts for a vagrant *frontalis* or *albicans*. Single White-fronted Geese occurring in 'odd locations' or notably early or late in the season also invite careful scrutiny.

An indication of just how easily these birds may be being overlooked can be illustrated by a recent experience of mine at the Slimbridge Wildfowl and Wetlands Trust reserve in Gloucestershire. There, on 15th February 2007, I found an 'odd'-looking adult goose among the European White-fronts. It had a squarer-shaped, darker head, prominent yellow orbital rings and a shorter and steeper-looking pink bill. The white on the forehead was also more extensive. Thus it had characters associated with an adult Lesser White-fronted Goose, except that it was just too big and slightly odd looking; almost like a Lesser White-front on steroids! The bird matched the appearance of an individual seen in the previous winter by the WWT staff and our common conclusion was that it was most likely a Lesser White-fronted/Eurasian White-fronted Goose hybrid. I photographed the bird and was to discover subsequently that I was the only person during that whole winter to see it. Was it only present for the few hours of my visit? I doubt it. I suspect it had been there for anyone who had expectations that flocks of geese contain interesting and rare vagrants, minding the fact that some are subtler in appearance than others! Expectation is vital in this game.

While there is still no absolute agreement as to the precise breeding ranges, practical identification criteria or (sub) specific status of the various forms of white-fronted goose nevertheless Richard Millington here presents the most up-to-date coverage of the variety and complexity of the beautiful White-fronted Geese.

Some will want to skim over the account and go straight to the key features, but for those who really want to get into the subject, this is the most in-depth account to be found anywhere, based on the author's typically thorough research as well as first-hand experiences of all the forms covered. The taxonomy is a vexing and complex subject and the conclusions here are tentative, inviting further investigation. Enjoy! *Martin Garner*

Geographical range - general

The white-fronted goose complex occupies a circumpolar breeding range, although it is absent from northern Europe and the range is interrupted in eastern North America. White-fronted geese breed in the Palearctic from the Kanin Peninsula, north-west Russia eastwards to easternmost Siberia. In the Nearctic, they breed in Alaska and Arctic Canada eastwards to north-west Hudson Bay, with an isolated population in western Greenland. All white-fronted geese are highly migratory and spend the winter at comparatively mild latitudes well south of their breeding range.

Vagrancy potential

Besides exceptional records of European White-fronted Goose *Anser albifrons albifrons* and Greenland White-fronted Geese *A. a. flavirostris* occurring outside of their normal winter ranges, there are at least three other forms of white-fronted goose which are likely to occur as vagrants in Western Europe and indeed have already been suspected in Britain at least. These are Gambel's White-fronted Goose *A. a. gambeli,* American White-fronted

Goose *A. a. frontalis* and Asian White-fronted Goose *A. a. albicans*. A brief summary of the vagrancy potential of each of these forms may be apposite:

Gambel's White-fronted Goose
A 'Perry River White-front' (*gambeli*) was present amongst the European White-fronted Geese at Slimbridge WWT, England (and shown to many visitors by Peter Scott) between January and March 1977. Two juvenile white-fronted geese in Oxfordshire from 3rd to 25th May 2004 were initially identified as Greenland White-fronted Geese. However their overall structure, plumage and behaviour (preferring rank, marshy habitat and upending to feed on aquatic vegetation) all support their identification as *gambeli*. (Ian Lewington pers comm.). The apparently late appearance was consistent with the normal northward migration of *frontalis* at the same latitude in North America (the migration of *gambeli* specifically is less well known). They appear to be the most likely vagrant White-fronted Geese to be occurring in Britain and are arguably the easiest to identify but have probably been overlooked.

American White-fronted Goose
There have been no claims of this form in the Western Palearctic. It is, however, a long-distance migrant of the Pacific and Central flyways of North America and should be considered a possible vagrant. It is closest in appearance to the Asian White-fronted Goose, and these two, while distinct, have population units which are very similar in appearance and are often collectively referred to as a single taxon: *frontalis*, or the 'Pacific White-fronted Goose'.

Asian White-fronted Goose
This form, from the Eastern Palearctic, has been suspected in Europe on occasion (including at Holkham, Norfolk in January 1999 (pers. obs.)).

All migrant geese exhibit some degree of vagrancy potential, and there are various mechanisms facilitating this. Spring migrants may overshoot the breeding grounds. Autumn migrants may be disorientated by adverse weather, causing some individuals to appear off-course. Frequently, 'lost' individuals of one species (especially young birds separated from their parents) will attach themselves to populations of another type of goose, and then follow these 'carrier species' to alien wintering grounds. The ability of some birds to return to their natural route has been demonstrated, but so has permanent 'adoption'.

White-fronted geese are as prone to abmigration as any other migrant goose. Within the range of a single subspecies, some birds are known to 'population hop', i.e. move from one population of birds to another. For example, individual *albifrons* ringed at Slimbridge WWT, England, have been seen in Italy, Greece and Macedonia in subsequent winters (Wernham *et al.* 2002). In southwest Europe, vagrant white-fronted geese occasionally reach Iberia. Three *flavirostris*, ringed in Greenland, have been recovered in eastern Canada, presumably carried there by Canada Geese (which also breed in western Greenland). Three colour-marked geese from the Cook Inlet, Alaska have been seen in Kansas (in December) and Texas (shot in November and December), so it could be that some Tule Geese (*A. a. elgasi*; see below) join the Central Flyway. Although it has been suggested that these birds may not have been bona-fide Tule Geese, it would appear that there is some interchange of geese between the Pacific and Central Flyways. Also in the USA, white-fronted geese frequently stray to the eastern seaboard, even reaching Bermuda (Raine 2003). Occasional white-fronted geese are seen associating with wintering flocks of other geese, which in Britain includes

Greylag *Anser anser*, Pale-bellied and Dark-bellied Brent Goose *Brant bernicla/B. hrota* and Pink-footed Goose *Anser brachyrhynchus*. These birds are usually identified as European or Greenland White-fronted Geese. Sometimes, a gathering of one form of white-fronted goose will attract some individuals of another form, though how they find each other is something of a mystery. They could be lost birds wandering alone until coming across others of 'their kind' or, as has been shown with vagrant *flavirostris* in Norfolk, they could be birds carried off-course by one species (Pink-footed Goose in the Norfolk instance), then 'jumping host' whilst at the wintering grounds.

The forms breeding in northern Canada and wintering as far south as Mexico (*gambeli* and *frontalis*) undertake amongst the longest migration of any geese in the world, and share their route with Snow Goose *Anser caerulescens* (a proven visitor to Europe). Greater awareness of their vagrancy potential and appearance will hopefully result in more records and greater understanding of their appearance and occurrence patterns.

Taxonomic history

The taxonomic history of the white-fronted goose complex is a fascinating one and, even though the subject has been addressed several times (e.g. Todd 1950, Mooij & Zöckler 2000), it remains a complicated issue. Indeed, a number of different arrangements have been proposed in the last decade alone, so it is useful to briefly review the taxonomic history of this species and its nomenclatural vicissitudes.

Despite being known to the ancient Egyptians in 2530 BC, White-fronted Goose *Anser albifrons* was first described to western science by Johannes Scopoli in 1769, from a specimen presumed to have been taken in northern Italy (Scopoli 1769). Nearly a century later, in 1852, Karel Hartlaub examined three specimens in the Berlin Museum (two juveniles said to have been taken in Texas and one adult said to have been taken in 'the south' of North America) and declared that they represented a different (North American) form of white-fronted goose (Hartlaub 1852). He named his discovery *Anser gambelli* but it has recently been argued that *gambeli* is more correct, and this is the spelling used hereafter. At around the same time, two juvenile white-fronted geese taken in North America (including the still extant 'type' from New Mexico) were named *Anser frontalis* (Baird, Cassin & Lawrence 1858).

Subsequent authors were rather reluctant to accept the existence of any distinct Nearctic form that was truly separable from *albifrons*, but, in 1916, two forms of white-fronted goose were discovered to be wintering in California, one of which was peculiarly large. A study of these geese (Swarth & Bryant 1917) concluded that the large birds (known then as 'Tule Geese') were of the subspecies *A. a. gambeli* (and the same as that described by Hartlaub 65 years earlier), while the smaller birds were of the subspecies *A. a. albifrons* (in accordance with a series of measurements published by Alphéraky in 1905). This was believed at the time to represent an extension of the wintering range of Hartlaub's mysterious *gambeli*, previously only known from east of the Rocky Mountains (i.e. the three Berlin Museum specimens). No breeding range was then known for these birds.

In 1929, Nagamichi Kuroda, who acknowledged the existence of the two forms as described by Swarth & Bryant (the circumpolar *albifrons* and the larger Californian-wintering *gambeli*), visited Berlin Museum in order to investigate the subspecific validity of *gambeli*. He measured the mounted specimens said to be Hartlaub's types, but regarded his new measurements of these specimens to be typical of *albifrons* and thereby invalidating the existence of *gambeli* (Kuroda 1929). There was a discrepancy here, as Kuroda believed the differences between his measurements and the larger ones of Hartlaub could not be easily explained. Something was amiss. Had Hartlaub's description really been based on the three birds Kuroda examined 77 years later, or had the original type specimens been substituted during the intervening time?

The middle of the 20th century was a busy time for students of white-fronted goose taxonomy. In 1948 a new form, Greenland White-fronted Goose *A. a. flavirostris,* was formally described for the first time (Dalgety & Scott 1948). These authors repeated the view of earlier authors that the American and Eurasian populations of *albifrons* were indistinguishable from each other. Just two years later, W. E. Clyde Todd published his belief, based on his study of a series of appropriate skins, that the smaller of the North American forms *was* in fact distinguishable from the *albifrons* of Europe. He deemed the name *A. a. frontalis* to be that most appropriate for this now identifiable subspecies (citing the source of the name to be Baird 1858). In the same paper, Todd supported the recognition of *gambeli* and addressed the mystery of Hartlaub's specimens, suggesting that Hartlaub had actually been accustomed to using the 'French inch' (somewhat larger than the English inch!). Thus, the metric equivalents of the original measurements were even larger than Kuroda had calculated in 1929, resulting in an even greater discrepancy (Todd 1950). Because he believed that the discrepancy between Hartlaub's original data and Kuroda's more recent measurements proved it, Todd unequivocally stated that 'there can be no question that the specimens in the Berlin Museum purporting to be his types are not his types at all.'

So now there were up to four forms of white-fronted goose: *albifrons, gambeli, frontalis* and *flavirostris,* yet other contemporary authors (e.g. Burturlin 1952) were still inclined to recognise fewer (although there was at least a belief that *albifrons* nested only to the Taimyr Peninsula, being replaced further east by *frontalis*). In July 1964, an expedition to the MacKenzie River delta, north-west Canada, discovered a form that was larger and darker than typical *frontalis* breeding in the taiga habitat of the Old Crow Flats. Some of these birds were collected alive and others were banded (and subsequently recovered along the Central Flyway), and the conclusion was that these birds conformed to the original description of *gambeli* (Elgas 1968). Since Hartlaub's original specimens were Central Flyway birds, this seemed a neat enough solution.

In 1975, Jean Delacour & S. Dillon Ripley again recognised *albifrons, frontalis* and *flavirostris,* but proposed an alternative scenario for the larger white-fronted geese occurring in North America, which did not encompass them all as *gambeli.* They did not consider the differences in Hartlaub's measurements of the specimens in the Berlin Museum to be so great as to imply that they were not the same as the specimens still present there, and they believed they remained valid; there had been no substituting of specimens after all. (Here it is worth remembering that, in 1929, Kuroda had been working under the assumption that the geese he was familiar with in eastern Asia were *albifrons*; only subsequently were they designated as *frontalis.*) Delacour & Ripley offered a new perspective on the problem and suggested that what all previous authors had overlooked was one simple fact: three populations of white-fronted goose existed on the mainland of North America. In addition to the tundra-breeding *frontalis* of the Arctic coast and the taiga-breeding *gambeli* of Yukon Territory, a third and separate form existed to the west of the main mountain ranges, the Tule Goose *A. a. elgasi* (Delacour & Ripley 1975). Although *elgasi* was assumed to breed in the taiga zone of Alaska, it was not until as recently as July 1979 that breeding Tule Geese were finally discovered at Redoubt Bay, on the west side of the Cook Inlet, in southern Alaska (Todd 1996).

This arrangement of five forms world-wide (*albifrons, frontalis, gambeli, elgasi* and *flavirostris*) is published in most of the modern literature (e.g. Cramp & Simmons 1977, del Hoyo *et al.* 1992) and is the subspecific delineation of the white-fronted goose complex most familiar to birders today. More recent studies have, however, questioned the validity of this subdivision of the complex, and Greenland White-fronted Goose at least appears to deserve specific status. Instead of being based on morphological characters alone, it is now proposed that subdivision based largely on the distribution of the main populations during their annual life cycles is preferable. On this basis, Mooij & Zöckler (2000) recognise the Asian population of *frontalis* as a separate form, *A. a. albicans*. Certainly it does seem sensible to factor in all the variables (e.g. breeding biology, habitat selection and migratory routes, in addition to morphology) when assessing the subdivision of the white-fronted goose complex, at least until, or if, genetic science can provide more evidence.

Current taxonomy and nomenclature

Here, six basic forms of white-fronted goose are recognised, but there is some evidence that dividing the complex even further (into eight or more population units) could be supported. For ease of reference, the six taxa referred to hereafter are:

- European White-fronted Goose *A. a. albifrons* (breeds in Russia, from the Kanin Peninsula to the Taimyr Peninsula; winters in Europe).
- Asian White-fronted Goose *A. a. albicans* (breeds in Siberia between the Khatanga River and Bering Strait; winters in south-west Asia).
- American White-fronted Goose *A. a. frontalis* (breeds in western and northern Alaska eastwards to at least Queen Maud Gulf; winters in western North America, Mexico and Texas).
- Gambel's White-fronted Goose *A. a. gambeli* (breeds in north-west Canada, from Old Crow Flats to Repulse Bay; winters in eastern Mexico, Louisiana and Texas).
- Tule White-fronted Goose *A. a. elgasi* (breeds in at least Cook Inlet, south Alaska; winters only in central California).
- Greenland White-fronted Goose *A. (a.) flavirostris* (breeds in western Greenland; winters in Ireland and north-west Britain).

Note that *frontalis* might be legitimately segregated into three sub-populations; one breeding from north Alaska to Canada (wintering from Texas to eastern Mexico), another breeding in west Alaska (wintering in California) and a third breeding in south-west Alaska (wintering south to western Mexico).

'Gambel's White-fronted Goose' is the preferred colloquial name for the form *gambeli*. For the sake of clarity (and because this has been the name used for the large Californian birds for the last 90 years) 'Tule White-fronted Goose' is used here for the form *elgasi* – contra Ogilvie & Young 1998, where *gambeli* is called 'Tule Greater White-fronted Goose' and *elgasi* is called 'Elgas's Greater White-fronted Goose'.

Some authors insert the name 'Greater' before White-fronted Goose (in order to prevent confusion with Lesser White-fronted Goose), but this is unnecessarily clumsy when the full names are used. The other English names used above accord with majority usage although, in the case of *albifrons*, the substitution of 'Russian' for 'European' may be equally apt (but note the use of 'Siberian' is inappropriate as both *albifrons* and *albicans* breed in Siberia). Also, in the case of *elgasi*, some authors prefer 'Taiga' rather than 'Tule' (e.g. Sibley 2000).

Note *gambeli* is sometimes regarded as synonymous with *frontalis* rather than with *elgasi* (but see below). The name 'Pacific White-fronted Goose' is usually used where authors regard *frontalis* and *albicans* as a single taxon, but note here they are treated as separate.

Of these six taxa, three (*albifrons*, *albicans* and *frontalis*) are tundra-breeding forms, favouring low-lying ground close to water, while *flavirostris* favours glacial plains and alpine bogs on plateaux up to 700 metres. Although *elgasi* does appear to be a taiga-breeding form, the breeding habitat of *gambeli* is less easily defined.

Quite how Greenland White-fronted Goose managed to lurk undiscovered for so long is truly a mystery, especially as it is nowadays considered such a singular taxon. Genetic investigation has shown that Greenland White-fronted Goose is distinct from American White-fronted Goose and may be regarded as a separate species (Paxinos *et al.* 2002). Greenland White-fronted Goose is treated as a full species by *Birding World* (see also Fox & Stroud 2002). European White-fronted Goose is a rather distinct form too. There is also evidence to suggest that *elgasi*, the taiga-breeding form of North America (perhaps along with *gambeli*) may deserve elevation to species status: Taiga White-fronted Goose.

Although it impacts little on modern taxonomic thinking, even today the controversy surrounding Hartlaub's original specimens of *gambeli* may not be settled. During the preparation of this paper in 2004, photographs of one of the specimens were kindly made available by the Berlin Museum. It is an adult, bearing numerous labels, including one recording that it had been collected in January 1828, at Alvarado. It seems that Alvarado in southeast Mexico may possibly be the locality it was taken, and not Alvarado in Texas as has been previously assumed. This may be significant, if only to help determine the true wintering range of *gambeli*. It is certainly worth reiterating that *gambeli* has always been a taxon that breeds, migrates and winters east of the main mountain chains of North America: it is a bird of the Central Flyway.

Breeding range, wintering grounds, and migration patterns

European White-fronted Goose *A. a. albifrons* winters almost exclusively in the Western Palearctic and, of the five recognised sub-populations, the Baltic/North Sea group are the birds which most European birders encounter. This unit consists of the birds from the most westerly breeding localities in northern Archangel and on the Kanin Peninsula, Kolguyev and Novaya Zemlya. They winter in the Netherlands, Belgium and England. Birds leave the breeding areas in September, reaching the Gulf of Finland by early October, where large numbers remain until December, although some move to the wintering grounds in October. The return passage commences from March in England, with most having left the Netherlands by early April; some stage in Estonia and others take a route to the east of Moscow, but all birds reach the tundra breeding grounds by late May (for greater detail, see Wernham *et al.* 2002). The other four sub-populations - the 'Pannonic', 'Pontic', 'Anatolian' and 'Caspian' groups (see Cramp *et al.* 1977) - winter in suitable habitats from south-central Europe to south-west Asia and breed on the Russian tundra. The total population size is about 1.3 million birds (Rose & Scott, 1997).

Greenland White-fronted Goose *A. a. flavirostris* breeds only in western Greenland, with the total global population of 33,000 birds nesting on alpine bogs and glacial plains between Nuuk (64°N) and Upernavik (73°N). Autumn migration commences in early September and birds migrate via Iceland in September to north-west Scotland and Ireland, arriving on the wintering grounds during October. At least one third of the population winters in

County Wexford, Ireland, from where they depart during the second or third week of April. Scottish birds leave a little later. Most birds fly direct to Iceland (one satellite-tracked bird completed the 1,000-mile journey from Wexford to Iceland in just 13 hours), staging there for three to four weeks before continuing on to Greenland in early May. The final part of their migration, directly over the Greenland ice cap, takes several more days and birds finally reach the nesting grounds between mid-May and early June (Fox & Stroud 2002).

Asian White-fronted Goose *A. a. albicans* breeds in Siberia, with the breeding range apparently abutting that of *albifrons* at the Khatanga River. The birds breeding on the tundra between here and easternmost Siberia winter in Japan, Korea and eastern China. The decreasing population was estimated at only 80,000 birds in 1990 (Mooij & Zöckler 2000). Migration timings are apparently similar to European populations.

American White-fronted Goose *A. a. frontalis* breeds on the tundra of North America with up to one million nesting between north-west Alaska and Arctic Canada. These birds follow either the Pacific Flyway (to winter in California and western Mexico) or the Central Flyway (to reach the gulf coast of Louisiana, Texas and eastern Mexico). Many of the latter birds stage on the border of Saskatchewan and North Dakota well into October before making a non-stop flight to the wintering grounds on the Gulf coast. Pacific Flyway *frontalis* may be subdivided into two populations: one breeding in west Alaska and wintering in California, the other breeding in south-west Alaska and wintering south to western Mexico. Breeding allopatry and temporal partitioning on the staging and wintering areas may even have resulted in phenotypic differences sufficiently pronounced as to qualify these two populations for subspecies recognition (Ely & Takekawa 1996). The northward migration in spring is rather weather-dependent, with birds revisiting staging areas on the way. Arrival time at the breeding grounds is dictated by the date of the thaw, which may not be until June.

Gambel's White-fronted Goose *A. a. gambeli* appears to have been found nesting in taiga habitat at several sites in north-west Canada, such as Old Crow Flats, Yukon Territory, the Perry River and Repulse Bay (Elgas 1968, Kuroda 1929, Gavin 1947). It is believed to winter in eastern Mexico, also Texas and Louisiana, but little is known of its migration strategy or status. A count of 7,990 birds at the Tamesi and Panuco Deltas, eastern Mexico, in the winter of 1980 has been quoted (del Hoyo *et al.* 1992). In fact, *gambeli* appears to be the longest-distance migrant of all the world's *Anser* geese.

Tule White-fronted Goose *A. a. elgasi* breeds near Anchorage in southern Alaska and the population may number fewer than 8,000 birds (Pacific Flyway Council 1991), although only half of the wintering population can be accounted for in the Cook Inlet Basin. Redoubt Bay and the Susitna area used to hold the greatest concentrations of nesting geese, but the slopes of Mount Denali may now be the core range. Radio telemetry is now being engaged as a means of establishing more precise data. Tule Geese depart from the breeding area during the second half of August before spending September at the staging sites (Malheur National Wildfowl Refuge and Summer Lake, Oregon). Many linger at Lower Klamath NWR, northern California through November, but over half the population over-flies the Klamath Basin, arriving in the Sacramento Valley, central California, in late September. (Timm, Wege & Gilmer, 1982). In spring, Tule Geese begin to leave the Sacramento Valley in early February and up to 2,000 arrive at the Klamath Basin by early March; the rest of the population (apparently mostly sub-adults) may stage elsewhere (Timm *et al.* 1982). Most set off again during April, reaching their taiga-zone breeding areas by the end of the month a journey of nearly 2,000 miles which can be completed in four days or less. Three colour-marked birds from the Cook Inlet have been seen in Kansas (December) and Texas (shot in

November and December), so it could be that some Tule Geese also join the Central Flyway. Although it has been suggested that these birds may not have been bona-fide Tule Geese, it would appear that there is some interchange of geese between the two flyways.

IDENTIFICATION

White-fronted geese were accurately depicted in almost field-guide detail in the 'Geese of Medum', an Egyptian frieze dated to 2530 BC. All forms of white-fronted geese are greyish-brown with, as adults, variable amounts of black barring on the belly and a white 'frontal shield' (bordered darker) at the base of the bill. The legs are orange, and the bill is pink or orange. Juveniles of all forms lack black markings on the belly and white on the head, have a dusky nail on the bill tip and show comparatively darker tails than do the adults.

Most birders are reasonably familiar with the identification of European White-fronted Goose *A. a. albifrons*, and Greenland White-fronted Goose *A. (a.) flavirostris*. These are the two forms which resemble each other least, and morphological characters indicate that *flavirostris* is in fact more closely related to the North American forms, particularly *gambeli*. Although some individuals may not be safely differentiated, the following accounts concentrate on characters that may be useful in the field identification of all taxa.

European White-fronted Goose A. a. albifrons

Familiarity with the European White-fronted Goose is the key starting point for Western Palearctic observers. They are a well-proportioned goose, rather compact-looking with a short neck and rather short, essentially pink, bill, which can be rather triangular-looking. Compared to other forms of white-fronted goose, they are the smallest and most compact. The head, neck and underparts have a rather cold, pale greyish tone and the brown tail has a noticeably broad white tip.

Key features of albifrons

- Smallest, most compact form, well-proportioned and rather short-necked
- Noticeably short, mostly pink bill
- Cold greyish plumage tones to head and breast
- Brown tail with particularly broad white tip
- Conspicuous off-white fringes to upperpart feathers giving a more barred appearance to upperparts

Greenland White-fronted Goose A. (a.) flavirostris

Greenland White-fronted Goose is larger and stockier than European White-fronted Goose with a usually obviously longer, more wedge-shaped bright orange bill (though different lighting conditions can some times render bill colour difficult to assess). The plumage is overall rather dark brown particularly over the head and neck compared with European White-fronted Goose. The tail is noticeably rather dark brown and has a clearly thin white 'fringe' at the terminal end of the tail. Many have particularly extensive black belly markings in adult plumage, though there is overlap in this feature. Historically, and like some of the North American forms, they have preferred marshy wetlands, hence the moniker 'Bog Goose' in Ireland. However more recently many have preferred similar habitats to those favoured by European White-fronted Goose including agricultural land, particularly managed grassland (Vinicombe 2003).

Key features of *flavirostris*

- Larger, bulkier and longer-necked than *albifrons*
- Clearly longer, more wedge-shaped, bright orange bill
- Dark brown plumage tones to head and breast
- Dark brown tail with only narrow white tip
- Buffish fringes to upperpart feathers contrast little, giving a more uniform appearance to upperparts

Asian White-fronted Goose *A. a. albicans*

Asian White-fronted Goose is, compared with European *albifrons,* a larger bird with a bigger bill; measurements indicate that it closely resembles *frontalis* in structure, though the bill may average a little smaller. It can appear quite solidly built, with a rather strong-looking head and neck. The plumage is basically similar to *frontalis*, being somewhat browner than *albifrons* and with a little more dark in the tail. Also, the bill frequently appears to be tinged orange. As *albicans* appears essentially similar to *frontalis*, most of the *frontalis* account can also be applied to *albicans*.

Key features of *albicans*

- Most likely to occur amongst wintering *albifrons* due to proximity of breeding range
- Larger than *albifrons*
- Larger bill than *albifrons*, and frequently has an orange tone
- Browner plumage overall
- Darker brown tail

American White-fronted Goose *A. a. frontalis*

This form is, on average, larger than *albifrons*, with a larger, heavier bill. The descriptions presented by Todd (1950) were rather scant; having compared a series of specimens (adults and immatures) he declared that, whereas the plumage of the European birds was greyish, the American birds were just as decidedly brownish. He found the difference especially well marked on the wings and wing-coverts, the latter being "pale mouse-grey in the European birds, but hair-brown in the American". Further, he states that the colour of the lower back and rump differed in a corresponding way "...in the one (*albifrons*) it is mouse grey; in the other (*frontalis*), chetura drab". Also the underparts differed in his series, showing an almost white ground colour in European, but strongly shaded with brown in American birds, while in the latter the throat and neck was "markedly browner" too. Although chemical or mineral staining might account for some of the perceived differences in plumage tones, American White-fronted Goose often does look a heavier bird in the field, inviting comparison with Greylag Goose. Also, there are other, more tangible field points to look for, such as the bill and tail. Rather than bright pink as in *albifrons*, the bill sometimes looks wholly or partly orange-tinged (Kaufman 1994). The tail (often held in a manner that makes it looks broad) is darker brown than on *albifrons* (which shows a broad grey-brown tail band) The white tip to the tail, though not as narrow as in *flavirostris*, can be reduced and is often rather neat. In comparison to *albifrons*, the white tip is narrower with less intrusion of white along the feather fringes.

Key features of *frontalis*

- Vagrancy potential to Western Europe unknown, though most likely to occur among geese originating from Greenland or Arctic Canada
- Big and rather ugly/scruffy-looking, with almost Greylag-like quality to overall appearance
- Larger bill than *albifrons*; bill colour variable, often with orange tone
- Browner plumage overall including upperparts, head, neck and belly (*albifrons* has whiter ground colour to belly)
- Darker brown tail with neat thin white tip (though not as narrow as *flavirostris*)

Tule White-fronted Goose A. a. elgasi

This form is very large, weighing at least 50% more than *frontalis* and with correspondingly long, broad wings. It is also very long-necked, has longer, thicker legs, and a longer bill. The disproportionately longer neck is conspicuous even in flight, and a 'more measured' wing-beat has been noted (and is apparent when flying alongside *frontalis*; RM pers. obs.). A detailed study by Bruce Krogman demonstrated that *elgasi* is morphologically distinct from *frontalis*, with the disproportionately longer bill being the single most important discriminating factor. In adult plumage, *elgasi* is a dark-looking bird; although it often shows less black on the breast than *frontalis*, it is browner overall, darker-backed, and with an extremely dark head and neck. The entire crown and nape is very dark umber brown, and compared to *frontalis* is darker as well as more brown (less grey)-toned (Krogman 1979). Also, the dark feathers surrounding the white frontal patch can be much blacker (Kuroda 1929). The whole plumage is often stained orange, most obviously on the white frontal patch, presumably due to chemical or mineral staining acquired whilst foraging in the waters it frequents. In addition, Tule Goose frequently shows a yellow (even orange) eye-ring (normally dull or greyish on *frontalis* and *albifrons*), but all forms of white-fronted goose can show this character, at least occasionally (e.g. Bailey 1928). Although it is less noisy than *frontalis*, and more often silent, the call is described as harsher and coarser, more stentorian, than the yelping call of *frontalis*. In winter, Tule Geese are usually found in pairs or discreet groups on ponds surrounded by heavy growth of tules (rushes) and willows, whereas *frontalis* is usually found in flocks in fields. The latter is a grazing goose, whereas Tule Goose prefers wet habitats and taller vegetation; it more often feeds on aquatic plants, up-ending to reach immersed food. In summer, Tule Goose nests in taiga (bushy) habitat by vegetated lakes, not on the open tundra like *frontalis*.

Key features of *elgasi*

- The largest form, outstanding in appearance next to *frontalis*, being 50% larger with longer legs, neck and bill
- Very dark upperparts, head and neck
- Blacker feathering around white frontal patch
- Prominent yellow or orange eye-ring
- Less black barring on breast and belly than *frontalis*
- Prefers marshy winter habitat with tules (rushes), feeds more on aquatic plants

Gambel's White-fronted Goose A. a. gambeli

Gambel's White-fronted Goose has been variously described as larger and darker than *frontalis* or slightly smaller and paler than *elgasi*. However, there is a weight of evidence suggesting its choice of habitat (taiga lakes in summer, wet marshland in winter) is similar to *elgasi*, and thus its morphological characters are also not surprisingly similar. Indeed, the following sentiment expressed in Ogilvie & Young (1998) speaks volumes: "Geographical location important in assessing likelihood of identification". During the preparation of this article, the author, along with Ian Lewington and Phil Barnett, examined all the white-fronted goose specimens in the collection of the British Museum of Natural History at Tring. Measurements of *gambeli* certainly approached those of *elgasi*. The bill is clearly long, broad-based and tapering to a fine tip, apparently pinched in behind the nail giving a 'teat-shaped' effect. Several of the skins are orange-stained, and in general appearance the plumage traits described for *elgasi* could also be seen (though were less extreme) in *gambeli*. Close scrutiny of the tail confirmed a pattern that was previously suspected: largely dark brown with a limited white fringe, closer in character to *flavirostris* than *albifrons*.

Key features of *gambeli*

- Probably the most likely vagrant form which has already occurred in UK
- Strikingly large size with long legs and neck
- Long and deep-based bill tapering to a fine tip; often orange-toned
- Prominent orange or yellow eye ring
- Dark tail with thin white fringe closer to *flavirostris* in pattern
- Prefers to feed on aquatic plants in wet habitat
- Overall appearance like a slightly smaller and paler version of the giant *elgasi*
- Tendency for less black on breast and belly than other forms (needs more research to confirm)

Acknowledgements

Special thanks are due to Peter Barker, Phil Barnett, Craig Ely, Mark Grantham, Kaj Kampp, Ian Lewington, Malcolm Ogilvie, Martin Reid, George Sangster, Frank Steinheimer and John Takekaw, the Natural History Museum, Tring and the Berlin Museum.

References

Bailey, A. M. 1928. Notes on Variations in the White-fronted Goose. *Condor 30*: 164–165.

Baur, R. D. 1979. Historical and status report of the Tule White-fronted Goose. Pages 44–55 in: Jarvis, R.L. & Bartoneck, J. C (eds), *Management and biology of Pacific flyway geese, a symposium*, Oregon State Univ Book Stores, Corvallis.

Browning, M. R. 1990. Taxa of North American birds described from 1957-1987. *Proc. Biol. Soc. Wash.* 103: 432-451.

Cramp, S. *et al.* 1977. *Handbook of the Birds of Europe, the Middle East and North Africa*. Oxford.

Dalgety, C. T. & Scott, P. 1948. A new race of the White-fronted Goose. *Bulletin of the British Ornithologist's Club* 68: 109-121.

Delacour, J. & Ripley, S. D. 1975. Description of a new species of the White-fronted Goose *Anser albifrons*. Amer. Mus. *Notivates* 2565, pp.1-4.

del Hoyo, J.; Elliot, A. & Sargatal, J. (editors). (1992). *Handbook of the Birds of the World. Volume 1: Ostrich* to Ducks. Lynx Edicions.

Ely, C. R., & Takekawa, J. Y. 1996. Geographic variation in migratory behavior of Greater White-fronted Geese (*Anser albifrons*). *The Auk* 113: 889-901.

Fox, A. D. & Stroud, D. A. 2002. '*Anser albifrons flavirostris* Greenland White-fronted Goose' in *BWP Update* 4: 65-88 (D. Parkin, ed)

Gavin, A. 1947. Birds of Perry River District, Northwest Territories. *Wilson Bulletin* 59: 195-203.

Godfrey, W. E. 1986. *The Birds of Canada*, National Museum of Canada, Ottawa.

Hartlaub, G. 1852. Description de quelgues nouvelles especes d'Oiseaux. Paris, *Rev. Mag* 2: 3-9.

Jarret, N. 1999. Sir Peter fixed it for me. *Wildfowl & Wetlands* 130:18-21.

Kaufman, K. 1994. Point/Counterpoint. 'Greenland White-fronted Geese - Over-Reported?' *Birding* 26: 380-382.

Krogman, B. 1978. The Tule Goose mystery - a problem in taxonomy. *American Birds* 32: 164-166.

Krogman, B, D. 1979. A systematic study of *Anser albifrons* in California. Pages 22-43 in: Jarvis, R.L. & Bartoneck, J. C (eds), *Management and biology of Pacific flyway geese, a symposium.* Oregon State University Book Stores, Corvallis.

Kuroda, N. 1929. On the subspecific validity of *Anser gambelli* Hartlaub. *Condor* 31: 173-180.

Madge, S., & Burn, H. 1988. *Wildfowl, an identification guide to the ducks, geese and swans of the world.* Bromley.

Moffit, J. 1926. Notes on White-fronted and Tule Geese in Central California. *Condor* 23: 241-243.

Mooij, J. H. & Zöckler, C. 2000. Reflections on the systematics, distribution and status of *Anser albifrons*. *Casarca* 6: 92-107.

Ogilvie, M. A. 1978. *Wild Geese.* Berkhamsted.

Ogilvie, M. & Young, S. 1998. *Photographic Handbook of the Wildfowl of the World.* London.

Orthmeyer, D. L., Takekawa, J. Y., Ely, C. R., Wege, M. L. & Newton, W. E. 1995. Morphological differences in Pacific Coast populations of Greater White-fronted Geese. *Condor* 97: 123-132.

Rose, P. M. & Scott, D. A. 1997. *Waterfowl Population Estimates, 2nd Edition.* Wetlands International Publication 44: 1-106.

Scott, P. 1961. *A Coloured Key to the Wildfowl of the World.* Slimbridge.

Swarth, H. S. & Bryant, H. C. 1917. *A Study of the races of the White-fronted Goose (*Anser albifrons*) occurring in California.* Univ. Cal. Publ. Zool. 17: 209-222.

Timm, D. E., Wege, M. L. & Gilmer, D. S. 1982. Current status and Management Challenges for Tule White-fronted Geese. *47th North American Wildlife Conference report*, pp. 453-463.

Todd, F. S. 1996. *Natural History of the Waterfowl.* San Diego.

Todd, W. E. C. 1950. Nomenclature of the White-fronted Goose. *Condor* 52: 63-68.

Vinicombe, K. 2003. Fresh Ansers. *Birdwatch* 128: 28-30.

Wege, M. L. 1984. Distribution and abundance of Tule Geese in California and southern Oregon. *Wildfowl* 35: 14-20.

Wernham, C.V., Toms, M. P., Marchant, J. H., Clark, J. A., Siriwardena, G. M. & Baillie, S. R. (eds). 2002. *The Migration Atlas: movements of the birds of Britain and Ireland.* London.

Brent Geese of four kinds: Dark-bellied Brent, Pale-bellied Brent, Black Brant and Grey-bellied Brant

Martin Garner

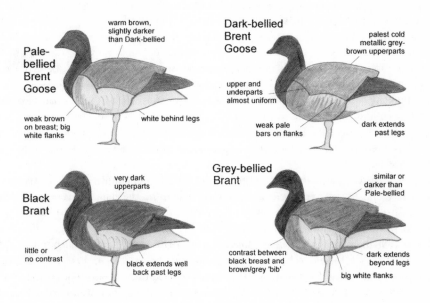

Pale-bellied Brent Goose
warm brown, slightly darker than Dark-bellied
weak brown on breast; big white flanks
white behind legs

Dark-bellied Brent Goose
palest cold metallic grey-brown upperparts
upper and underparts almost uniform
weak pale bars on flanks
dark extends past legs

Black Brant
very dark upperparts
little or no contrast
black extends well back past legs

Grey-bellied Brant
similar or darker than Pale-bellied
contrast between black breast and brown/grey 'bib'
dark extends beyond legs
big white flanks

Diagram by Martin Garner

I suppose insatiable curiosity is essential to discovering new things. When Anthony McGeehan first told me about a creature called the 'Grey-bellied Brant' of the Canadian High Arctic, he was describing something I had never seen or heard of before. No photos or illustrations appeared anywhere. Yet as I began to read and research it seemed that some, including leading biologists and taxonomists, believed that such a creature existed. To me it was near-mythical and therefore, of course, all the more fascinating. As I continued to research the subject it became quite obvious: with Ireland hosting almost the entire world population of the only other goose population occupying the Canadian High Arctic (some 20,000 Pale-bellied Brent), the occasional occurrence of the Grey-bellied Brant in Ireland should be a foregone conclusion. I didn't have to wait long.

One particular morning in April 1998 I decided to make a concerted effort to go and 'look for' Grey-bellied Brant. It felt more like serendipity than sagacity. Within literally one minute of arriving at Dundrum Bay and scanning through the first flock of Brent I locked eyes onto a candidate bird. It was this bird that returned to be seen in the same area three years later. In 1998 the bird produced almost no interest from sceptical observers, but following some championing of the Grey-bellied cause, the 2001 occurrence resulted in an immediate twitch from Britain's hard-core top listers. For the first time I also experienced the awesome potential of the video and stills digiscoping revolution. Having successfully twitched the bird, Messrs Batty, Hackett, Lowe and Webb returned to my house and it was

121

while reviewing the video footage on my television (and not birding in the field!) that the revelation was first confirmed. It was not one bird, but a full-blown family including identifiable female Grey-bellied Brant and five young. You just couldn't have written the script!

Over a five-year period in Northern Ireland I personally found examples of all four varieties of Brent, and it remains arguably the only place in the world where this can readily be done.

Geographical range and status

In line with the BOURC's own taxonomic guidelines (but *contra* its own classification) the Brent Geese are here treated as three separate species, with the fourth, 'Grey-bellied' Brant, as not yet assigned taxonomic status while research is ongoing (see below).

Dark-bellied Brent Goose *Branta bernicla* breeds in northwest Siberia, mainly on the Yamal, Gydan and Taymyr peninsulas and on islands in the Kara Sea. It winters on both sides of the North Sea and English Channel, from Denmark to France and in south-east England (between Lincolnshire and Devon), with some also wintering along the Atlantic coast of France.

Pale-bellied Brent Goose *Branta hrota* occurs in two different populations in the Canadian Arctic. Those breeding in the Canadian Low Arctic winter on the eastern seaboard of North America. Those that breed in the Canadian High Arctic, from Melville Island eastwards, winter mostly in Ireland. Populations also occur in northern Greenland, Spitsbergen and Franz Josef Land, which winter in Denmark (Jutland) and northeast England (Northumberland).

Black Brant *Branta nigricans* breeds in the north-west Canadian Arctic to Alaska, and in north-east Siberia westwards to the Taymyr peninsula. It winters on both sides of the North Pacific, southwards to Baja California in the east and the Yellow Sea in the west.

Grey-bellied Brant (*Branta* sp., unassigned) breeds on Melville and Prince Patrick Islands in the western Canadian High Arctic. The breeding grounds are therefore to the north of Black Brant and to the west of the High Arctic population of Pale-bellied Brent. They winter almost exclusively in Puget Sound, western USA (in particular at Padilla Bay, Washington). Grey-bellied Brant is the least abundant of all the Brent Geese and has been declining, with an estimated 15,000 birds in 1988 but only 4,000-8,000 birds by the turn of the century (Hagmeier 2000). Thanks to recent implementation of shooting restrictions in Puget Sound, this decline may have been slowed, but other factors (such as disturbance from increased human recreation, lack of alternative winter feeding grounds and relatively low breeding productivity due to their harsh nesting environment) may still be adversely affecting their numbers.

Taxonomy

Despite past uncertainty, the current taxonomic situation is clear: Black Brant, Dark-bellied Brent Goose and Pale-bellied Brent Goose are three closely related but separate species. They each breed and winter independently and are identifiable in all plumages. Additionally, limited analysis of the DNA of Black Brant and Pale-bellied Brent Geese has revealed that these two species are more distinct from each other than Ross's and Snow Geese (per Debenedictis 1991). The DNA of Dark-bellied Brent Goose has not been investigated.

There is no widespread intergradation between the three species. Birdwatchers may be confused by the commonly repeated sentiment that the various populations of Brent

Geese freely interbreed. Statements such as 'Three populations…with little range overlap in winter, but intergrade freely where breeding ranges meet' (Sibley 2000) are, in fact, complete conjecture and simply cannot be upheld. In reality, Brent geese normally only breed with the same birds that they winter with, since they form life-long pairings and are mated prior to arrival on the breeding grounds. Indeed, the fact that they travel in family parties and are readily observable in their temperate wintering grounds means that it is very easy to see the exact relationships and pairings of individual birds. Naturally enough, like almost all wildfowl, there is occasional hybridisation between congeners, most especially between Black Brant and Dark-bellied Brent Goose. Hybrid pairings between displaced vagrant Black Brants and Dark-bellied Brent Geese, and their resulting offspring, have been reported in Britain and the Netherlands.

The taxonomic status of Grey-bellied Brant is currently the subject of an ongoing scientific study, as part of a major project investigating the DNA and morphology of the whole Brent Goose complex (Hugh Boyd in litt.). Interestingly, some other recent genetic work (Shields & Cotter 1998) resulted in the following statement: '…not only is the Grey-bellied Brant of Melville Island genetically differentiated from the other two Brants, but also none of its unique mtDNA fragment patterns can be derived from either of the other two Brants. This suggests a non-hybrid origin for the Grey-bellied Brant as well as temporal and reproductive isolation.' Also, Reed et al., in the definitive The Birds of North America (Poole & Gill 1998), designate Grey-bellied Brant as 'Western High-Arctic Brant' and the account reads as follow: 'A fourth group (no subspecies designation), breeding in w. North American High Arctic, is distinct from both hrota and nigricans in plumage, range and genetics…This group constitutes the fourth stock in North America'. Amongst the possible scenarios might be that Grey-bellied Brant is a distinct population formed by long-past introgression between the other Nearctic forms of Brent, or that it represents a darker geographical variant of Pale-bellied Brent Goose. However, according to present knowledge, it is not a hybrid population, but appears to be a separate ancestral form of Brent (e.g. Shields 1990).

Vagrancy potential

Black Brant is a rare, but now annual, vagrant to the UK, with approximately 200 records, although given the longevity of geese and their faithfulness to known wintering sites, the actual number of individuals involved has probably been far fewer. Indeed, most records refer to lone adults which could well be regularly returning birds. The mechanism for their arrival to our shores in the winter is clear: some birds cross the Atlantic from the Nearctic with Canadian Pale-bellied Brent and others cross the western Palearctic region from Siberia with Dark-bellied Brent. This means that western Europe gets Black Brant from both ends of its range.

Grey-bellied Brant is a very rare but previously overlooked vagrant that has a very recent history of discovery in the UK. In April 2001, a family party of seven Grey-bellied Brant was found in the Dundrum Bay/Tyrella Beach area of Northern Ireland. This group consisted of a large, darker-plumaged and aggressive (presumed) male, a more subtly plumaged female (that could be easily overlooked as a Pale-bellied Brent Goose) and five juveniles. The male appeared to be the same individual that was seen at Dundrum in April 1998 (Garner 1998). It is not certain whether this is the same bird that was involved in records at Greyabbey Bay, Strangford Lough, in November 1999 and Newcastle/Dundrum in January-February 1992 (McGeehan 1992). This last record was thought at the time (based on the available literature) to be a hybrid, until George Sangster suggested it could be a Grey-bellied. A second apparent pairing at Dundrum in April 2001 consisted of an obvious male Grey-bellied Brant paired to an unidentified female Brent goose that was indistinguishable from Pale-bellied Brent. Meanwhile, another pair of birds found nearby in Killough Harbour appeared very similar to each other and rather like Pale-belled Brent, but with a brown-toned belly-pattern extending to the vent. While some of the details of these observations may prove only incidental, it is perhaps worth noting that, in two of the pairs, the larger males were also the obviously darker-plumaged birds with broader collars.

It is fascinating to note that there are over 50 records (relating to about a dozen individuals) of Black Brant in Ireland, while up to ten Dark-bellied Brent geese are seen there annually, with similar numbers staging in Iceland (Gauker Hjartarson in litt.). All of these presumably end up on the Pale-bellied Brent Goose (Canadian High Arctic) breeding grounds, although no hybrids have yet been recorded. Conversely, despite some assertions that it was probably a hybrid, the 1998 Dundrum Bay Grey-bellied Brant (referred to above) has reappeared mated to an identifiable female Grey-bellied Grant. It seems self-evident that the increased number of sightings has been facilitated by the increased awareness of the field appearance of Grey-bellied Brant and that this form has probably been occurring more frequently, but undetected, in Ireland. For example, the female and the five young of the Dundrum Bay pair in 2001 could otherwise easily have gone undetected amongst the Pale-bellied Brent. The increase in awareness has led to Grey-bellied Brent being reported annually in Ireland since then, and in 2006 one was reported on Britain's east coast (Hutt and Taylor 2006) with Pale-bellied Brent. Further confirmation of the ability of Grey-bellied Brent to reach Western Europe as genuine vagrants came from a colour-ringed Grey-bellied Brant that was seen staging in Iceland on 15th May 2001. It had been ringed on Prince Patrick Island in the previous summer (Gunnlauger Petursson pers. comm.)

The occurrence of Brent Geese in Ireland from as far west as Melville Island has already been established from ringing recoveries (Ruttledge 1976 & 1977) and it is not inconceivable that some of these recoveries actually involved Grey-bellied Brant. We can surely expect more records of this taxa in the Western Palearctic while the unfolding taxonomic debate will be watched with interest. The problem of occasional hybrids means that it is individuals occurring with Pale-bellied Brent Geese of likely Canadian origin which will be taken the most seriously.

IDENTIFICATION

Dark-bellied and Pale-bellied Brent Geese

The separation of Dark-bellied and Pale-bellied Brent Geese is usually quite straightforward. Apart from being very slightly larger and (as the name implies) distinctly paler on the belly and flanks, Pale-bellied Brents are noticeably and diagnostically browner on the upperparts than Dark-bellied Brents, which are ashy grey in comparison. Juveniles of all four species show pale tips to the wing coverts, secondaries and tertials and lack the white neck patch, but are still separable using the same criteria.

Black Brant

Black Brant is (again as the name implies) darker overall than both the Brents, but also paler in parts than both. Given reasonable views, picking out an adult Black Brant from a flock of Dark-bellied or Pale-bellied Brent Geese (or both) is not too problematic; any bird showing the requisite suite of characters should stand out from the crowd. In all three species, the coloration of the upperparts is the key.

124

The identification of Black Brant has been well documented already (e.g. Madge & Burn 1988 and McGeehan 1992), but a summary of the main pointers seems timely. Lone individuals usually appear rather stockier than their companions, and often noticeably dumpier with an apparently thicker neck and somewhat domed forehead. All these are subtle, individually variable, features, but nevertheless many observers agree that vagrant Black Brants do exhibit a character all of their own. The diagnostic plumage patterns may contribute towards these apparent structural differences, as Black Brant is a bird of stark contrasts. The mantle and scapulars are far darker and browner than the ashy grey upperparts of Dark-bellied Brent, and blacker than Pale-bellied Brent, while the lower breast and belly are similarly coloured, so only in good light is any real contrast with the black upper breast visible. An isolated, strikingly pale flank patch is the best single field point on a suspected Black Brant. The flank feathers are white with contrasting dark bases, but the broad white tips of the overlying feathers largely obscure the dark portions of the underlying ones and thus produce the overall extent and whiteness of the flank patch. The larger rear flank feathers do usually exhibit bold blackish crescentic markings that can break up the pattern. Perhaps as a result of the darker surrounding body tones, Black Brants also seem to show a 'snowy' rear-end in which the rear vent and undertail coverts appear gleaming white. In addition, the white neck-collar tends to be far more prominent (typically deeper, broader and with well-developed 'rivulets' linking the upper and lower borders) than on either of the Brents and nearly always joins across the front of the neck and frequently extends further around the back of the neck.

First-winter Black Brants can, like the two Brents, be aged by the pale tips to their wing coverts, secondaries and tertials. They resemble first-winter Dark-bellied Brent Geese, but are much darker above and below, with contrasting white tips to the flank feathers and, often, a more well-developed neck collar.

Although Siberian Black Brants may appear a little paler below than the Nearctic birds, their separation as a distinct form (*orientalis*) is arguable. In this respect, comparison of vagrant Black Brants on the east coast of England (of Siberian origin) with those in Ireland (from Canada) reveals little difference.

The very few presumed hybrid birds (usually presumed Dark-bellied x Black Brant) that have been documented appear to show various mixed characters of the parent species.

Grey-bellied Brant
In simple terms, Grey-bellied Brant falls somewhere between Black Brant and Pale-bellied Brent Goose in general appearance. The following description is an initial attempt to document the field appearance based primarily on observations of Grey-bellied Brant in Puget Sound, British Columbia.

Grey-bellied seems to be the most variable of all the Brent geese with some paler birds being apparently indistinguishable from Pale-bellied Brent and darker individuals which approach Black Brant in appearance (Hugh Boyd pers. comm.). Typically, however, the overall appearance of Grey-bellied Brant is close to that of Pale-bellied Brent Goose, but with more darkly pigmented underparts. It should be stressed that the belly colour is not pure grey, but varies from brown to brownish-grey, and this darker area often tends to extend to the area between the legs or just beyond (approximately in line with the rear flank feathers). This coloured 'bib' is not as extensive or as dark as on Black Brant, and there is always an obvious contrast between the dingy belly and the lower border of the black chest. A key feature for telling an identifiable Grey-bellied Brant from Pale-bellied Brent is that, with careful observation, the area just posterior to the legs should be seen to be brown-toned, and often similar in extent to that on Dark-bellied Brent Goose. Note that some juvenile/first-winter Pale-bellied Brent Geese can show a tawny-brown colour here, but these are normally in the company of identifiable adults. The flanks are pale, although the dark bases to the largest rear flank feathers can be obvious and may 'link' with the brown-toned lower belly. On many Grey-bellied Brants, the dark portion of the underparts can show a pattern of tight transverse barring (formed by the contrast between the dark feather bases and the narrow pale tips), with this pattern extending towards the flanks. On other birds the belly is more uniformly dark, contrasting strongly with the paler flanks.

The colour of the upperparts of Grey-bellied Brant varies from being similar to Pale-bellied Brent (mid-brown, with slightly darker feather centres and paler fringing creating a lightly barred effect), to being darker and more uniform. Black Brant, although variable, are usually darker still, whilst Dark-bellied Brent Geese tend to show greyer-toned upperparts. The collar varies from being similar to that of Pale-bellied Brent, to being more obvious and, on many birds, approaching that of Black Brant in both height and extent. The lower part of the white band may (just) meet across the front of the neck (but not at the rear), and the white 'rivulets' running up the neck sides can be quite tall.

First-winter Grey-bellied Brants are similar in appearance to adults, but have the age-diagnostic off-white tips to all the wing-coverts, secondaries and tertials. They also exhibit looser-looking plumage and, as post-juvenile moult progresses through the first winter, have a tendency to look 'patchy' on the underparts as the unmoulted (juvenile) darker belly feathers often contrast sharply against the newer (adult-like), paler feathers. Many young birds retain obvious off-white fringes to the scapular feathers well into the late winter (similar to some Pale-bellied Brent, but unlike most young Black Brant).

Key features

Dark-bellied Brent

- Underparts show dark pigmentation extending beyond rear of legs
- Upperparts a cold metallic grey tone, paler than the upperparts of Pale-bellied Brent
- Flank feathers have the thinnest white tips of all forms, creating least contrast with the upper-and underparts
- White collar variable in extent; can be small or large and occasionally joined at the front

Pale-bellied Brent

- Underparts show no dark extending beyond legs (except coffee tone on fresh juveniles)
- Upperparts a warm and brown tone, typically appearing slightly barred
- White spider necklace small and usually confined to sides of neck

Black Brant

- Belly extensively blackish, with pigmentation extending well beyond legs
- Upperparts very dark brown-black
- Little contrast between black neck sock and dark brownish-black upper breast

- Flank patch strikingly white, sandwiched between the very dark upper-and underparts
- White necklace nearly always joined at front and typically the most extensive of all the forms of Brent/Brant

Grey-bellied Brant

- The most variable. Pale birds like Pale-bellied but with brownish extending beyond legs. Dark birds like 'pale-plumaged' Black Brant
- Upperparts warm brown, like Pale-bellied or slightly darker
- White necklace variable, often joined at front

References

Bloomfield, A. & McCallum, J. 2001. Changing fortunes of the Black Brant. *Birding World* 14: 66–68.

Boyd, H. & Maltby, L. S. 1979. The brant of the western Queen Elizabeth Islands, N.W.T. Pp. 5–21 in *Management and biology of Pacific Flyway geese, a symposium* (R. L. Jarvis and J. C. Bartonek, eds.). Oregon State University Book Stores, Corvallis.

Boyd, H., Maltby, L. S. & Reed, A. 1988. Differences in the plumage patterns of Brant breeding in High Arctic Canada. Canada Wildlife Service Program. Note 174.

Buckley, P. A. & Mitra, S. S. 2003. Three geese resembling "Gray-bellied Brant"/ "Lawrence's Brant" from Long Island, New York. *North American Birds* 56: 502–507.

DeBenedictis, P. A. 1991. A.B.A. [American Birding Association] checklist report. *Birding* 23:190-196.

Delacour, J. & Zimmer, J. T. 1952. The identity of *Anser nigricans* Lawrence 1846. *Auk* 69: 82–84.

Garner, M. & Millington, R. 2001. Grey-bellied Brant and the Dundrum conundrum. *Birding World* 14: 151-155.

Garner, M. 1998. Brent Crosses. *Birdwatch* 78: 29–32.

Hagmeier, K. 2000. The conservation conundrum of Grey-bellied Brant. *British Columbia Waterfowl Society's Marshnotes*. Spring 2000, pp 4–6.

Handley, C. O. 1950. The brant of Prince Patrick Island, Northwest Territories. *Wilson Bulletin* 62: 128–132.

Hutt, A. & Taylor, G. 2006. The apparent Grey-bellied Brant in East Yorkshire. *Birding World* Vol. 19 pp 113-117

McGeehan, A. 1992. Black Brant: a goose worth watching. *Irish Birding News* 2: 91-99.

Madge, S. & Burn, H. 1988. Wildfowl. *An identification guide to the ducks, geese and swans of the world.* Helm Publications.

Manning, T. H., Hohn, E. O. & Macpherson, A. H. 1956. The birds of Banks Island. National Museum Canada Bulletin. No. 143, *Biology Service No. 48.* Ottawa

Martin, J. 2002. From the Rarities Committee's files: Unusual Brent Geese in Norfolk and Hampshire. *British Birds* 95: 129-136.

Ogilvie, M. A. 1978. *Wild geese*. T. & A. D. Poyser, Berkhamsted, U.K.

Reed, A., Davison, M. A. & Kraege, D. K. 1989a. Segregation of Brent Geese *Branta bernicla* wintering and staging in Puget Sound and the Strait of Georgia. *Wildfowl* 40: 22–31.

Reed, A., Stehn, R. & Ward, D. 1989b. Autumn use of Izembek Lagoon, Alaska, by brant from different breeding areas. *Journal of Wildlife Management* 53: 720–725.

Reed, A., Ward, D. H., Derksen, D. V. & Sedinger, J. S. 1998. Brant (*Branta bernicla*). In *The Birds of North America*, No. 337 (A. Poole and F. Gill, eds.). The Birds of North America, Inc., Philadelphia, PA.

Rutteledge, R. F. 1975. *Irish Bird Report* 23: 43–37.

Rutteledge, R. F. 1976. *Irish Birds* 11: 65–67.

Shields, G. F. 1990. Analysis of mitochondrial DNA of Pacific Black Brant. *Auk* 107: 620–623.

Shields, G. F. & Cotter, J. P. 1998. Phylogenies of North American geese: the mitochondrial DNA record. Pp. 405–411 in Biology and management of Canada Geese (D. H. Rusch, M. D. Samuel, D. D. Humburg, and B. D. Sullivan, eds.). Proceeds. International. Canada Goose Symposium., Milwaukee, WI.

Sibley, D. 2000. *The North American Bird Guide.* New York.

Wynn, R. 2002. Brants: the hybrid problem. *Birdwatch* 118: 16–18.

White-cheeked Geese – Canada Goose and Arctic Goose
A new approach to their taxonomy and identification

Martin Garner

To anyone who has taken a family walk around a park lake populated with Canada Geese and discovered the joys of shoes and child's buggy bedecked in green slimy goose-poo, the fact that these 'honkers' struggle to inspire interest among the British birding public comes as no surprise. However, in North America they really are truly 'wild geese' with many undertaking phenomenal migrations, breeding in hostile environments and eluding our best attempts to understand their variety and complexity. Indeed the Canada Goose may represent THE BIRD (when considered as just one species) which demonstrates the single greatest level of variation of any bird species in the world. The Giant Canada is the largest form of goose in the world and the little '*minima*' Cackling Canada one of the smallest and there is a great complex of forms in between. Wild Canada Geese occur every year in the UK as vagrants, and yet their specific origins and identification remain a mystery that is only very slowly beginning to be resolved and understood, with many wrong assumptions and blind alleys regularly stymieing our progress. For those who like to be involved in 'discovery' during their birdwatching, there is perhaps no greater challenge than the taxonomy and identification of vagrant Canada Geese in the UK.

Current taxonomy

The two taxonomic decision-making bodies in North America (the American Ornithologists Union) and the UK (the British Ornithology Union Records Committee) recently split the Canada Goose (hereafter White-cheeked Goose) complex into two species. The split simply divided the eleven already familiar and most frequently assigned subspecies into large and small-bodied birds as follows:

Greater Canada Goose *Branta canadensis* with subspecies

- *canadensis* (Atlantic)
- *interior* (Interior or Todd's)
- *maxima* (Giant)
- *moffitti* (Moffit's)
- *parvipes* ('Lesser')
- *fulva* (Vancouver)
- *occidentalis* (Dusky)

Cackling Goose or 'Lesser Canada Goose' *Branta hutchinsii* with subspecies

- *hutchinsii* (Richardson's)
- *leucopareia* (Aleutian)
- *taverneri* (Taverner's)
- *minima* ('Cackling')

The limits of this arrangement were immediately obvious to those familiar with the subject. For example, in terms of nomenclature, what is familiarly known as the Lesser Canada Goose (ssp. *parvipes*) is now a Greater Canada Goose though some individuals are reportedly indistinguishable from Taverner's Canada Goose (ssp. *taverneri*) which is now a Lesser Canada Goose!

The identification of vagrants in the UK seems to become more of a conundrum with each winter's new arrivals. Many vagrants simply do not fit the described 'classic' appearance of the prescribed forms as set out in this 'new' framework of taxonomy. Additionally, the vagrancy potential of some forms that are suggested to occur here, such as *parvipes* and *taverneri*, are not, based on the available literature, really likely candidates for vagrancy to Western Europe. So what is going on?

One step back - an overview of White-cheeked Geese

As well as being the most varied in appearance, White-cheeked Geese are the most widely distributed geese in North America. Broadly speaking, the larger-bodied birds are found mostly in interior North America in the southern part of the breeding ranges and have the shortest migration distances. Progressively northwards and toward the harsher arctic climates the birds become smaller and it is these populations that migrate the greatest distances. To understand speciation and potential vagrancy it is very important to be aware of some aspects of their breeding biology and behaviour. White-cheeked Geese typically breed alone or in small and localised colonies. They pair for life and most young (particularly females) return to breed in the same place that they hatched. They also have specific population flyways, faithfully using the same staging and wintering locations year after year. Occasionally, environmental factors cause them to change wintering locations, in which case the whole of the population is involved. With this basic understanding it is not difficult to see, for example, that reported widespread intergrading between two populations is actually pretty unlikely if they pair for life, go back to their natal site to breed, and hang out with their own 'kin' all year round, even though most do mix with a variety of other forms on the wintering grounds. The fictitious spectre of 'widespread intergradation', based nearly always on unproven supposition and guesswork, has similarly affected the taxonomy of most Holarctic species of geese.

The problem of too little data

In the twentieth century, taxonomists have made several attempts to make sense of vast range and seemingly infinite variety of White-cheeked Geese, proposing between eight and twelve subspecies and between one and four different species. The core problem that has beleaguered these efforts is the poverty of data. For example John Aldrich, who reviewed the taxonomy in 1946 and cemented our contemporary understanding of the eleven subspecies, used only 359 specimens, of which only 28 were from the breeding grounds. All subsequent taxonomic arrangements have been built on the same limited data and have therefore repeated the same assumptions and have arguably perpetuated a poor overview of the true situation. With such a tremendous variety, vast range and the inaccessibility of large areas of the northern breeding grounds, perhaps we should not be surprised that taxonomic arrangements to date seem to have failed to match what is actually observable in the field.

Harold Hanson's taxonomy

Harold Hanson's lifetime's work on the Canada Geese (Hanson 2006) is unequivocally monumental in its scope and in its conclusions. It already has its plaudits and critics alike, both of whom are left secretly trying to fathom whether Hanson's work really does usher in a whole new understanding of these wild geese. The first volume of a two-part work was published in 2006 and is perhaps of greatest interest to observers in the Western Palaearctic as it covers the eastern taxa, i.e. those most likely to occur on this side of the Atlantic. The second volume covering the western taxa was published in 2007. Hanson died in 2003 having spent fifty years of his life working on this project. He concluded that the White-cheeked Geese can be divided into six different species (not two) and in Volume I a total of 78 new subspecies of *canadensis* and 84 new subspecies of *hutchinsii* are presented. That's just for starters!

White-cheeked Geese with six species (after Hanson):

- Canada Goose *Branta canadensis*
- Giant Prairie Goose *Branta maxima*
- Ontario Goose *Branta "lawrensis"*
- Arctic Goose *Branta hutchinsii*
- Aleutian Goose *Branta leucopareia*
- Cackling Goose *Branta minima*

With such radical conclusions it is important to assess his credibility. Hanson is most well known for the rediscovery of the Giant Canada Goose ('*maxima*'), which was considered extinct for most of the latter part of the twentieth century. It is a touch ironic that '*maxima*' had never been recognised by the AOU until their recent, and arguably already out-of-date, two-way species split. In comparison to Aldrich's 359 specimens, of which only 8% were from breeding grounds, Hanson used 1800 specimens, of which 60% had come from the breeding grounds.

Hanson, broadly speaking, makes the case that each local population is essentially reproductively isolated from other populations and evolves in response to its own particular environments into a different subspecies. Until now, UK observers have had to try to make each vagrant fit one of only eleven alternative subspecies and, in doing so, have reached some strange conclusions. But Hanson's more definitive description of all the possible populations gives us a much greater chance of making sense of these vagrants. For example, consider the riddle of the darker-breasted *hutchinsii* seen in the UK. The naming of such birds as 'good' *hutchinsii* has been repeatedly questioned because the description of classic *hutchinsii* is of a silver-breasted bird. However this classic 'type' is based on a specimen from Melville Island, in the western Canadian High Arctic. Hanson ably demonstrates that there really are darker-breasted populations that are consistent in appearance and look exactly like some of the birds occurring in the UK, as well as paler-breasted populations which nest nearby. Hanson's dark-breasted Fox Basin Arctic Geese (ssp. *baffinensis*) from southern Baffin Island fit some of our birds very nicely!

Many of Hanson's conclusions are well tested while others are unproven hypotheses based on positive results elsewhere. His book requires a Herculean change in the way we look at Canada Geese, and it cannot be lightly dismissed, as frightening as it may seem.

Indeed I believe it will become the *sine qua non* for future research, identification, taxonomy and, crucially, conservation of the White-cheeked Geese, whether all his work is validated or not. With that view in mind here is a preliminary 'new approach' to the way we could be heading with identifying vagrant Canada Geese in Britain and Western Europe.

Suggested identification of Canada Goose and Arctic Goose using Hanson

Of the six species proposed by Hanson, only two, Canada Goose and Arctic Goose, are likely to have occurred as vagrants in the UK. Cackling Canadas and birds showing characters of the Giant Prairie Goose have also been reported in the UK, but these are, for the time being at least, considered to be probably introduced or escaped birds.

This matches the currently accepted view, now that Lesser Canada Goose (Arctic Goose is surely a better name) has been added to the British list, but Hanson can now help us go further in defining which races are involved. The identification process of a potential vagrant should be in two steps. Firstly, the bird needs to be confirmed as a White-cheeked Goose and not a hybrid! Secondly, there needs to be a careful assessment of size in comparison with other geese. To this effect a bird should fit into the following categories:

'Large Canada Geese'

Obviously larger than Pink-footed or Greenland White-fronted Geese and maybe appearing the same size as, or even larger than, Greylag Geese. In my view, using Hanson, this narrows the choice down to two subspecies of Canada Geese, *'canadensis'* and *'interior'*. Of these, *canadensis* is a shorter-distance migrant with a flyway along the eastern seaboard that suggests that it is a less likely vagrant than *interior*. The latter is also a large Canada Goose, but slightly darker than *canadensis* with a tendency to have darker buff fringes to the upperparts. There are some individuals with *interior*-like characters in the feral UK population, but it is also highly likely to occur as a vagrant. It is important to note that *interior* is at the LARGE end of White-cheeked Geese.

'Intermediate Canada Geese'

Approximately the size of Pink-footed Goose but with some slightly larger and some slightly smaller. This is easily the hardest group to assess, due to the range of sizes between 'smaller intermediates' and 'larger intermediates'; birds at the extremes of this range might be mistakenly placed in one of the other categories. However, they are distinguished from the generally smaller Arctic Geese usually (but not always) by their obviously longer, shallower/ thinner-looking bills and longer-looking bodies and longer legs. It was concerning these birds that I found Hanson to be most enlightening. He presents a variety of intermediate-sized Canada Geese breeding in the sub-arctic zones of Baffin Island and northern Hudson Bay. Their field characters include white cheeks that are variously darker flecked to unmarked and varying degrees of dark throat bars and pale neck rings in combination with variously darker or paler-plumages. It is these types which seem to easily fit the appearance of birds that have been incorrectly assumed to be *taverneri* and *parvipes* in the UK. However the breeding range and migration strategy of Hanson's 'intermediate' Canada Geese makes them much more likely as vagrants than these western forms that are sometimes claimed. I am not sure whether we will ever be able to assign every vagrant seen in the UK to a specific population but we can at least have Hanson's populations on our radar during the coming winters – particularly the darker-cheeked *hunti*, the slightly paler *suttoni*, the shorter-billed *charcoti* and the paler-breasted *soperi* and *davisi*.

'Arctic Geese'

If a bird is more or less as small as a Barnacle Goose it will probably be one of the races of Arctic Goose. Some 'intermediate geese' may be just as small but Arctic Geese are also similar to Barnacle Geese in structure, with a noticeably compact shape and rather short and triangular-looking bills. Small geese with longer, thinner bills than a Barnacle Goose will not be Arctic Geese and should be put in the 'intermediate goose' category. Hanson demonstrates there is considerable variety in the appearance of Arctic Geese that could reach the UK. These include plainer dark-breasted birds (e.g. *frobisheri* which could recall *minima*), dark-breasted birds with pale neck rings (e.g. *baffinensis*) and classic silver-grey-breasted birds (e.g. *kumlieni*). This goes a long way to explaining some of the perplexing variety of so-called '*hutchinsii*' we have been encountering in the UK. Note that it is not unusual for Arctic Geese to have dark throat bars.

In the early stages of gaining a 'corporate consciousness' as regards to the types of vagrant White-cheeked Geese we get in the UK, it may be a struggle in some cases to distinguish (using Hanson) whether an individuals falls into the Canada Goose or Arctic Goose category due to the smaller size of some Canada Geese. It is also clear from Hanson that much more detailed information should be gathered whenever a potential vagrant is found which may help us discover if there are particular sub-populations that turn up regularly as vagrants. In this way we can begin to look for patterns. These details include:

- Upperpart and underpart plumage (described in details relative to other areas of plumage)
- Dark throat line (extent and degree)
- Dusky tips on white cheeks (presence or absence)
- Pale/white collar at base of neck sock (extent – front and back – and degree of presence)
- Bill shape

Great care should be taken to describe as accurately as possible all plumage and structural details of any given individual whose circumstances suggest it could be a wild vagrant White-cheeked Goose.

This is by no means a full endorsement of Hanson. I have used his scientific names as they give a useful point of reference where they match some of the phenotypes we find in Western Europe. His work leaves as many questions as answers, and some of his conclusions are highly speculative. Nevertheless his overall thesis makes much greater sense of the appearance of many of the vagrants we see. Thus the real challenge of Hanson is that it forces us to go right back to basics and start from scratch. What better invitation for the pioneering birder? We can all contribute!

References

Hanson, H.C. 2006 *The White-Cheeked Geese: Taxonomy, Ecophysiographic Relationships, Biogeography, and Evolutionary Considerations. Vol 1* Eastern Taxa Avvar Books. California, USA

Hanson, H.C. 2007 *The White-Cheeked Geese: Taxonomy, Ecophysiographic Relationships, Biogeography, and Evolutionary Considerations. Vol 2* Western Taxa Avvar Books. California, USA

Ducks to Raptors

Female-type Blue-winged Teal and Cinnamon Teal

Martin Garner

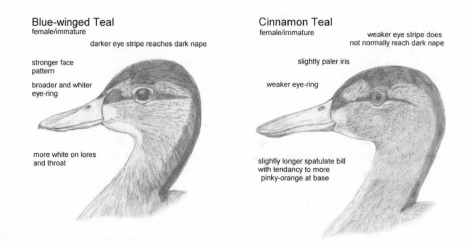

Blue-winged Teal
female/immature

darker eye stripe reaches dark nape

stronger face pattern

broader and whiter eye-ring

more white on lores and throat

Cinnamon Teal
female/immature

weaker eye stripe does not normally reach dark nape

slightly paler iris

weaker eye-ring

slightly longer spatulate bill with tendancy to more pinky-orange at base

Diagram by Emily Garner

In the late 1970s, a recently discovered Blue-winged Teal would most certainly have been declared an escape by Eric Hardy, the doyen of Merseyside birding. At the same time, some of the birds claimed to be Blue-winged Teal were really just relatively plain-faced Garganey. One such individual even tripped up the late Peter Grant at the Abbey Pool, Tresco (Isles of Scilly) in October 1984. As for Cinnamon Teal I saw at least three obvious escapes in the 1980s and the exotic gaudiness of males meant they never featured in straw polls of predicted vagrants!

Times and perspectives change. It now seems we know less than ever about vagrancy and what might occur and why (see Andy Stoddart's section 'Bird movements and vagrancy'). Is the prospect of Cinnamon Teal reaching the Western Palearctic as a genuine vagrant really so unrealistic? Perhaps we should at least carefully identify and monitor the presence of Cinnamon Teal in apparently 'wild settings' and be prepared for our perspectives to change once again in the future.

Geographical range

The Blue-winged Teal *Anas discors* has a breeding range extending right across North America from southern Alaska and British Columbia to south-west Newfoundland, south to northern Texas. It is a long-distance migrant, wintering as far south as northern Argentina and Chile (Rohwer *et al.* 2002). The Cinnamon Teal *A. cyanoptera* has a much more restricted breeding range in western North America from southern British Columbia, southern Alberta and SW Saskatchewan, south to Northern California. It is also a shorter-distance migrant than the Blue-winged Teal with some overlap between northern breeding areas and southern wintering areas, wintering from California, south to Central America with occasional records from northern Columbia, Venezuela and Ecuador (Gammonley 1996).

Vagrancy potential

Blue-winged Teal is a well-established vagrant to the Western Palearctic. There have been approximately 300 accepted records in the UK up until the end of 2006. Autumn records show a western bias to their distribution, but spring records can occur anywhere. This seasonal difference is usually considered to validate the hypothesis that these birds arrive directly from the Nearctic during the autumn and at least some of them spend the winter in southern Europe or north Africa and head back north on spring migration. As the species is commonly kept in waterfowl collections, the issue of escape likelihood does arise; however the recovery of an immature male bird ringed in New Brunswick and shot in Suffolk on 9th October 1971, as well as other Canadian ringed birds in the Outer Hebrides and County Offaly, Ireland, demonstrates that some, at least, are genuine vagrants.

In contrast, the Cinnamon Teal has yet to be accepted as a genuine vagrant in the Western Palaearctic by National Records Committees. With the recent increase of vagrant birds occurring in Britain with a native distribution essentially in western North America it seems entirely possible for the occasional Cinnamon Teal to reach Western Europe. There are many sight records across eastern North America (Sibley 2000) including records from Quebec, Nova Scotia, and New York (Gammonly 1996, Palmer 1976). Vagrants have also reached Hawaii to the west (Madge and Burn 1988). An adult male Cinnamon Teal at Loch Tuamister, Lewis, Outer Hebrides from 13th May to 16th June 2004 was only accepted onto Category E of the British List, but the possibility of it having been a genuine vagrant, with exceptional supporting cast of other wildfowl of North American origin in the same spring (Scott 2004), is very real. Between 1990 and 2004 approximately 25-35 Cinnamon Teal were reported 'in the wild' in Britain, which is an average of about three per year (anon 2004). A number of these involved long-staying and even breeding individuals, obviously suggesting that they were escaped birds. However, it is important, as with all potentially vagrant wildfowl, that each record is viewed on its own merits with due attention to the wider perspective of occurrence patterns.

IDENTIFICATION

The remarkable similarity between female Cinnamon and Blue-winged Teal, and the obvious identification pitfalls, were first dealt with by Ian Wallace and Malcolm Ogilvie in *British Birds* in 1977 (see Wallace and Ogilvie 1980). At that time, Cinnamon Teal was only considered to be a problem escape and not a potential vagrant. The difficulty of identifying these species is vividly illustrated by the only record of a Blue winged Teal to be ringed in Britain. This bird, trapped and ringed as a male (immature or eclipse adult) at Abbotsbury Swannery, Dorset on 23rd October 1979, was subsequently shot at Hautebut, Somme, France on 22nd February 1981 as an adult male Cinnamon Teal! Clearly this individual also raises the question of whether it was an escape or genuine vagrant.

Size and structure
Cinnamon Teal averages slightly larger than Blue-winged Teal, though this is perhaps likely to be of little use in the field. More importantly (and usefully) the bill of Cinnamon

Teal is typically about 10% longer and often has the appearance of being more spatulate (recalling a 'mini-Shoveler') due to greater length, expanded tip, overlapping bill flanges and corresponding slightly more pinched-in appearance towards the base.

Head pattern

The main features for distinguishing between the species in juvenile and female plumages are to be found in the head pattern. The differences are subtle and there is some overlap, so great care should be taken to note as many of the following features as possible: Cinnamon Teal typically have an overall much warmer-toned face with an almost orange/rusty wash as the background colour. The pattern is generally much blander as the features are less contrasting than on Blue-winged Teal. The dark eye stripe is thin and does not extend to the dark nape. The pale eyelids are thin and relatively inconspicuous. The pale areas of the loral spot and throat area are relatively small in size and pale yellowy-cream in colour. On Blue-winged Teal the loral spot and throat area are white, large and conspicuous while the pale eyelids are thicker and more obvious. Typically, the dark supra-loral spot on a Cinnamon Teal appears more-or-less to join with the dark forehead, forming a continuous dark area across the forehead region, whereas on Blue-winged Teal this spot is usually divided from the dark forehead by a conspicuous pale line. This difference is most noticeable when the birds are seen head-on. Together, all the facial features give the juveniles and females of each species a subtly distinct appearance, which becomes more familiar with practice.

Bare parts

There appear to be subtle differences in the bare part colours, which are not absolute but can be apparent and helpful on some individuals. Many Cinnamon Teal have fairly obvious orangey pink along the rim of the upper mandible while the iris pattern tends to be a warm hazel colour. On Blue-winged Teal there can be some orangey pink on the bill but it is so subtle that usually the whole upper mandible appears blue-grey only. The iris on Blue-winged Teal is a colder grey brown colour.

Key points in identifying juveniles and females

	Cinnamon Teal	Blue-winged Teal
Face colour	Warmer tone, background colour rusty-washed brown	Cooler tone, background colour off-white
Extent of dark eye stripe	Obviously thinner, does not reach dark nape	Thicker, extends to and joins dark nape
Eyelids	Thinner and pale, upper one almost lacking	Thicker and white, usually very obvious
Colour and size of pale loral spot and throat patch	Yellowy-cream, small and indistinct	White, large and conspicuous
Supra-loral spots	Dark spots join across dark forehead	Dark spots separated from forehead by pale line

Colour of rim of upper mandible	More obvious pink-orange	Less obvious pink-orange, con-colorous with rest of bill
Iris colour	Paler warmer hazel-brown when catches light	Darker grey-brown, duller and hard to see

Pitfall of eclipse male Blue-winged Teal

There is a potential pitfall in confusing eclipse male Blue-winged Teals for juvenile/female Cinnamon Teals. For example, an eclipse drake Blue-winged Teal on Unst, Shetland in September 1983 stirred up much debate in regard to its identity. Originally accepted as a female/immature Blue-winged Teal, it took five circulations of the record at BBRC to finally conclude that the similarities to Cinnamon Teal, as noted in published photographs, were due to the fact that it was actually an adult male Blue-winged Teal in eclipse plumage (Garner & Lansdown 1991).

Adult male Blue-winged Teals have longer bills than females making them very close in length to the bills of female Cinnamon Teal. They also tend to have warmer plumage tones and blander face patterns, which can be very Cinnamon Teal-like. The key is to check the leg colour and speculum pattern to confirm the age and sex of the bird. In females the speculum pattern is dull and rather colourless with only a weak, broken, white upper border. In males the speculum is a bright metallic green with a broad curving solid white bar on the upper border. In the case of the Unst bird, the wing pattern demonstrated that it was a male, while the presence of yellow legs, at a time when juveniles would have had dull greyish legs, indicated, among other features, that it was an adult male in eclipse plumage. Had it been an adult male Cinnamon Teal, it would also have had an obvious bright yellow or red-coloured iris.

References

Anon, 2004. *Birding World* 17: 201.

Gammonley, J. H. 1996. Cinnamon Teal (*Anas cyanoptera*). In *The Birds of North America*, no. 209 (A. Poole & F. Gill, eds.). Acad. Nat. Sci., Philadelphia, PA, and Am. Ornithol. Union, Washington, D.C.

Garner, M. S. & Lansdown, P. 1991. Blue-winged or Cinnamon Teal? *British Birds* 84: 285-287.

Madge, S. & Burn, H. 1988. *Wildfowl*. A. & C. Black, London.

Palmer, R. S. 1976. *Handbook of North American Birds. Vol. 2: Waterfowl. Pt. 1.* Yale Univ. Press, New Haven, CT.

Rowher, F. C., W. P. Johnson, & E. R. Loos. 2002. Blue-winged Teal (*Anas discors*). In *The Birds of North America*, no. 625 (A. Poole & F. Gill, eds.). The Birds of North America, Inc., Philadelphia, PA.

Scott, M. 2004. The Cinnamon Teal on the Outer Hebrides - a new Western Palearctic bird? *Birding World* 17: 200-201.

Sibley, D. A. 2000. National Audubon Society *The Sibley Guide to Birds*. Chanticleer Press, NY.

Wallace, D. I. M., and M. A. Ogilvie. 1980. Distinguishing Blue-winged and Cinnamon teals, in Sharrock, J. T. R., ed. *The Frontiers of Bird Identification*, pp. 267-271. British Birds, Ltd., Biggleswade, U.K.

Female-type Green-winged and Baikal Teals
Martin Garner

The Green-winged and Baikal Teal are an intriguing brace of dabbling ducks. While the female Green-winged Teal teeters at the edge of the 'unidentifiable' realm, the Baikal Teal teeters on the brink of 'unacceptable'. Being a natural optimist I want to haul both of them back from the edge. Some female Green-winged Teals can be identified as surely as eclipse drakes. A number of Baikal Teal in the Western Palearctic have been genuine vagrants and what a 'beautifully formed' (Latin meaning of *formosa*) vagrant duck the males are!

For those who want to take a longer look at wildfowl in the hunt for these things, a female *Anas* sp. at Seaforth, Merseyside in May 2006 provided a salutary lesson that there is much to be discovered. Quickly heralded as a female Baikal Teal, it soon became evident that while the face pattern seemed exceptional, the overall structure and plumage were closer to Teal (indeed Green-winged Teal). While the identification of this particular bird may never be unequivocal, it provided the necessary perspective that female Teals, though rarely studied, have the potential to include some much sought-after vagrants and that knowing speculum patterns is a key to correct identification.

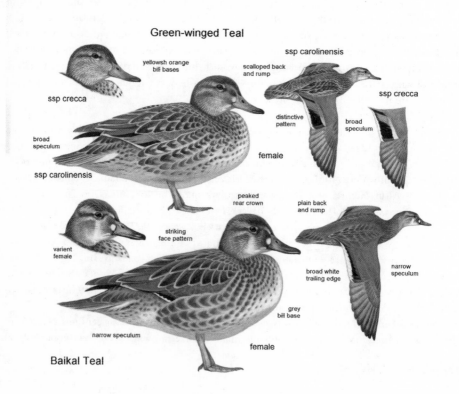

Geographical range

The Green-winged Teal *Anas carolinensis* breeds throughout North America (apart from the high arctic) south to northern California and northern New England. The species winters as far south as Central America and the West Indies.

Baikal Teal *Anas formosa* breeds in the forest zone of northern and north-eastern Siberia from the Yenisey basin to Kamchatka. It is a migratory species which winters in Japan, Korea and northern and eastern China. Only recently Ogilvie and Young (1998) estimated the total world population at 75,000 following a rapid decline chiefly due to massive over-hunting. However, more recently it has apparently made a phenomenal recovery with huge monospecific flocks numbering up to 400,000 birds found wintering in Korea. The BBC has filmed these huge flocks as one of the great wildlife spectacles of the world.

Vagrancy potential

Green-winged Teal is a frequent visitor to Western Europe averaging about 25 records of drakes annually in Britain and Ireland. The presence of unidentified and overlooked Green-winged Teals in female-type plumages has to be assumed and is probably the most overlooked of vagrants in the UK. In a comparable species, the Blue-winged Teal *Anas discors*, it is the drab females and immature plumages that outnumber the adult males in breeding plumage reported in the UK.

There has been the occasional hint of possible female Green-winged Teal whenever a female clearly accompanies a vagrant drake. For example, a "pair" of teals including a drake Green-winged Teal was at Flamborough Head, Yorkshire in late April 2005. Unfortunately both birds only stayed a few minutes before being flushed, the female being hardly looked at. There were no other Teal in the area.

Vagrant Baikal Teals have been found on the Pacific coast of North America from Alaska to California. The species has now surely also established itself as an occasional vagrant to the Western Palearctic with a number of records of note. An apparent first-winter male Baikal Teal at Minsmere, Suffolk from 18th November 2001 seemed an obvious candidate for vagrancy. A first-winter female shot in Denmark on 24th November 2004 finally settled the arguments when it was found to have an isotope signature for which the simplest explanation is that the bird originated in Siberia (Fox *et al.* 2007). However, evidence for true vagrancy was established as early as 1836 when five birds were obtained in the Saone Valley, France, pre-dating any known introductions into Europe (Cramp *et al.* 1977). Perhaps it should come as no surprise that these were also found in the month of November! The evidence clearly indicates that Baikal Teal can, and do, arrive occasionally in Western Europe and have been doing so for a long time.

As with Green-winged Teal, most male Baikal Teals are straightforward enough to identify while the potential for females and juvenile males to go unnoticed seems self-evident.

IDENTIFICATION

Although the following text will focus on various aspects of separating Green-winged from Baikal Teals in the less distinct juvenile and female plumages, some of the detail can also be applied to separating Green-winged from Eurasian Teal *Anas crecca*. One aspect of plumage well worth focusing on for all these species is that of the colourful specula. In many cases, with practice, the differently patterned speculums provide one of the easiest ways of identifying otherwise rather difficult (=similar) looking individuals but there are other differences that are also worth checking for.

Structure

Baikal Teal is not dissimilar in head and bill size to Eurasian and Green-winged Teal, the bill of Baikal Teal averaging less than two millimetres longer★ and slightly thinner. The head is somewhat squarer and more peaked at the rear crown ("fuller-naped and thicker-necked" - Eldridge and Harrop 1992). However, the most obvious structural difference is in body length, particularly at the rear end, such that Baikal Teal normally look obviously longer-bodied, longer-winged★★ and, especially, longer-tailed than Eurasian/Green-winged Teal.

Measurements (in mm) of female teals (taken from Palmer 1976)

	Bill length*	Wing chord**
Green-winged Teal	34.2-36.1	185-189
Baikal Teal	36.0-38.0	201-214

Plumage

Scapular feathers

The scapulars feathers on any individual dabbling duck vary to some extent in shape and size but, in very broad terms, juvenile and female Baikal Teals have scapulars that are typically plain-centred and pointed, whereas Green-winged and Eurasian Teal have scapular feathers that are typically rounded and obviously marked internally with pale, orangey-buff-coloured, wavy crossbars and crescents. These differences are more difficult to judge in juveniles because many of the scapular feathers of juvenile Baikal Teal are short and rounded, like Eurasian/Green-winged Teal, until they are replaced by the more pointed scapulars of first-winter plumage. To make matters worse, juvenile Eurasian/Green-winged Teal have scapulars that show some of the features of Baikal Teal (!) with some being slightly pointed and fairly plain, only becoming round-ended and internally patterned in subsequent plumages. On adult female Baikal Teal, the scapulars average longer and are more obvious, some individuals even having very long, lanceolate scapulars as on adult males. Furthermore, the scapulars are normally plain-centred on Baikal Teal; they may show a simple pattern of a single buff internal cross-bar, but, if so, this is usually less obvious than on most adult female Eurasian/Green-winged Teal.

Rump and back pattern

In female Baikal Teal, the back and rump feathers are relatively plain, pale, brownish-grey, with faint paler fringing in young birds. The exception is a row of upper tail coverts which have dark centres and paler buff fringes which produce a dark 'band' between the rump and tail. In female Eurasian/Green-winged Teal the appearance of the back and rump is quite different and essentially consists of blackish feathers (sometimes with paler internal marks) with obvious pale greyish fringes, producing a very scaly or scalloped effect.

Underwing

Differences in underwing pattern between Baikal Teal and Green-winged/Eurasian Teal are slight. In all three species, the smaller underwing coverts are relatively dark, contrasting with the rest of the paler underwing, particularly the whitish mid-wing bar/panel formed by the greater underwing coverts. In all plumages of Baikal Teal these smaller underwing coverts are uniformly dark but in Eurasian/Green-winged Teal these dark feathers have pale fringes, at least in the autumn while the plumage is fresh. This difference becomes less obvious as the winter progresses; as the pale fringes wear away, the underwing pattern becomes progressively more similar to that of Baikal Teal.

Facial pattern

On adult female Baikal Teal the facial pattern is typified by a bright white loral spot, emphasised by a dark surround, and a bright white chin and throat. In addition, a white vertical spur (variable in its conspicuousness) extends up from the throat towards the eye and about 15% of females (Palmer 1976) have a dark line running from the gape and forming a bridle, but this can be broken and inconspicuous (Eldridge & Harrop 1992). The rest of the head pattern is relatively subdued and usually lacking such an obvious dark cheek stripe as on female Garganey and some Green-winged Teal. A thin line between the bill base and eye and a broader supercilium behind the eye both tend to be quite deep cinnamon buff in colour and add to the cryptic face pattern. The white loral spot can be somewhat obscured in summer and the full distinctiveness of the face pattern reduced at distance with only the loral spot being outstanding (Eldridge & Harrop 1992).

The facial pattern of juvenile Baikal Teal can be closer to some congeners with a more conspicuous Garganey-like cheek stripe on a greyer face and an absence of a vertical white spur. However the white loral spot is usually still conspicuous. Some juveniles can have a remarkably similar face pattern to some female Eurasian and, especially, Green-winged Teals.

Female and juvenile Eurasian Teals usually have a much more subdued facial pattern lacking the bright whites of the loral spot, throat and spur found in Baikal Teal and instead having a much simpler pattern of buff and grey-brown tones broken by a weak dark eye-stripe and paler supercilium. There is some variation, with some birds showing a slightly stronger face pattern with a weak cheek stripe, or a vague pale spur and pale loral spot, but not normally like that of adult female Baikal Teal.

Female Green-winged Teal vary somewhat more than Eurasian Teal. Some have a very similar facial pattern to Eurasian Teal but many have a much stronger facial pattern that includes a prominent pale loral spot and strong Garganey-like cheek stripe (as first indicated by Millington (1998)) and even occasionally a pale spur (Martin Reid pers. comm). Indeed, well-marked birds are sometimes mistaken for Garganey by North American birders even though a prominent pale loral spot has long been known as a feature of Green-winged Teal. Schioler (1925) illustrated all the Eurasian/Green-winged Teal plumages in great detail and painted a female Green-winged Teal with a striking face pattern of a kind that would be unfamiliar to British observers. Palmer (1976) wrote in the description section of female Green-winged Teal:

"... Quite often with unmarked circular white area at side base of bill (such as is typical of the female Baikal Teal)."

However when considered more carefully, the loral spot and chin/throat region on Baikal Teal are generally brighter, whiter and, combined with the white spur, form incongruent patterns contrasting with the rest of the head plumage with its rich, almost rusty buffs and browns. Obvious pale loral spots on Green-winged and Eurasian Teals, when present, tend to be more buff-toned in keeping with the ground colour of the rest of the facial pattern.

Specula

Much useful information can be gained by studying the shapes and patterns of specula which can greatly aid identification. In Green-winged and Eurasian Teals there are important age- and sex-related differences in the speculum patterns.

Width of speculum

This is a crucial point. Within the genus *Anas* there is variation in the arrangement and structure of the upperwing feathers between the different species and this affects the width of the speculum. The most obvious example of this is between Garganey and Eurasian Teal. In Garganey the white-tipped greater coverts are much closer to the trailing edge of the wing than in Eurasian Teal so the speculum on a Garganey is obviously narrower than on a Eurasian Teal. The same is true on female Baikal Teal. The greater coverts lay closer to the trailing edge, so the speculum on female Baikal Teal is considerably narrower than on a Eurasian and Green-winged Teal. This can be admittedly difficult to assess on flying birds but when at rest (in profile) it is relatively easy to assess the speculum width relative to the rest of the wing.

Upper border to speculum

The pale tips of the greater coverts form a bar, which creates the pale upper border of the speculum. On female Baikal Teal this pale bar is a solid deep cinnamon-orange/brown colour and is relatively narrow. Importantly it is of even colour and width all along its length. In Eurasian Teals the greater covert bar is obviously different to this. It varies according to age and sex, but is typically quite extensively white, broader, and, often, more wedge-shaped as it widens from the inner to outer section of the greater coverts. It is thinnest and of most even width in young females and broadest and most wedge-shaped in adult males. The speculum of Green-winged Teal differs, on average, from both Baikal Teal and Eurasian Teal when birds of the same age and sex are compared. In general, the upper border of the speculum on Green-winged Teal is thinner and of more even width along its length than on Eurasian Teal. Colour differences in the greater covert bar have long been documented (Phillips 1923; Schioler 1925) with Green-winged in all plumages having more cinnamon-orange present in the greater covert bar than Eurasian Teal (nine out of ten birds identifiable according to Phillips 1923).

The thinner, more even, width of the greater covert bar of Green-winged Teal compared to Eurasian Teal has not previously been well documented. Although the colour of the greater covert bar can be helpful (but see below), the shape of it can be a more significant difference in all ages, including adult males, and would seem to be another useful character in the identification of vagrant 'teals' in general. The differences become very apparent when comparing flight shots of Eurasian and Green-winged Teal. In a flock of Eurasian Teal, many of the birds will show a rather broad, wedge-shaped upper border to the speculum. It appears mostly whitish and obviously broader than the white trailing edge. However in a flock of Green-winged Teals the upper borders are thinner and produce a more parallel pattern with the white trailing edge which is of similar width. These differences can also be useful for identifying trickier moulting or eclipse adult male Green-winged Teals when the well-known differences from Eurasian Teal are less obvious.

It is important to note that there is overlap in the colour of the greater covert bar between Green-winged and Eurasian Teal with some Green-winged Teal showing a very similar amount of white as Eurasian Teal in similar plumage (Noel Wamer pers. comm.). This renders it particularly difficult to identify female Eurasian Teals in a North American context.

Adult male Green-winged Teal have a narrower, parallel-sided upper border to the speculum, which can be mostly orange-coloured. Adult male Eurasian Teal have a broader, mostly white and more wedge-shaped speculum.

White trailing edge to speculum

All three species have a white trailing edge to the speculum. The exact shape of white on each feather tip affects the width and overall appearance of the white trailing edge. The amount of white also varies with the age and sex of the individual. In general the broadest white trailing edges are found in adult male Baikal Teals, on some appearing more like prominent long rectangular blocks of white on the rear wing and extending well into the speculum. Conversely in Eurasian and Green-winged Teals it is the immature females that have the broadest white and adult males which have the least white in the trailing edge.

In female Baikal Teal the upper edge of the white tip of each secondary feather is more squared off or even convex. The overall effect is of a more solid 'block' of white with a straight-looking line along its upper edge. This long 'block' of white is usually very obviously wider than the cinnamon-brown greater covert bar, by as much as two or three times.

On Green-winged and Eurasian Teals the shape of the white tip of each secondary feather is, on average, more concave (with much less white on the inner web) creating more of a 'U' shape of white at the feather tip. The overall result is a slightly more wavy upper edge to the white. The width of the trailing edge to the speculum is different between Green-winged and Eurasian Teals, with Green-winged having, on average, a slightly broader pale line than Eurasian Teal of the same age/sex (Scott 1999, pers.obs.). The combination of narrower, richly coloured greater covert bar and broader white trailing edge means that some female Green-winged Teal (particularly immatures) show a superficially similar pattern to Baikal Teal. In reality, the distinctive differences in patterns of speculums between Baikal Teal and Eurasian/Green-winged Teal are not too difficult to distinguish once the patterns are properly understood.

Pattern of green and black in speculum

On female Baikal Teal, the green and black pattern in the speculum typically makes a line of green and a line of black, both parallel to the pale upper and lower borders and both extending across most of the speculum. The green line does broaden slightly towards the inner section of the wing but there is still a broad portion of black in that area. The green colour is often a slightly darker, bronzy-green (making it harder to see), and it extends onto between six and nine out of the ten secondaries; birds with only six green-marked secondaries are probably immatures and have very restricted green on the inner secondary feathers.

On Eurasian and Green-winged Teal, the variation in the green and black pattern of the speculum varies considerably but the general pattern, in both species, is for the inner speculum to be mostly green (making a discrete 'block' of colour, not a long narrow line) and the outer speculum to be mostly black. The number of green-marked feathers varies between three and nine out of ten (*contra* Cramp *et al.* 1977) depending, to some extent, on age and sex; adult males have the most green and immature females have the least green. This green is a brighter, more 'teal-green' (sometimes looking metallic blue) than the darker bronzy-green of a Baikal Teal. In addition to showing more green in their inner speculum, Eurasian and Green-winged Teal also show less black there. The amount of black on the inner secondary feathers varies from none (in adults) to quite an obvious subterminal margin (most often in immature females). Hence a problem teal with no black in the inner speculum could only be Green-winged/Eurasian Teal, not Baikal Teal.

Although the differences in the black and green patterns in the speculum may help us to distinguish Baikal Teal, there are apparently no obvious differences in these patterns between Eurasian and Green-winged Teal.

Bare parts

Female Baikal Teal has a dark grey bill, which is more grey-blue towards the base. Green-winged and Eurasian Teals have slate-coloured bills which usually show a pink or orange/yellow colour to varying degrees at the base combined with some dark spotting. It has been suggested that, on average, Green-winged Teal may have less orange-yellow colouring at the base of the bill compared to Eurasian (Millington 1998).

The leg colour of female Baikal Teal is described as bluish or yellowish-grey (Phillips 1923). On young birds, the leg colour appears to vary, with some being flesh-coloured (pers. obs., Eldridge & Harrop 1992). The leg colour of Eurasian Teal varies from olive-grey to grey-brown (Cramp et al. 1977), grey-green to drab (Witherby et al. 1939) or greenish to brownish-grey (Phillips 1923), being on average typically greyish. Green-winged Teal has paler legs than Eurasian Teal having been described as darkish, lead-coloured to olive-greenish (Palmer 1976) and pale brown to grey-fawn (Witherby et al. 1939). In fact a search of photos on the Internet reveals that many Green-winged Teal have quite obviously pale legs ranging in colour from olive-green though flesh to even yellowish.

Adult male Green-winged Teal – extra feature

Besides the well-documented differences between Green-winged Teal and Eurasian Teal in adult male plumage such as:

- White vertical stripe at front of breast and lack of white horizontal stripe (scapular band) above flanks
- Reduced/absent cream borders (especially upper) of green facial blaze
- Darker overall due to finer, more densely packed vermiculations on body
- Deeper pink wash on breast

There is also one other feature, which could be used even in eclipse plumage, or with tricky moulting individuals:

- Narrower, parallel-sided upper border to speculum, which can be mostly orange-coloured (broader, mostly white and more wedge-shaped in Eurasian Teal)

Key features of female/ immature Baikal Teal (compared to Green-winged Teal)

- Longer-bodied
- Scapulars typically rather long and pointed and mostly plain-centred
- Back and rump mostly plain brownish-grey
- Speculum narrow, covering less than one-third of the inner wing and obviously thin at rest
- Bill base blue-grey

- Small underwing coverts always wholly dark, lacking obvious pale fringing
- Greater covert bar particularly thin and wholly cinnamon-orange
- White trailing edge to secondaries often appears as solid block of white
- Facial pattern with bright whitish loral spot usually against strongly rufous-toned background. Beware though that some Green-winged Teals can appear confusingly similar especially when comparing fresher juvenile/first-winter plumages.
- Speculum pattern consists of parallel black and green lines both extending
- across most of the width of the speculum. A broad area of black always shows on the inner speculum feathers.

Key features of female/immature Green-winged/Eurasian Teal (compared with Baikal Teal)

- Short-bodied, compact structure
- Scapulars typically rather short and rounded with pale internal barring
- Back and rump with scaly appearance due to pale-fringed black feathering
- Speculum broad covering nearly half of inner wing, obvious at rest
- Bill base colour varies from pinkish to orange to yellow
- Small underwing coverts blackish with pale fringes when fresh (autumn), more uniform dark when worn (spring onwards)
- Green area of speculum makes a block of colour mostly on the inner speculum which may show no black subterminal line.

Key features of female/immature Green-winged Teal (compared with Eurasian Teal)

- Narrower, parallel-sided and more extensively orange-toned greater covert bar
- Stronger face pattern, more often with pale loral spot and more conspicuous dark cheek stripe

References

Cramp, S. et al. 1977. *Handbook of the Birds of Europe, the Middle East and North Africa. Vol 1.* Oxford.

Eldridge, M. & Harrop, A. 1992. Identification and Status of Baikal Teal. *Birding World* 5: 11.

Fox, A. D., Christensen, T. K., Bearhop, S. & Newton, J. 2007. Using stable isotope analysis of multiple feather tracts to identify moulting provenance of vagrant birds: a case study of Baikal Teal *Anas formosa* in Denmark. *Ibis* 149:3 622-625.

Millington, R. 1998. The Green-winged Teal. *Birding World* 11: 430-434.

Palmer, R. S. 1976. *Handbook of North American Birds. Vol. 2.* Yale University Press, New Haven, CT.

Phillips, J. C. 1923. *A natural history of ducks. Vol. I.* Houghton Mifflin. Boston.

Sangster, G., Knox, A. G., Helbig, A. J. & Parkin, D. T. 2002. Taxonomic recommendations for European birds. *Ibis* 144: 153–159.

Schioler, E. L. 1925. *Danmarks Fugle 1.* Copenhagen: Nordisk Forlag.

Scott, M. 1999. Identification of female Green-winged Teal. *Birding World* 12: 81.

Witherby, H. F., Jourdain, F. C. R., Ticehurst, N. F. & Tucker, B. W. 1939. *The Handbook of British Birds. Vol. 3.* Witherby Ltd., London.

Stejneger's, White-winged and Velvet Scoters
Martin Garner

A serendipitous happening got me hooked on these beasts! A fortunate encounter with a female Velvet Scoter in Belfast Loch (where the species is not common) was followed a week later by a close encounter with female White-winged Scoters in British Columbia. I was quickly taken aback with how different the latter species looked, much more like a Surf Scoter in head and bill shape. Indeed because of the similar head and bill profiles, North American birders sometimes need to distinguish carefully between female White-winged and Surf Scoters (when white secondaries are obscured) by the distribution of feathering at the bill base, a scenario unlikely to unfold when comparing female Velvet and Surf Scoters (cf. Kaufman 1990). Like Black Scoter, it is only adult male White-winged and Stejneger's Scoter which have so far been identified in the Western Palearctic. Awareness of the possibilities of identifying female and immature males will greatly increase the likelihood of finding a national 'first' among the tribe *Mergini* – the Sea Ducks.

Taxonomic status

In Europe and North America, these were formerly treated as three separate species (Dwight 1914) but then subsumed into one species *Melanitta fusca* comprising three subspecies: *M. f. fusca* of Europe and western Russia, *M. f. deglandi* of North America, and *M. f. stejnegeri* of Siberia and eastern Asia (e.g. Cramp & Simmons 1977; AOU Checklist of North American Birds, 7th edition). In Russia, they have been treated for some time as two species, *Melanitta fusca* and *M. deglandi*, the latter comprising two subspecies, *M. d. deglandi* and *M. d. stejnegeri* (e.g. Dementiev & Gladkov 1967; Stepanyan 2003). In Britain the BOURC more recently followed the Russian split (Collinson *et al.* 2006), but it is reasonable to argue they did not go far enough.

Declaring new taxonomic positions for these taxa may sound presumptuous, but by simply applying established criteria (Helbig *et al.* 2002) it is clear that these three forms display more than sufficient criteria for them all to be classified as full species. They are well-defined biological and evolutionary species. It is anticipated that any DNA/phylogenetic studies will further establish this taxonomic position.

All three taxa are diagnosable in the field and exhibit differences at all ages and in all plumages (e.g. Dwight 1914, Witherby *et al.* 1944, Cramp & Simmons 1977, Gardarsson 1997, Garner 1999, Garner 2004). They also appear to be reproductively isolated: they have essentially separate breeding and wintering ranges, and there is no evidence of interbreeding or clinal variation. Thus, according to the criteria proposed by Helbig *et al.* (2002), they can justifiably be classified as three separate species:

Velvet Scoter *Melanitta fusca* (Linnaeus 1758)
White-winged Scoter *M. deglandi* (Bonaparte 1850)
Stejneger's Scoter *M. stejnegeri* (Ridgway 1887)

There is no clear precedent for an English name for *stejnegeri*. Potential English names include: 'Asian/Siberian White-winged Scoter' (which seems a laborious concoction and would necessitate 'American White-winged Scoter' for *deglandi*); 'East Siberian Scoter' (as per Dementiev & Gladkov 1967, but is perhaps too general and could equally be applied to other scoters in East Siberia); and 'Hump-nosed Scoter' (the closest anglicised translation of the Russian '*Gorbonosyi turpan*' (per Mike Wilson), although this is used generically to include both *deglandi* and *stejnegeri*). Stejneger's White-winged Scoter could be used but is again rather clumsy. Stejneger's Scoter is used here (being precise and distinctive) after the Norwegian zoologist, Leonhard Hess Stejneger (pronounced "Stayneger"), who made pioneering discoveries in northeast Siberia and whose name has already been given to the taxon.

Geographical range

There are three forms of scoter which show white feathering on the inner wing. They each have separate breeding areas and their normal wintering ranges do not overlap. Velvet Scoter *Melanitta fusca* breeds in northern Europe and Asia east to the River Yenisey at least. The species winters from the Baltic to the North Sea and eastern Atlantic Ocean. Small numbers also winter in the Black, Caspian and Mediterranean Seas. The breeding range of White-winged Scoter *Melanitta deglandi* is confined to north-western North America from north-west Alaska to Hudson Bay and south to southern Manitoba. The species winters south to California along the Pacific coast and to South Carolina along the Atlantic coast. Stejneger's Scoter *Melanitta stejnegeri* breeds in eastern Asia from Altai (River Yenisey?) eastwards to Kamchatka and south to northern Mongolia. Its wintering range is along the Asian Pacific coast south to China (Collinson *et al.* 2006).

Vagrancy potential

Velvet Scoter in North America
Velvet Scoter has reached Greenland (Witherby *et al.* 1944), and thus seems a likely potential vagrant to North America.

White-winged Scoter in Western Europe
Iceland is the only country so far in the Western Palearctic with confirmed records of White-winged Scoter. Since the first, at Arnarfjordur, northwest Iceland, in June 1993, there have been five accepted records, all in the period May to July including one adult male, which paired with a female Northern Eider (Kolbeinsson *et al.* 2001). There have also been several records of White-winged Scoter (*deglandi*) in north-east Asia (Dementiev & Gladkov 1967).

Stejneger's Scoter In Western Europe
There have been four extralimital records of Stejneger's Scoter in Europe, two of which were initially misidentified, perhaps suggesting that others have been overlooked. The records, all of adult males, are as follows: Baie de Somme, northern France, 4th December 1886 (recently re-identified specimen: Jiquet 2007); Kemio, southwest Finland, May to June 1996 (Lindroos 1997); Iceland, April to May 2003 (Garner *et al.* 2004); Gdansk Bay, Poland, 10th March 2007 (photographed, Dorota Lukasik pers.comm.).

Stejneger's Scoters in North America
Until recently there were no records of Stejenger's Scoter in North America. In early June 2002, while leading a bird tour to Gambell, Alaska, Jon Dunn, Steve Howell and Gary Rosenberg found a 'White-winged' Scoter swimming off the northwest tip of St Lawrence Island. They had witnessed a small, but consistent, spring passage of White-winged Scoters in late May and

early June in each of the previous twenty-five years they had collectively led tours to Gambell, but this was the first time that a swimming bird had been found there. JD was the first to notice that this male-plumaged bird had 'black' flanks, unlike normal *deglandi* White-winged Scoters from the mainland. The bird remained off the point for at least three days (2nd-4th June), and photographs were taken by GR. Shortly thereafter, GR photographed normal *deglandi* in the interior of Alaska, from which differences in bill coloration and structure were noticed. Further direct comparison of the photographs of the Gambell bird with photographs of *stejnegeri* in a photographic guide of the birds of Japan confirmed that the Gambell bird was an example of Stejenger's Scoter.

This record was subsequently pre-dated when a photograph was discovered of an adult male Stejneger's Scoter taken at Cape Nome, Alaska, by Brad Bergstrom on 30th May 2001 (Garner *et al.* 2004). Given this overlooked record and the fact that most birds are seen only in flight off Gambell (see above), it seems likely that Stejneger's Scoter actually occurs more commonly in North America.

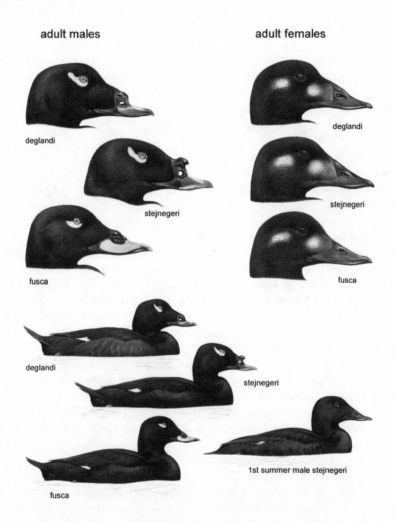

adult males   adult females

deglandi

stejnegeri

fusca

deglandi

stejnegeri

fusca

deglandi

stejnegeri

fusca

1st summer male stejnegeri

IDENTIFICATION

The most important identification characters are the patterns and colours on the bill, the colour of the flanks in adult males, the shape of the head and bill profile, and the shape and pattern of the feathering at the base of the bill in all plumages. The latter is covered in detail under 'Adult females', but the pattern is basically the same for both sexes and all ages. The consistent differences in the head and bill profiles between all three taxa, in both males and females, clearly suggest differences in skull morphology, which would be additionally relevant to the taxonomic debate. Differences in the trachea structure between *fusca* and *deglandi/stejnegeri* have already been established (Cramp & Simmons 1977).

Adult males

Velvet Scoter is relatively straightforward to separate from the other two taxa. It has an essentially yellow–and–black bill, with the yellow or yellow–orange colouration extending well back along the sides of the upper mandible almost to the feathering at the bill-base. This pattern is not found in the other two taxa. The forehead and bill profile lacks an obvious knob at the base of the bill (there is just a slight swelling) and so presents a relatively neat, concave curve from the bill tip to the forecrown. Additionally, the white sub-ocular mark (or 'teardrop') is the least striking of the three taxa; it lacks the obvious upswept 'tail' found in the other two forms. Less than 1% of *stejnegeri* and *deglandi* show a similarly shaped sub-ocular mark (and these are probably immature males).

White-winged Scoter has a predominantly pinkish-red bill, with yellow or orange tones confined to the nail and the area of the culmen adjacent to the basal knob. The bill often looks uniform pinkish-red. A black line runs along the cutting edge and broadens slightly at the tip, either side of the nail. Also, the red area on the bill usually has a convex rear edge. The forehead and bill profile appears 'stepped' due to an obvious knob at the base of the bill. This basal knob shows a downward slope towards the tip of the bill and is half-covered by a forward protrusion of feathering, so that half appears feathered and the other half bare. The nasal cavity is normally oval-shaped. The white sub-ocular mark has an obvious, strongly upswept 'tail'. The flanks are brown (unlike the other two forms on which the flanks are black) and contrast with the black breast, rear end and upperparts.

Stejneger's Scoter has a bill pattern similar to White-winged Scoter, but with a narrow yellow 'lick' along the rim of the bill. The black along the bill rim (lamellae) does not extend to a lateral expansion either side of the nail, as it does on White-winged Scoter, so the bill looks more uniformly red and not 'interrupted' by black. Also, the the bill has a concave rear edge although this is variable and not diagnostic of all individuals.

The forehead and bill profile are subtly, but clearly, different from White-winged Scoter. The profile from the mid-crown to the knob at the base of the bill is flatter on Stejneger's Scoter, whereas on White-winged Scoter it is stepped and the forehead is more obviously squared. There is also no forward protrusion of feathering over the knob at the base of the bill, so the forehead feathering stops more abruptly at the basal knob. The basal knob itself is quite variable, but looks more 'square' in shape as it is essentially flat-topped, with an almost vertical front edge, but it has a variable overhanging protuberance (which may perhaps become more pronounced with age). The taller basal knob on some individuals can create the impression that the forward section of the bill is shorter than in White-winged Scoter.

The nasal cavity is usually circular, less oval than on White-winged Scoter, although this is subtle and probably of limited use in the field. The white sub-ocular mark is similar to that of White-winged Scoter, although on average has a slightly thicker 'tail', but there is overlap. The flanks are black in fresh plumage, with the feather fringes fading to brown in worn plumage, as in Velvet Scoter. This creates a pattern of scattered dark brown marks within the black flanks but not an obviously brown-pigmented block as in White-winged Scoter.

Some literature (e.g. Stepanyan 2003) has indicated differences in the pattern of black on the culmen between White-winged and Stejneger's Scoters but, in fact, the amount of black is variable in both. Study of specimens at the British Natural History Museum has confirmed that individuals of either form can have black bleeding forward from the basal knob and black 'dividing' lines on the culmen, or an entirely yellow/orange surface to the culmen.

Key features of adult males

Velvet Scoter
- Bill colour yellow to yellow-orange (no red tones) extending furthest back to feathering at bill base
- Bill with only slight swelling
- Head and bill profile a smooth concave curve
- White sub-ocular mark lacks tail
- Flanks black

White-winged Scoter
- Bill colour predominately pinkish-red with black line running full length of bill rim and yellow present adjacent to bill knob
- Red area on bill has a convex rear edge
- Feathers protrude forward over top of basal knob
- Nostril cavity oval-shaped and more prominent than Velvet Scoter
- A three-step bill and head profile with raised basal knob which slopes down towards the bill tip
- White sub-ocular mark with obvious up-swept tail
- Flanks extensively brown

Stejneger's Scoter
- Bill colour similar to White-winged Scoter but with diagnostic yellow lick along the bill rim
- Red area on bill has a concave, or straight, rear edge
- Flat-topped basal knob on bill with vertical front edge and variable overhanging protuberance
- No forward protrusion of feathering on top of basal knob
- Nostril cavity circular-shaped, 'see-through' and most prominent
- Head and bill profile subtly different, flatter from mid-crown to basal knob, lacking the stepped profile of White-winged Scoter
- White sub-ocular mark with obvious up-swept tail
- Flanks black (mottled brown when worn)

Adult females

Velvet Scoter has only a very slightly swollen base to the culmen (reflecting that of the male) so that the forehead and bill profile forms a neat, if slightly 'broken', shallow concave curve from the bill tip to the forecrown, combined with a generally quite rounded crown profile. On some, the forehead feathering can be held more vertically, such that the head appears rather squarer. The pattern of feathering at the bill base is diagnostic. The feathering runs in a line from the gape towards the nostril, but falls clearly short of the nostril (c. 6-8 mm behind the nostril; Cramp & Simmons 1977). The foremost tip of the feathering reaches a point level with the nasal cavity, but not below it.

White-winged Scoter has a more obviously swollen central culmen than Velvet Scoter which produces a somewhat 'stepped' forehead and bill profile. The overall profile is deeper and more wedge-shaped, with a more solid, squarer-looking head. The pattern of feathering at the bill base is diagnostic. The feathering protrudes over the swollen part of the culmen and envelopes the bill base with broad ovate or squarish patches. Importantly, the feathering on the top of the culmen extends forward (often in a triangular shape), which is not found on Velvet or Stejneger's Scoters. The feathering behind the nostril cavity comes closer to the nostril than in Velvet Scoter (c. 1-4 mm behind the nostril; Cramp & Simmons 1977) and reaches a point which is in line with the lower edge of the nasal cavity or obviously below it. There is a tendency for some, particularly young, female White-winged and Stejneger's Scoters to show larger white face patches than on Velvet Scoters.

Stejneger's Scoter has a flatter forehead and bill profile with an almost straight line running from the mid-crown almost to the bill tip. This is very different to White-winged Scoter, which shows a more obvious squared forehead and obvious swelling over the culmen thus creating a stepped profile. The pattern of feathering on the bill sides is similar to that of White-winged Scoter but the feathering does not protrude forward over the culmen. Together with the difference in forehead and bill profile this produces the most 'Roman-nosed' or Eider-like profile of the three.

Key features of adult females

Velvet Scoter
- Head and bill profile gently concave with only slight swelling at bill base
- Feathering at bill base runs in diagonal line from gape towards nostril, falling clearly short of nostril
- Most rounded head shape (of the three)

White-winged Scoter
- Head and bill profile a subtle three-step wedge, with an obvious swollen bill base (closer to Surf Scoter than Velvet)
- Feathering at base of bill is extensive, enveloping bill base with broad patches that almost reach nostril
- Triangle-shaped extension of feathering on top of basal swelling
- White face patches particularly large in some (young) females

Stejneger's Scoter
- Head and bill profile forms an almost straight line from mid-crown to bill tip, producing the most Roman-nosed profile (lacks swelling of White-winged)

- Feathering at base of bill is extensive, enveloping bill base as on White-winged Scoter
- Lacks extension of feathering on top of basal swelling
- White face patches particularly large in some (young) females

Immatures

Immature females can be aged by their extensively pale bellies and indistinct, pale greyish-brown fringing to the upperparts (especially the wing coverts). Some immature female White-winged and Stejneger's Scoters have particularly large and striking white facial spots, more so than most Velvet Scoters of a similar age. Immature males also have pale bellies, with the black feathering beginning to appear within the body plumage during the first winter, although the moult timing is very variable between individuals (Dwight 1914). Features such as the white sub-ocular mark, flank colour and shape of the bill-base knob develop gradually, so are of limited use in the identification of young birds. However, the pattern of colouring on the bill, which is diagnostic in adult males, can appear quite quickly and thus facilitate identification. Specifically, the yellow 'lick' on the male Stejneger's bill can appear during its first winter. At close range, the shape of the feathering around the bill base, similar to that described for females, is also diagnostic at an early stage.

References

Collinson, M., Parkin, D. T., Knox, A. G., Sangster, G. & Helbig, A. J. 2006. Species limits within the genus *Melanitta*, the scoters. *British Birds* 99: 183-201.

Cramp, S. & Simmons K. E. L. Eds. 1977. *The Birds of the Western Palearctic. Vol. 1.* Oxford.

Dementiev, G. P. & Gladkov, N. A. Eds. 1967. *Birds of the Soviet Union. Vol. 4.* Jerusalem.

Dwight, J. 1914. The moults and plumages of the Scoters, genus *Oidemia* (*Melanitta*). *Auk* 31: 293-308.

Gardarsson, A. 1997. Korpönd að vestan. *Bliki* 18: 65-67.

Garner, M. 1999. Identification of White-winged and Velvet Scoters – males, females and immatures. *Birding World* 12: 319-324.

Garner, M., Lewington, I. & Rosenberg, G. 2004. Stejneger's Scoter in the Western Palearctic and North America. *Birding World* 17: 337-347.

Gilroy, J. J. & Lees, A. C. 2003. Vagrancy theories: are autumn vagrants really reverse migrants? *British Birds* 96: 427-438.

Gooders, J. & Boyer, T. 1986. *Ducks of Britain and the Northern Hemisphere.* London.

Helbig, A. J., Knox, A.G., Parkin, D.T., Sangster, G. & Collinson, M. 2002. Guidelines for assigning species Rank. *Ibis* 144: 518-525.

Jiquet, F. 2007. Siberian White-winged Scoter, New to France. *Ornithos* 14: 38-42.

Kaufman, K. 1990. *Advanced Birding.* Houghton Mifflin. Boston.

Kolbeinsson, Y., Prainsson, G. & Petursson, G. 2001. Sjaldgaefir Fuglar a Islandi 1998 [Rare birds in Iceland in 1998]. *Bliki* 22: 21-46.

Lindroos, T. 1997. *Rare Birds in Finland 1996.* Alula 3: 160-169.

Madge, S. & Burn, H. 1988. *Wildfowl.* London.

Palmer, R. S. 1976. *Handbook of North American Birds. Vol 3.* London.

Phillips, J. C. 1922-1926. *A Natural History of the Ducks.* New York.

Proctor, B. 1997. Identification of Velvet and White-winged Scoters. *Birding World* 10: 56-61.

Iráinsson, G. & Pétursson, C. 1997. Sjaldgaefir fuglar a Islandi 1995. *Bliki* 18: 23-50.

Sangster, G., Collinson, M., Helbig, A. J., Knox, A. G., Parkin, D. T. & Prater, T. 2001. The taxonomic status of Green-winged Teal *Anas carolinensis. British Birds* 94: 218-226.

Sangster, G., Hazevoet, C. J., van den Berg, A. B. & Roselaar, C. S. 1997. CSNA-mededelingen Dutch avifaunal list: taxonomic changes in 1977-97. *Dutch Birding* 19: 21-28.

Stepanyan, L. S. 1990. *Conspectus of the ornithological fauna of the USSR.* (In Russian) Moscow.

Stepanyan, L. S. 2003. *Conspectus of the ornithological fauna of Russia and adjacent territories (within the borders of the USSR as a historic region).* (In Russian) Moscow.

Witherby, H. F., Jourdain, F. C. R., Ticehurst, N. F. & Tucker, B. W. 1944. *The Handbook of British Birds. Volume III.* London.

Common and Black Scoter

Martin Garner

Common Scoters are present in huge numbers at certain points around our coasts but are often beyond telescope range and therefore frequently go unscrutinised. To get sufficiently clear views of scoters it is important to seize the opportunities wrought by the occasional close offshore flock, overland migrants in the summer, or storm-blown waifs in the autumn and winter. I have tried to make it a practice to chase down every locally occurring inland Common Scoter and although I have so far failed to find a female or immature Black I have left satisfied that all birds studied have proved to be identifiable as definitely Common Scoters. The first British claim of a female or immature male Black Scoter will come some day soon…to whoever is better prepared than I was on one October day in the early 1980s when the female-type 'Common Scoter' on a small pool on Tresco, Isles of Scilly received little more than a cursory glance.

Geographical range

Black Scoter *Melanitta americana* breeds in northern Asia, east of the Lena/Yana watershed, and in North America, where there are essentially two disjoint populations centred on Alaska and northern Quebec. The species winters along the Pacific coasts of Asia and North America and along the Atlantic coasts of North America from Newfoundland to the Gulf of Mexico with the largest concentration around New Jersey (Palmer 1976; Sibley 2000).

Vagrancy potential

There have already been eight records of Black Scoter in the UK and a further five from the Netherlands (3), Denmark (1) and Spain (1). Records have occurred from September to May but with a concentration in winter from November onwards. Given that all vagrants so far seen in Western Europe have been adult males, the possibility that some females and immatures are being overlooked seems very high. There have also been two records of Common Scoter *Melanitta nigra* in Greenland (Palmer 1976) and it is perhaps a little surprising that Common Scoter has not yet been recorded along the north-eastern seaboard of North America.

Taxonomy of scoters

In a paper published back in 1914 Henry Thurston illustrated not three but six species of scoter (see Dwight 1914). Under the genus of *Oidemia* the six recognized species were:

Oidemia americana = Black Scoter
Oidemia nigra = Common Scoter
Oidemia fusca = Velvet Scoter
Oidemia deglandi = White-winged Scoter or American White-winged Scoter
Oidemia stejnegeri = Stejneger's Scoter or Asian White-winged Scoter
Oidemia perspicillata = Surf Scoter

Since then the genus has changed to *Melanitta* and, for "western" ornithologists at least, the six species were lumped into three during the early to middle part of the twentieth century. With some bird forms there have been genuine discoveries during the last couple of decades concerning biology, behaviour and morphology (including molecular data) that have caused former subspecies to be elevated to species status. Examples such as Taiga Flycatcher, Balearic Shearwater and Hume's Warbler spring to mind. However some taxonomic changes are more of a pendulum swing simply reflecting current trends rather than new information, and this is certainly more the case with the scoters. Past authors such as Dwight fully recognized the very significant differences in bill structures, feathering around the bill base and some plumage differences that caused them to see specific status for these birds as axiomatic. More recently the BOURC split Black Scoter and 'American' White-winged Scoter (Collinson *et al.* 2006), and the criteria used are largely the same as those evident in Dwight (save for the difference in courtship call between Common and Black Scoters). Russian ornithologists have had these species splits in place for many years. The current taxonomic situation under the BOURC is as follows:

Melanitta americana = Black Scoter
Melanitta nigra = Common Scoter
Melanitta fusca = Velvet Scoter
Melanitta deglandi (with subspecies *deglandi* and *stejnegeri*) = American and Asian White-winged/Stejneger's Scoter
Melanitta perspicillata = Surf Scoter

For further discussion on the taxonomy of White-winged and Stejneger's Scoters, see those species accounts.

IDENTIFICATION

It was not long ago that only adult male Black Scoters were considered identifiable in a vagrant context. Indeed, all records so far in Western Europe have been of adult males. Following excellent short papers by Alderfer (1992) and Waring (1993) it became increasingly clear that some examples of both females and immatures should also be identifiable. While hybridisation between the two species is so far unknown (Collinson *et al.* 2006) I have come across a photograph of a single male bird from Korea in winter that does appear to be intermediate in bill pattern between the two species; the base of its bill is like that of a Black Scoter but the reduced height of the bill base and the more extensive area of yellow (extending towards the bill tip) is more suggestive of Common Scoter. Whether it represents an odd male Black Scoter or a hybrid individual is unclear.

It will take clued-up observers making the most of close views to identify the next Black Scoters in Europe so, for those inspired to try, here is an analysis of some of the key characters to look for.

Adult males

In January 1992 I went to see an adult male Black Scoter in St Bride's Bay, Dyfed. This was only the fourth British record of a species I had long wanted to see in the UK. I ended up having fantastic views of this individual in the company of a couple of hundred Common Scoters. It showed quite a number of interesting differences from the Common Scoters, both in plumage and behaviour, which inspired me to look even more carefully at these birds subsequently in Canada.

The most important and well-known difference is in the shape and colour pattern on the bill. In both species, the bill is black with a yellow area on the upper mandible. The difference is in the extent to which this yellow (or yellow-orange) colour covers the swelling at the base of the bill (the 'basal knob'). In Black Scoter, the basal knob is completely covered by yellow, creating a yellow 'dome', hence their colloquial names of 'butterbill' and 'coppernose'. In Common Scoter, the yellow is typically restricted to the flat section of the upper mandible with only a thin yellow line extending back over the top of the basal knob, which therefore looks mostly black when viewed from the side. Beware though that, in some males, this yellow line can be so extensive that, in a head-on view, it can appear to cover the basal knob thus becoming more similar in appearance to Black Scoter (such birds have been suggested to be younger/second calendar-year-males, e.g. Cramp & Simmons 1977). A clear side-view may be needed to confirm whether the sides of the basal knob are entirely yellow (Black Scoter) or at least partly black (Common Scoter).

The problem is, most scoters don't come close enough to see these details well. When watching birds bobbing about at some distance on the sea, many male Commons can appear to show big yellow patches at the base of the bill which can mimic the appearance of male Black Scoter. Under these conditions it's very easy to be fooled!

While watching the Dyfed Black Scoter I noticed straight away that it sat higher on the water showing more body than the Common Scoters, a feature that also made it look a little larger. It also cocked its tail more frequently than the male Commons, and the tail was clearly shorter than its companions. One of the most striking features, however, was a distinctive pattern of behaviour. I observed the bird suddenly leave the other scoters, which were a couple of hundred yards offshore, and head straight for the shore by itself. It proceeded to swim all the way to the breaking surf and, after diving and feeding here for several minutes, headed back out to the flock. To confirm this was not just a one-off action, it repeated this behaviour several times during a three-hour period of watching. I have since noted in Canada that Black Scoters often enjoy feeding close inshore, much more so than their European counterparts. Another generic name for all scoters in North America, which reflects this behaviour, is 'Surf Duck'. While the bird of recent winters in Colwyn Bay, North Wales may not have been so obliging, I still think that any approachable or surf-feeding scoter is worth checking with particular care.

Key features of adult males

- Prominent yellow-orange 'dome' stuck onto bill base, with no black at sides
- Orange colour tends to be in lower section of 'dome' (on Common Scoter the orange is often in upper section or spread all over)
- Sits higher on water and looks bulkier
- Thicker-necked and shorter-tailed
- Penchant for feeding in or near the surf
- Eye ring tends to be bluish-grey, not yellow
- Bill tip with more prominent nail (very close views required!) and nostrils nearer bill base

First-winter males

One of the peak times of discovery of Black Scoters in Western Europe has been during the early winter so, although my experience and observations are limited to November and December, they may well be apposite. At this time, first-winter males of both species still show the brown tones of their juvenile plumage and therefore tend to look very female-like. This appearance persists until they moult into blacker adult-like feathering. The timing of this moult varies greatly between individuals; in some birds it is beginning to show through in early winter but other first-winter males retain their 'brown' female-like appearance even into the spring (see Dwight 1914).

Given good views, first-winter males, even in the female-like plumage, can be aged and identified by studying their bills. At a glance the bills may appear to be just uniformly greyish but careful scrutiny will show that, in both species, the young males have a grey-green or mustard-coloured patch where the orange/yellow of adulthood will eventually appear. Crucially, the shape of this patch mirrors the pattern on adult birds; on young male Black Scoters the whole patch butts up to the bill base whereas on young male Common Scoter it is centred on the middle of the culmen with a thin line extending back to the bill base. If carefully observed, the pattern is diagnostic. It would be easy to suggest that first-winter male Black Scoters are being overlooked in the UK during November and December except by those taking a careful second look for this grey-green or mustard-coloured patch, and assessing its shape, on female-like birds. Later in the winter, the patch becomes more yellow and more conspicuously raised as the presence of black feathering in the plumage (indicating a young male bird) also increases.

Key features of first-winter male Black Scoter

- Grey-green/mustard-coloured patch over bill base in November/December mimics the pattern on adults, becoming more yellow and more raised as the winter progresses
- Bill tip with more prominent nail
- Typically steeper forehead and squarer head shape
- Possibly with different pattern of dark and light on head compared to Common Scoter (see description of females)

Females and juveniles

While sceptics may argue that you can't identify this plumage of Black Scoter in the field, I would disagree. I have closely examined a number of more obliging female/juvenile Common Scoters and, in each case, I have eventually been able to confirm to my satisfaction that they were definitely Common Scoters rather than Black Scoter. I am confident that if a real female Black Scoter gave obliging views that it should be identifiable.

All of the key features are around the head and bill. Compared with Common Scoter, the bill of a Black Scoter is a little 'lumpier'-looking in profile and on average, slightly shorter with a more swollen base and prominent 'hooked' nail. Black Scoter also tends to have a steeper forehead and flatter crown producing a squarer head shape.

Look out too for differences in the extent of black on the nape. In Common Scoter this is relatively narrow and tapers to a point when seen from behind but in Black Scoter it is broader (hence more extensive in side-view) and more round-ended or 'squared-off' in rear-view. I have not tested this sufficiently to note any degree of overlap, but I think it could be a useful feature in general.

Waring (1993) noted that approximately 10% of adult female Black Scoters, mainly in spring and summer, can show extensive yellow markings on the bill. Female Common Scoters can show some yellow in the nostril cavities and a smaller patch in the middle of the culmen but otherwise do not show such extensive yellow. Juveniles of both species tend to have the palest cheeks while, typically, adult females tend to have darker cheeks with dusky streaking throughout, contrasting less with the dark cap. Common Scoters in juvenile and female-type plumages often show a dark smudgy curve extending vertically below the eye. This feature tends to be much less prominent on juvenile and female-type Black Scoters.

Key features of female and juvenile Black Scoter

- Lumpier bill, often with a slightly swollen base and prominent hooked/arched nail
- Typically steeper forehead and squarer head shape
- More dark patterning on sides of nape
- Dark cap may end as a squared-off or broad rounded line on the nape, not tapered as in Common
- 10% of adult females show extensive yellow on bill
- Cheeks tend to be cleaner with a less obvious dark vertical cheek mark

Female/juvenile Common Scoter

smooth bill profile
evenly curved crown,
commonly with dark
verticle 'sickle' below eye

Female/juvenile Black Scoter

lumpy bill profile
with prominent arched nail.
squarer head shape, more
dark visible on sides of
hind neck

Diagram by Martin Garner

Rear head view

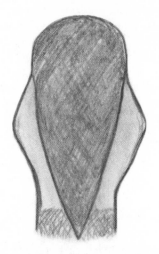

female/imm Common Scoter
<u>tapered</u> at hindneck

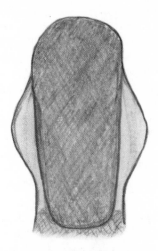

female/imm Black Scoter
<u>squared-off</u> at at hindneck

often lumpy
forehead

yellow
eye-ring

always some
black at sides
of bill

thinner
neck

male Common Scoter

golden globe
stuck on
bill base

dull bluish
eye-ring

thicker
neck

male Black Scoter

These features are obviously subtle and require prolonged and close views. The prize of finding more of these birds will fall to those who go the extra mile in checking and double-checking those scoters that give close views.

References

Alderfer, J. 1992. Immature Black Scoters. *Birding World* 5: 193-4.

Collinson, M., Parkin, D. T., Knox, A. G., Sangster, G. & Helbig, A. J. 2006. Species limits within the genus *Melanitta*, the scoters. *British Birds* 99: 183-201.

Cramp, S & Simmons, K. E. L. (eds.) 1977. *The Birds of the Western Palearctic. Vol. 1*. Oxford.

Dwight, J. 1914. The Moults and Plumages of the Scoters, genus *Oidemia* (*Melanitta*). *Auk* 31: 293-308.

Garner, M. 1989. Common Scoter of the nominate race with extensive yellow on bill. *British Birds* 82: 616-618.

Palmer, R. S. 1976. *Handbook of North American Birds. Vol. 3*. London.

Waring, D. 1993. Identification Forum: female Black Scoter. *Birding World* 6: 78-79.

Canvasback, Pochard and Redhead

Martin Garner

A putative male Redhead at Martin Mere WWT reserve in winter 1979 intrigued me enough to encourage a visit to the reserve. The bird proved to be a hybrid but I did photograph some of the captive Redhead with a brownie camera in the hope of eventually finding one in the UK! Since then I have been fortunate enough to add Ferruginous Duck, Lesser Scaup and Ring-necked Duck to my self-found list, but the two much rarer *Aythya* vagrants continue to elude me. Up until the mid 1990s, the identification of Redhead and Canvasback in Britain was largely hypothetical: there were no records of either species. Since then there have been several records and some tricky identification challenges. As vagrant *Aythya* ducks have the capacity and potential to turn up just about anywhere in the country, including your local village pond, they remain a great winter target species, and I do wonder if females could still be easily overlooked except by those clued up. Good hunting!

Geographical range

Redhead *Aythya americana* and Canvasback *A. valisineria* are both Nearctic species while Pochard *A. ferina* breeds widely across the Palearctic region from Britain, east to Mongolia and western China and winters within and south of the breeding range to sub-Saharan Africa and the Pacific coast of Asia.

The core breeding range of Redhead is across the prairies of central North America and marshes of the western USA, occurring much more locally and sporadically to the north and south of the core range and east to the Great Lakes Basin as far as the extreme south of Quebec. There is a disjunct breeding population in Alaska. The winter range of Redhead overlaps with the southern limits of the breeding range and extends right across the southern half of the USA and Mexico. Birds regularly occur on the Atlantic coast from New York southwards, with the largest concentration along the coastline of the Gulf of Mexico. It is, however, rare in the extreme north-east of Canada with only three records for Newfoundland prior to a remarkable arrival of ten birds at St. John's in late September 2005 (B. MacTavish pers. comm.)

The core breeding range of Canvasback is across the prairie and parklands of north-west North America. The species winters mostly to the south of the breeding range, across the southern half of the USA and Mexico. Winter concentrations are at widely scattered sites and movements are greatly affected by the severity of winter weather. There are casual records from the Atlantic coastline of north-east Canada and regular wintering records from Massachusetts to central Florida.

Vagrancy potential

The breeding ranges of both Redhead and Canvasback are considerably further west than many of the other Nearctic wildfowl, such as Lesser Scaup, Ring-necked Duck, American Wigeon, and Green and Blue-winged Teals, which regularly reach western Europe. Hence, they are likely to occur here much less frequently and this is reflected in the currently small number of records. Both species have nevertheless occurred in an apparently wild state in Iceland and Britain, with Redhead also having reached Ireland and records of Canvasback from the Netherlands and Germany too. There have also been reports of both species which have obviously involved individuals that had escaped from captivity.

While the males of the three sibling species are stunning birds in full red, black and grey breeding plumage, their partners look considerably less inspiring. It is not surprising therefore that the 'brown' plumages of Pochard are not generally the focus of intense study by birdwatchers in the UK! However, such a lack of interest in female and juvenile Pochard may well result in individuals of the two rare sibling species being overlooked.

IDENTIFICATION

While the identification of the males of these three species is generally straightforward, the presence of individuals with apparent hybrid characters is both very real and problematic (e.g. Vinicombe 2003; Vinicombe 2008) Any claim of an apparently vagrant male Canvasback or Redhead should be thoroughly checked to ensure that overall size and shape (especially of the head), iris colour, bill pattern and the tone of grey on the back and flanks all match the normal appearance of the species. Not surprisingly the challenge of separating 'brown' examples in female and juvenile plumages of these species (including Pochard) remains a testing challenge. Despite some very helpful identification resources on the subject in recent years, they can still cause real problems. This situation can be readily illustrated by erroneous claims of female Canvasback in England and Ireland during autumn 2004, and a female Redhead-like *Aythya* on Shetland in November 2006. Indeed, the first accepted female Redhead in Scotland was, on first views, described as "a bird that looked to all intents and purposes like a female Pochard" (Scott, Gillon & Rivers 2004). Furthermore, while Pochard is roughly intermediate in appearance between the other two, its particular similarity to Canvasback in some plumages led Palmer (1975) to write "Identifying young birds; also adults in late summer, may be very difficult, if in fact possible".

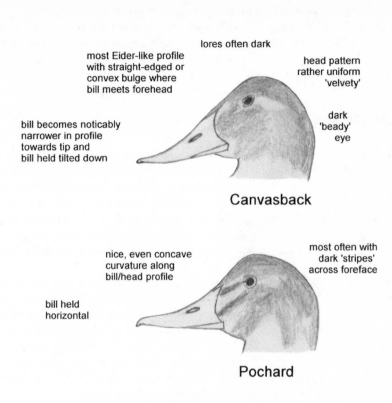

most Eider-like profile
with straight-edged or
convex bulge where
bill meets forehead

lores often dark

head pattern
rather uniform
'velvety'

bill becomes noticably
narrower in profile
towards tip and
bill held tilted down

dark
'beady'
eye

Canvasback

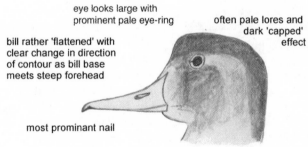

nice, even concave
curvature along
bill/head profile

most often with
dark 'stripes'
across foreface

bill held
horizontal

Pochard

eye looks large with
prominent pale eye-ring

often pale lores and
dark 'capped'
effect

bill rather 'flattened' with
clear change in direction
of contour as bill base
meets steep forehead

most prominant nail

Redhead

Diagram by Martin Garner

Learning female-type Pochard

It is no surprise that 'brown' Pochard tend to get no more than a cursory glance much of
the time. However, the training for counterfeit checkers in the American Treasury is not in
the appearance of the varieties of counterfeit notes, but in absolute familiarity with the real
dollar bill. Counterfeit checkers know the weight, texture and patterns of real dollar bills
so well that it is easy to spot even the best forgery. This is a great philosophy. Reapplied to
the identification challenge of these three species of *Aythya* ducks in brown plumages, the
best way to find the rarer ones is to get to know the variation in the appearance of Pochard

inside out, particularly that of summer females and fresh juveniles with their all-black bills. It is also important to be familiar with the effects of diving and feeding behaviour on such things as head shape and bill/head profile. Lack of real familiarity with some of these things has led to some Pochard in Britain and Ireland being misidentified as the rarer species.

The work of learning the Pochard will also reap real benefits for picking out interesting hybrids (which can be present in many larger flocks of *Aythya* ducks). It will also put diligent students ahead of the pack when it comes to finding and correctly identifying the really rare female or juvenile Redhead or Canvasback in the UK.

Redhead

Structure
Redhead is intermediate in size between Pochard and Canvasback. Compared to the other species in this group, it has a solid, chunky profile due to the way it typically sits higher on the water with a rather squared head shape, near-vertical forehead and frequently cocked tail (which often reveals whitish in the undertail coverts). Indeed it is more distinctive from the other two than they are from each other.

The most critical feature is the head shape. In profile the forehead rises steeply (almost vertical at times) above the bill base, rising to a high point on the crown, which peaks in front of the eye and therefore is further forward than in the other two species. The crown is mostly flattened, or only slightly domed. As a result, the whole head shape tends to be squarer.

Plumage
The familiar plumage of female Pochard, as seen through most of the winter months, with a grey body contrasting strongly with the brown breast, is sufficiently different from most Redhead plumages not to present too much of a problem. However the possibility of Pochard in the more uniformly brown juvenile and summer female plumages (the latter sometimes from February), and some Redhead-like *Aythya* hybrids, means that subtler characters must be carefully recorded to discern a genuine Redhead.

Redhead tends to have the darker, most uniform patterning of all three species. The head is rather uniform with a distinct dark cap and nape contrasting with an often rather uniform paler 'face' (thus recalling female Common Scoter). The palest areas are around the bill base and an obvious pale eye-ring which highlights a large-looking eye and has a pale line extending out from the rear [not shown in the drawing]. Importantly, the area adjacent to the bill base on Redhead is usually pale and plain and lacking the one or two dark 'tramlines' which, on most female Pochards, run diagonally back from the bill base and divide the pale region behind the bill. Also, the loral bulge of feathering at the bill base is least obvious on Redhead although this is feature is of marginal value as an identification aid.

The most noteworthy feature of the body plumage is a distinct lack of contrast between the breast and flanks unlike on winter-plumaged female Pochard and Canvasback, in which the contrast is strikingly obvious. The overall plumage tone of the body varies from rather uniform brown to more variegated with many pale fringes to the feathers. The more variegated individuals include some with broad grey fringes to the back and flank feathers, which can give the overall effect of a dull, grey-lookingbody and producing a subtle contrast with the darker, slightly more uniform breast. However, this body coloration is not as strikingly grey as on most winter-plumaged female Pochard.

The frequently cocked tail of female Redhead usually reveals the presence of some extent of white in the undertail coverts unlike in Pochard and Canvasback where the tail is usually held depressed and the pattern of the undertail coverts is not discernable.

Bill shape and pattern
There is a distinct break in the profile of the head at the bill base caused by the steep forehead. Structurally the bill is rather flattish with the most prominently 'hooked' large nail of all three species, although the latter is not an easy feature to see. The pattern of the bill typically appears as a duller version of the male's, being mostly mid-grey with a sharply demarcated 'dipped-in-ink' black tip and a blue-grey subterminal band or bar which is straight (not U-shaped as in Pochard). The colour of the bill base is slightly paler blue-grey than on female Pochard and so the black nostril groove tends to be more outstanding. Note, however, that the bill can be totally blackish in summer females and early-season juveniles.

Key characters of female-type Redhead

- Squat, chunky *Aythya* which sits high on water with cocked tail revealing whitish undertail coverts
- Squared head shape, with a steep forehead and flattish crown which peaks in front of eye
- Distinct dark cap and nape with a plain pale area at the bill base
- Body plumage variable in tone but typically rather uniform and lacking much contrast between the breasts and back/flanks
- A more 'flattened' bill rising only slightly at bill base, and a forehead/bill profile with a distinct change of angle where the steep forehead rises from the bill base
- Bill can be all-black in summer females and early juveniles, though the black 'dipped in ink' tip with a thin, straight (not U-shaped) blue-grey subterminal bar is a key feature when present.
- Slightly paler blue-grey bill base with more outstanding black nasal groove
- Loral bulge either slight or absent

Canvasback

Structure
Canvasback is the largest of the three species and also has the longest bill and a long 'ropy' or muscular-looking neck, particularly when the bird is alert. The long neck is also a significant feature of birds in flight, being outstanding compared with the other two species. It has the most triangular-shaped head with the peak of the crown the furthest back, often appearing to be behind the eye. The long black bill is frequently held at an angle tipped down from the horizontal and in profile is noticeably thin towards the tip and deep at the base. Where the bill and forehead meet, the contour, in profile, is either straight or even with a slight convex bulge. This bulge can create a detached look, rather like an ill-fitting crowned tooth next to the gum! The large body can sometimes have a somewhat hump-backed profile.

Plumage
The head plumage is generally rather uniform-looking with a soft, velvety, brown appearance and, while it can show a bit more patterning in the foreface, this area is most often uniformly dark as opposed to pale (Redhead) or striped (Pochard). The eye has a tendency to look

a little smaller and beadier than in Pochard. The loral area bulges out against the bill base making a convex curve that is more prominent than in the other two species, though this can be difficult to use as an identification feature. In winter plumage, female Canvasbacks have the palest greyish-white back and flanks of all the three species, which creates the greatest contrast with the dark sooty-brown breast. The demarcation line between the breast and flanks is also further forward and makes a more sloping angle compared with the other two species in which this line is located further back and is more vertical.

Bill pattern
The bill is always wholly black.

Key characters of female-type Canvasback

- Largest, with long muscular neck (useful in flight too), sometimes with slightly hump-backed profile
- Head shape is the most triangular, with the peak of the crown often behind the eye
- Head plumage rather uniform, velvety brown often with rather plain, dark foreface
- Palest grey-white back and flanks in winter with strongest contrast with sooty-brown breast
- Long, black bill, with deep-based and thin-tipped profile (hence the most triangular), held tilted slightly down
- Sloping angle to the demarcation line between the breast and flanks
- Nostril groove more conspicuous
- Loral bulge more prominent

Pochard

Structure
Pochard is slightly smaller than the other two, but the size difference is subtle. The most important identification feature is the bill and head profile. On relaxed birds there is a neat and continuous concave curve from the tip of the bill to the forecrown. The crown is usually neatly domed and, on average, peaks just above the eye (further forward than on Canvasback), giving a well-proportioned feel to the head/bill and eye. The tail is usually held depressed, hiding the undertail coverts and lacking the cocked tail more typical of Redhead.

Plumage
The warm-brown head is frequently marked by a paler area bordering the bill, which is broken by one or two dark diagonal lines running back from the bill base and creating a vaguely 'striped' effect over the foreface. In comparison, female-type Redhead is usually plain and pale in this area while in female-type Canvasback it is usually plain and dark. Both of the rarer species can show dark lines here but it is more the exception than the rule and, likewise, a few Pochard may lack these dark marks and have a plainer pattern here. In winter plumage, the warm, dark-brown breast contrasts strongly with the grey back and flanks, while the dividing line between the breast and flanks is vertical.

Bill shape and pattern

The bill pattern has previously been highlighted as a key identification feature for distinguishing between these species but it is common for juvenile and summer-female Pochard to have all-black bills, so other criteria, especially the bill and head profile, are more reliable tools for identification. When not all-black, the bill pattern of female-type Pochard is dark-grey or blackish with a black tip and a blue-grey subterminal band. Critically, both the black tip and the blue-grey subterminal band have a curved edge extending back along the bill sides so the subterminal band becomes clearly U-shaped. The nostril groove is more concolorous with the dark grey or blackish bill base and is therefore less outstanding than on Redhead.

Key characters of female-type Pochard

- Subtly the smallest of the three species, with a well-proportioned head on which the domed crown peaks approximately above the eye
- Forehead/bill profile of an even and gentle concave curvature along its length
- Head with one or two dark stripes straddling the paler foreface is a common pattern
- Bill black in summer-females and juveniles, otherwise dark grey base with black tip that bleeds along bill sides creating U-shaped blue-grey subterminal band
- In winter, strong contrast, and vertical dividing line, between the dark brown breast and flanks
- Nasal groove less conspicuous
- Loral bulge medium

References

Bolt, D. 2001. The Redhead in Glamorgan. *Birding World* 14: 495-496.

Garner, M. 2006. Identification of Redhead and Canvasback - with emphasis on female and immature plumages. *Birding Scotland* 9: 8-17.

Lonergan, P., Mullarney, K. & Harrop, H. 2007. Identification of Redhead in Europe. *Birding World* 20: 113-124.

Madge, S. 1991. Separation of Canvasback and Redhead from Pochard. *Birding World* 4: 365-368.

Mowbray, T. B. 2002. Canvasback (*Aythya valisineria*). In *The Birds of North America*. No 659 (A. Poole & F. Gill, eds.) The Birds of North America, Inc., Philadelphia, P.A.

Palmer, R. 1975. *Handbook of North American Birds*. Vol.3. Yale.

Scott, C., Gillon, K. & Rivers, S. 2004. The female Redhead on Barra, September 2003 to April 2004 - the first Scottish record. *Birding Scotland* 7: 130-135.

Vinicombe, K. 2003. The identification of a hybrid Canvasback × Common Pochard: implications for the identification of vagrant Canvasbacks. *British Birds* 96: 112-118.

Vinicombe, K. 2008. Redhead. *Birdwatch* 189. March 2008 31-34

Woodin, M. C., & Michot, T. C. 2002. Redhead (*Aythya americana*). In *The Birds of North America*. No 695 (A. Poole and F. Gill, eds.) The Birds of North America, Inc., Philadelphia, P.A.

Northern, American and Pacific Eiders
Martin Garner

I first became interested in looking for Northern Eider (ssp. *borealis*) following the report of a bird on Anglesey in the early 1980s, which I looked for but failed to see. In January 1985 during a long-distance 'hitch and twitch' to see Ross's Gull and Desert Wheatear in the far north of Scotland I discovered an immature-male Eider with an obvious orange bill base off John O'Groats. I had to wait another twelve years before finding a classic Northern Eider off Portrush, Northern Ireland in November 1997. This inspired me to try and work out key features for identifying these birds and led to the discovery of the regular wintering and occasional summering of Northern Eiders in north Donegal. Similarly keen-eyed observers have seen at least three adult male Northern Eiders in Shetland since 1989. In the winters of 2006 and 2007 a number of birds showing characters of Northern Eider were discovered in northeast Scotland though, rather disconcertingly, these included a ringed male which had hatched in a nearby colony in the 1980s. A maximum of 14 male Eiders with sails were seen around the Ythan Estuary in autumn 2007 (Chris Gibbins pers. comms.). Research is still ongoing but it's entirely possible that Northern Eiders originating in the Arctic occasionally summer and breed in northwest Europe as has been suspected in Donegal (pers. obs.). The presence of summering King Eiders and Surf Scoters, themselves likely originating from similar areas of the Arctic, is normal in the same region of Scotland. I suspect that there are Northern Eider genes in some of the populations of Eider in the north of Ireland and in northern Scotland, but this hardly invalidates looking for these birds and expecting occasional influxes in harsh winters. There is yet much to be discovered.

Taxonomy

The classic (yet unfinished) work *Handbook of North American Birds* by Ralph Palmer gives a good idea of the complexities which face the observer when dealing with the 'Common Eider' *Somateria mollissima*. While Palmer lists a number of subspecies, the lack of good factual information from remote breeding areas, different opinions on subspecific naming of some populations and the suggestion of intergradations between almost every form makes for a daunting subject.

In trying to make sense of some of the complexities, it is easiest to view all the birds breeding in the Arctic region of the North Atlantic (i.e. Svalbard, Iceland, Greenland and north-east Canada) as of similar form and to refer to them collectively as *borealis* (after Cramp & Simmons 1977). The main reasoning behind this approach lies in the shared morphological feature of white sails on the back that can be found among adult males, and which generally distinguishes them from the southerly North Atlantic populations of *mollissima* and *faeroeensis*. However, it is important to be aware that *borealis* is not uniform across its range, which makes it more difficult to isolate key criteria by which vagrants may be identified, and therefore to realise that some individuals from the range of *borealis* may not be identifiable as vagrants.

Of interest to taxonomists and field birders alike is a study by Livezey (1995). He suggests that the Common Eider is actually four species: *S. v-nigrum* (Pacific Eider), *S. borealis* (Northern Eider), *S. dresseri* (Canada/American Eider) and *S. mollissima* (European Eider). The identification text which follows uses these splits if only for ease of reference.

Geographical range

Northern (or Boreal) Eider breeds in Arctic regions from Baffin Island and north-east Canada to Greenland, Iceland and Spitzbergen and possibly further east. Eiders from all these localities have been shown to move significant distances south to escape the harsh Arctic winter (see Vagrancy potential). American Eider, already suggested to be worthy of specific status (Livezey 1995), breeds along the coasts of north-east Canada and the United States of America from Labrador to Maine. Pacific Eider breeds along the Arctic and Pacific coasts of north-east Siberia and north-west Canada and Alaska. There is some evidence in the past that the Pacific Eider has reached southern Greenland and has occurred amongst the huge swarms of wintering wildfowl there (Palmer 1976).

Vagrancy potential

The Northern Eider appears to occur annually, probably in small numbers, off the northern coasts of Britain and Ireland, and should be expected even further south, although at present there is only one accepted British record, of a tideline corpse. The origin of these birds remains uncertain but, in terms of movement and migration, birds from Canada, Greenland, and maybe Spitzbergen, could all occur in Britain and Ireland. Birds from Southampton Island in the Canadian Arctic have been radio-tracked to southern Greenland. Ringed birds, which have bred in East Greenland, have subsequently been found wintering, and even breeding, in Iceland. There are also ringing recoveries of birds from Spitzbergen wintering in Iceland. However, the Icelandic population seems to be highly sedentary overall, and is augmented in the winter months by large numbers from further north. Therefore the birds that could potentially occur in Britain could have travelled considerable distances.

Birds showing characters of American Eider have been suspected on the Western Isles of Scotland and in North Donegal. There is the suggestion that *dresseri* readily hybridise with *borealis* in Labrador, Canada (e.g. Palmer 1976) although this needs to be verified.

While investigating the subject of the origins and identification of Eiders it became apparent that there was real potential for Pacific Eiders to mix with Northern Eiders off the Canadian Arctic and occasionally abmigrate bringing them into the North Atlantic. Coincidentally, not long after the publication of 'Northern Eiders in Scotland - are they being missed?' (Garner & Farrelly 2005), Bruce MacTavish found Newfoundland's first Pacific Eider mixed in with flocks of wintering Northern Eiders. While it might surprise some, the potential for this stunningly beautiful duck to reach Western Europe seems very real.

IDENTIFICATION

Eider flocks are routinely scrutinised for the presence of stunning male or subtle female King Eiders. However, it is likely that the lack of awareness has lead to the rarer forms (or even species!) of Eider being overlooked. One of these, the Northern Eider (ssp. *borealis*) has recently been demonstrated to occur regularly in northern Scotland and off the north of Ireland. The other two remain unproven but very exciting possibilities! Features such as scapular sails, the shape of the bare loral region in both sexes, orange bill tones and extra green facial patterning are clues to finding these rarer taxa.

A word about 'white sails'

All male eiders have two stiffer modified long scapulars. They are the same feathers that give male King Eiders their permanently erect black sails. On the southern forms *mollissima* and *faeroeensis* they don't normally form more than a slight bump above the contour of the back. So far it seems that only vagrant forms to Western Europe from further north and west have obvious white sails. These sails are triangular in shape, looking rather like a dolphin's dorsal fin (or the 'wings' from one of granny's butterfly cakes!) and are presently considered to be a guarantee of Arctic or Nearctic origin.

A word about bill colour and frontal lobe shape

This is a complicated subject! What is important to note is that in *mollissima* the bill colour can vary quite considerably from being very dull olive-grey to bright and yellowy-looking (usually a kind of mustard tone). Similarly the shape of the frontal lobes varies from fine and pointed to broader and more rounded. In addition, observers should be aware that the appearance of the lobes varies according to the angle of observer from the bird, appearing more rounded from in front and above and more pointed in profile and from other oblique angles. Confusingly, the colour and shape also varies within *borealis*. There is a cline in colour from east to west, birds in the east (Svalbard and some in Iceland) with olive-grey bills and birds in the west (Greenland and north-east Canada) with increasingly bright and orangey bills. The shape of frontal lobes also vary in *borealis* populations from fine and pointed to slightly broader and round-ended to some extent, with variation probably most pronounced in the Icelandic population. Leg and foot colour usually mirrors bill colour in that birds with dull olive bills have dull yellowy-olive legs while birds with the brightest yellow or yellow-orange bills tend to show the brightest yellow-coloured legs and feet.

Identification process

Bearing in mind some of the tricky issues mentioned above, and the notes on range and movements, the following is an overview of the main distinguishing characters. The criteria apply largely to adult males, as female and immature males do not normally display sufficiently clear features to identify vagrants. However some immature male and female Pacific Eiders are identifiable, and it is possible that females exhibiting brown sails are identifiable as of Arctic/Nearctic origin.

Northern Eider (ssp. *borealis*)
Northern Eiders are variable in appearance depending on their origins. Birds from north-east Canada and Greenland have the brightest orange bill bases while those from Iceland and Spitzbergen have duller bills. Some of the birds which winter in Iceland, at least, have a distinctive bright orange bill base, though many have duller bill colours, which will not readily distinguish them from British birds (*mollissima* and *faeroeensis*) on bill colour alone.

The two key characters of this form are the colour of the bill base and the presence of white sails on the back. Those birds with a truly orange bill base (i.e. the colour of the fruit!) are striking in appearance. However many Northern Eiders have a bill colour considerably duller and close to matching typical British birds.

Key features of adult male Northern Eider (unless otherwise stated)

- Bill colour is variable with some having gorgeous bright orange base
- Prominent white triangular sails on the back not normally found in other European populations (this is the most important character)
- Black cap often has a straight lower edge
- Head shape tends to be squarer with steeper forehead
- Breast can be a richer, deeper salmon colour
- Females can have diagnostic small brown sails

American Eider (ssp. *dresseri*)

This potential vagrant from North America is most easily identified by its rounded frontal lobes that almost reach the eye and a line of green running horizontally underneath the black cap. Classic *dresseri* are straightforward to identify, having large rounded frontal lobes quite unlike other forms of Eider occurring in the Atlantic (only Hudson Bay's *sedentaria* is similar). In *dresseri* these lobes vary in colour from greyish through greenish to bright orange, the latter particularly in the winter and early spring. The bill and head profile can be particularly distinct on some individuals with a high peaked forecrown sloping down to the rear crown and, sometimes, a bill with a distinct kink near the tip, unlike on other forms of Eider. Any Eider seen with particularly broad frontal lobes should be immediately checked for the presence of green running horizontally below the black cap (i.e. underneath the eye) as the combination of these two features is highly indicative of *dresseri*. Other features to look for on an American Eider include white sails on males and brown sails on females, and the fact that the black line separating the white face and frontal lobes is thinner than in any of the other races and is normally more parallel-sided due to the lateral expansion of the broad frontal lobes.

Key features of adult male American Eider

- Obviously broad frontal lobes with wide rounded ends which seem almost to reach the eye
- Green extending to form a horizontal line below the black cap
- High peaked forecrown and kinked bill tip on some
- Thin black loral line which is parallel-sided or bulging in the middle and not tapering to a fine point as in *molissima* or *borealis*
- Usually obvious white sails (not so vital if all other features noted)

Pacific Eider (ssp. *v–nigra*)

The large size of the male Pacific Eider with a heavy-looking vivid orange bill, very short, pointed, frontal lobes and a green line running horizontally below a deeply curved black cap combine to produce a very distinctive bird. As in male King Eider, many male Pacific Eiders have a black V pattern over the throat. Female Pacific Eiders, like the males, have particularly short frontal processes and a very prominent bulge of feathering at the base of the bill, which together with a weighty bill often held tilted down make them quite distinctive compared with females of other forms of Eider. Their distinctive, if subtle, appearance, especially compared to other females among the Eider taxa, could well make them identifiable as vagrants.

Their size and most spectacular appearance (of the males) makes this the most different of the Eider forms and may mean this is the best candidate for separating as a species in its own right.

Key features of adult male Pacific Eider (unless otherwise stated)

- Bill wholly bright orange and often held tilted down
- Short and very thin and pointed frontal processes
- Obvious green line running horizontally below the deeply curved lower edge of the black cap
- Obvious white sails on some (but some populations seem to completely lack sails)
- Normally distinct black 'V' on throat (not always present and not essential for identification)
- Larger size compared with accompanying Eider
- Females have very short frontal processes and most prominent bulge of feathering at bill base

European Eider
ssp mollissima

slight variation in width of frontal processes

some variation in bill colour from olive to mustard yellowish

area below black cap is white

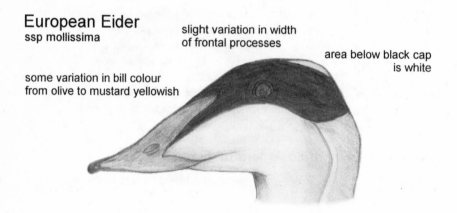

Northern Eider
ssp borealis

some individuals have squarer head shape with more vertical forecrown and narrow frontal processes pointed at end

many have orange tones over bill base

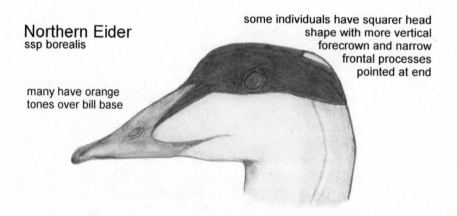

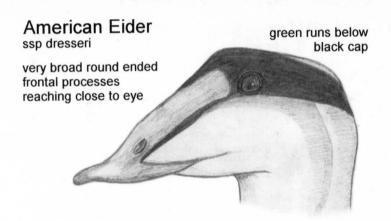

American Eider
ssp dresseri

very broad round ended frontal processes reaching close to eye

green runs below black cap

Pacific Eider
ssp v-nigra

large droopy bright orange bill with very short frontal processes

green runs below black cap

deeply curved lower edge to black cap

Diagram by Emily Garner

References

Andrews, I. J. & Naylor, K. A. 2002. Records of species and subspecies recorded in Scotland on up to 20 occasions. *Scottish Birds* 23: 61-116. SOC, Musselburgh.

Cramp, S. & Simmons K. E. L. (eds.) 1977. *The Birds of the Western Palearctic. Vol. 1.* Oxford.

Donald, C. 1995. Eider showing features of the race *S. m. borealis.* In *Shetland Bird Report* 1994, Shetland Bird Club.

Garner, M. & Farrelly, W. 2005. Northern Eiders in Scotland - are they being missed? *Birding Scotland* 8: 4-15.

Livezey, B. C. 1995. Phylogeny and evolutionary ecology of modern seaducks (Anatidae: Mergini). *Condor* 97: 233-255.

Palmer, R. J. 1976. *Handbook of North American Birds. Vol. 3 Waterfowl* (Part 2). Yale.

Pennington, M., Osborn, K., Harvey, P., Riddington, R., Okill, D., Ellis, P. & Heubeck, M. 2004. *The Birds of Shetland.* Christopher Helm, London.

Black, Red and Black-eared Kites

John McLoughlin

Having formerly had the ignominious title of 'highest rejection rate' of any species assessed by the BBRC, Black Kite remains a challenging identification to secure in Britain, even for otherwise thoroughly experienced observers. My dewy-eyed recollection of those long journeys to Tregaron and Aberystwyth in mid-Wales to 'see the kites' has been supplanted with the rapid reappearance of the Red Kite across a much greater area of the British countryside in recent years. This is an unquestionably delightful sight but adds a new and challenging element to the identification of vagrant Black Kites. Young Red Kites in their first year are not always as straightforward to identify as the adults. But that's only the start! Red and Black Kites occasionally hybridise with each other as well as with Buzzards, producing confusing-looking offspring. There has been more than one well-photographed yet unidentified 'kite' in recent years. Now a new quest waits for those with a pioneering spirit. The eastern Black-eared Kite has clearly demonstrated its ability to reach Western Europe and, while winter juveniles will remain outstanding in appearance, perhaps individuals with less obvious plumage have so far gone undetected. A candidate first-summer Black-eared Kite occurred in Finland in June and July 2006. Johnny Mac prepares us to 'learn the kites' with his thorough knowledge of the subject and its pitfalls. *Martin Garner*

Geographical range

The nominate form of Black Kite *Milvus migrans migrans* breeds across much of continental Europe, particularly Spain, France and Germany though it is absent from north-west Europe and Scandinavia. The European population winters mainly in Africa.

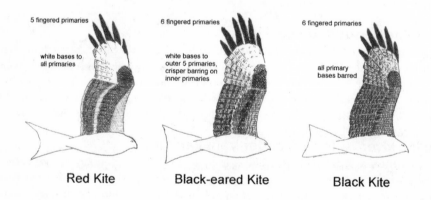

Red Kite   Black-eared Kite   Black Kite

Diagram by Mick Cunningham

Black-eared Kite *Milvus (migrans) lineatus* breeds widely from Western Siberia to China and Japan. Birds from the western parts of the range migrate long distances to winter in southern Asia as far west as Iran and Iraq. Note that Black Kite and Black-eared Kite are treated as distinct species by various authorities (e.g. Sibley & Monroe 1990; Rasmussen & Anderton 2005; Ferguson Lees & Christie 2005).

Vagrancy potential

Black Kite is an annual vagrant to Britain and the majority of individuals appear in spring. These overshooting spring migrants are adults or sub-adults, i.e. third calendar year or older. Most Black Kites leave their European breeding grounds in the early autumn. As a result, Black Kites seldom occur in the UK at this time of year and records of juveniles are very rare. Only two out of 360 accepted Black Kites in the UK up to 2006 have been reported as being juveniles (BBRC Reports) and both were in late August/September. A Black Kite appearing later than this should immediately ring alarm bells as to the possibility of it being a Black-eared Kite. Events in 2006 highlighted the potential of birds of this eastern form (or species) arriving into north-west Europe, with two birds identified as showing characters of Black-eared Kite, one in Finland and another in Britain; both were immature birds.

IDENTIFICATION

Kites are elegant raptors with a loose and buoyant flight that is distinctive amongst European birds of prey. Their long tails are used as aerial rudders, twisted and turned in a seemingly effortless continuum as they soar overhead. Given good views, identification of birds in flight is relatively straightforward but distance or poor light can hamper a correct diagnosis. The variability of viewing conditions is a well-known factor affecting the identification process. But other less understood variables associated with age and moult can also confuse observers, even with good views.

Ageing of raptors is an integral part of the identification process and observers should routinely try to assess the age or state of moult of any raptors they see. The key here is to practise on the commoner species. The identification process should then be easier when the appearance of the next large bird of prey starts to pose awkward questions. Although kite identification within a familiar context is relatively straightforward, a stray raptor viewed in isolation can prove to be a difficult call.

Black Kite versus Red Kite

The identification of a vagrant Black Kite (hereafter BK) in Britain is now complicated by the success of the Red Kite (hereafter RK) reintroduction scheme. Hundreds of young RK have been dispersing widely across the country in recent years. Perhaps surprisingly it is in first-year plumage that RK provides its own pitfall and therefore confusion with BK. Conversely, older BK can also be mistaken for RK.

Pitfall of juvenile/first-calendar-year Red Kite

In first-calendar-year plumage RK differs from adults in both plumage and structure. A juvenile RK is paler than the adult with sandy and buff tones to its plumage. The underparts are buff brown rather than the deep rufous colour shown by adults. From underneath a young RK shows a contrastingly paler body in comparison with the dark underwings. A useful ageing feature is the prominent pale tips to the greater coverts on both the upper- and underwings. Additionally, the upperwings have broad pale tips to the median secondary coverts creating a prominent pale bar which is generally paler and more prominent on RK compared to BK. The rusty tones to the brown upper tail should also point towards RK. Note that, from underneath, the RK tail is paler, almost white, with a dark subterminal band.

A young RK has shorter wings than an adult and, importantly, a shorter tail. By the spring and summer of the second calendar year, the tips of the juvenile tail feathers, often especially the outer ones, have been subjected to heavy wear for several months and can produce a strikingly square-ended shape to the tail. In a nutshell, a flying, worn juvenile RK can convey a very different jizz to the one presented by an adult RK. This is essentially one of a "stubbier" bird with shorter wings and a less well-forked tail.

In summary, a young RK has a duller plumage and a shorter tail with a shallower fork than an adult RK. The subtly different structural features produce an appearance, at least superficially, similar to BK and so the risk of misidentifying a second-calendar-year RK in spring as a BK is very real.

Given good views from below, certain features will help point straight to RK. The warm-toned lesser and median coverts line the inner wing, whilst the white bases to the primaries create a pale translucent wedge in the outer wing. Crucially, the outer wing shows five fingered primaries creating a narrower hand compared to BK.

Black Kite

Essentially BK is a bolder bird, stockier than RK and therefore not as rangy and harrier-like in flight. Compared to other confusion species such as Marsh Harrier the BK flies on flatter and slightly 'hunched' wings which have more prominent primary fingers. The details of the well-fingered 'hand' also provide a difference from RK. In BK the hand is broader, with six prominent primary tips, producing a squarer-ended wing tip. The underwing also lacks the prominent pale primary window which is such an obvious feature of RK, being at most a diffuse and less contrastingly pale patch.

Overall the BK has a darker plumage than RK with less contrast in the appearance of the upperparts due to less pale fringing. However, the upperwing panel created by the pale fringes to the median coverts can be very prominent, matching RK in some individuals. Be aware also that a good proportion of adult BK also show a significant rufous tone to the body, and older adults in particular have very pale heads. The tail, as well as virtually lacking an obvious fork, is dull brown above and completely lacking the rufous tones shown by RK.

An older (third-calendar-year plus) BK in worn plumage could be mistaken for a RK. A late-summer BK in active primary moult would show fewer than six prominent primary fingers. Combined with the warm rufous underparts that many BK possess this could cause confusion!

Fresh juvenile BK can appear quite strikingly varicoloured due to the prominent pale tips to the wing coverts and the pale streaks on the underbody. It should be less problematic distinguishing these from RK, although their racial identification must now also be considered; it could be a Black-eared Kite from the east!

Juvenile Black-eared Kite

This form is larger and broader-winged than the "Western" (nominate race) Black Kite. The prominent dark cheek patches are evident in close views. The heads of adult birds are dark, unlike the paler-headed western birds, whilst the eye is dark at all ages. Juvenile and second-calendar-year Black-eared Kites are very similar to BK but they can be separated on a suite of characters which includes the structure, and the pattern on the undersides, of the primaries. The following criteria were developed by Dick Forsman (Forsman 2003).

The most obvious features shown by this form are the prominent white bases to all the outer four or five primaries. At least P10 to P7 or P6 in most individuals have clear white primary bases, which can be very obvious in the field. The inner primaries P5 to P1 also show whiter, less muddy, bases with clearer, more defined, barring than shown by BK. The effect is to create a white block in the hand of the wing which is much more prominent than shown by BK and in some individuals can produce the translucent effect that is so obvious in RK. The possibility of hybrids must always be carefully considered and, with a pair of Black x Red Kites nesting in Scotland in recent years could present a problem for identification.

Although both forms show six fingered primaries, Black-eared Kite has a more eagle-like wing, the primary fingers themselves being relatively longer in Black-eared Kite than in BK. Crucially in Black-eared Kite P5 is longer, being two-thirds the length of P6, compared with the shorter P5 in BK, which is only half the length of P6. The longer P5 in Black-eared Kite effectively 'squares' the wing tip off resulting in a slightly broader, less pointed hand.

The pale head and dark face mask of juvenile and second-calendar-year Black-eared Kite is similar in appearance to BK; both forms also share the feature of pale streaks on the body. However, Black-eared Kite often shows a paler ventral area contrasting with the rest of the underparts and underwing.

Key features

Black Kite
- Upperwing with a paler carpal bar, sometimes prominent
- Six fingered primaries, with long P5 creating a broader hand than in Red Kite
- Primary bases paler than rest of underwing but heavily barred creating a diffuse light window
- Some birds have some white on the underside of the outer one-three/four primaries and are thus more similar to Black-eared Kite

Red Kite
- Upperwing with a prominent broad, pale carpal bar
- Five fingered primaries creating a narrower hand
- Primary bases of underwing white, only lightly barred, and creating a large and prominent light window
- Rusty or rufous tones to the upper tail

Black-eared Kite
Very similar to Black Kite but with the following main differences:
- Outer primaries, especially P8 and P7, relatively longer
- P6 even longer thus creating squarer wing tip and broader hand
- White bases to outer primaries (P10-P6) more similar to Red Kite
- Inner primaries more crisply barred than Black Kite

References

Badley, J. & Hyde, P. 2006. The Black-eared Kite in Lincolnshire: a new British Bird. *Birding World 19: 465-470.*

Crochet, P. A. 2005. Recent DNA studies of Kites. *Birding World* 18: 486-488.

Forsman, D. 1999. *The Raptors of Europe and the Middle East*. London.

Forsman, D. 2003. ID of Black-eared Kite. *Birding World*. 16: 156-160.

Ferguson Lees, I. J. & Christie, D. A. 2005. *Raptors of the World: A field guide*. London.

Sibley, C. G. & Monroe, B. L. 1990. *Distribution and Taxonomy of Birds of the World*. New Haven, USA.

Ramussen, P. C. & Anderton, J. C. 2005. *Birds of South Asia: The Ripley Guide*. Lynx Edicions.

Ringtail harriers (inc. Marsh Hawk)
John Martin

The question of whether the 'Hen Harrier' of North America has occurred in Britain and Western Europe has been the subject of much controversy. An old and hotly debated claim of one at Cley, Norfolk from October 1957 to April 1958 was followed by a number of claims, including two from the Isles of Scilly in October 1967 and 1979. Then a well-watched and photographed juvenile bird on the Isles of Scilly from 22nd October 1982 to 9th May 1983 seemed to be the real deal. However this was shortly followed by a paper by Peter Grant published in *British Birds* in 1983 entitled "The Marsh Hawk Problem". This confirmed the presence of rufous juvenile Hen Harriers in the European population which seemed to set an axe to the root of all claims of vagrant Marsh Hawks. However, for those observers who have championed the 1982/83 bird, the long-drawn-out campaign is finally over. Following the clarification of some features in recent years, the most recent Scilly bird has been accepted as a Northern Harrier by the BBRC and recently added to the British list by the BOURC. Here John Martin skilfully presents the key features of juveniles in readiness for the next potential juvenile Marsh Hawk in Britain, which hopefully will not be so contentious as those in the past! *Martin Garner*

Geographical range

Northern Harrier *Circus (cyaneus) hudsonius*, sometimes referred to by the old North American name 'Marsh Hawk', is the Nearctic race of Hen Harrier *Circus (cyaneus) cyaneus*, although it is perhaps better treated as a separate species. It breeds widely in North America from Alaska to Newfoundland, as far south as 30° north in Baja California in the west and Pennsylvania in the east. It winters from southern Canada south to northern South America, with a proportion of the population comprising long-distance migrants. It is declining across much of its range, though remains locally common.

Vagrancy potential

It was once thought that long-distance flights over water by broad-winged raptors were impossible. However radio tracking has shown that such birds are capable of remarkable feats of endurance. For example a juvenile Honey Buzzard, on its first migratory flight, was tracked as it flew for at least four days over the Atlantic (www.roydennis.org). With the recent acceptance of a juvenile on the Isles of Scilly from October 1982 until June 1983 it is anticipated that further vagrant Northern Harriers could reach us, though they are likely to remain very rare.

IDENTIFICATION

Ringtail harriers are a difficult group of birds to identify but fall into two pairs in terms of size, build and in particular wing structure. Northern Harrier not surprisingly forms one pairing with the closely related Hen Harrier, while Montagu's and Pallid Harriers make up the other. Structurally, Northern Harrier is very similar to Hen Harrier in terms of its relatively broad wings with five fingers at the tip, which give both of them a heavier flight than the two smaller species. The smaller Montagu's and Pallid Harriers share narrower wings and four fingers at the wing tip and have a lighter, more buoyant, flight action. The identification of the three European taxa is particularly well covered in Forsman (1999).

Separation from Hen Harrier

Northern Harrier shows subtle but consistent differences in plumage from Hen Harrier in both juvenile and adult male plumages, though adult females appear very similar. Juveniles are perhaps the most likely age class to occur in Britain and the notes below will concentrate on separating juvenile Northern Harrier from Hen Harrier. It is assumed here that a careful check of age, plumage and structure has already eliminated the possibility of both Montagu's and Pallid Harrier.

Ageing

Ringtail harriers are relatively straightforward to age. Autumn juveniles will be in rather fresh plumage with no signs of moult. Adult females are superficially similar in plumage pattern but, in September and October, they would be near the end of their complete moult, often showing gaps in the primaries and secondaries. The primaries of juvenile Hen and Northern Harriers are somewhat narrower and more pointed at the tips than the broad and rather square-ended fingers of adult females, which also have slightly broader wings, especially on the inner hand. Juvenile Hen Harriers also differ from adult females in details of plumage. Juveniles show largely dusky secondaries (contrasting with the paler primaries), darker brown upperparts (lacking grey tones) with warm feather edging and a more strongly contrasting head pattern. Any ringtail harrier in autumn with distinctly orange-toned underparts will be a juvenile, adults being creamy or whitish with distinct dark streaking. Juvenile Hen Harrier often shows rich ochre or rufous tones to the distinctly streaked breast and belly (though some individuals are more cream- or buff-toned here) while juvenile Northern Harrier has a largely unstreaked cinnamon to deep orange breast and belly, like that of Montagu's or Pallid Harrier. It is the combination of broad wings and five fingered primaries (ruling out Pallid/Montagu's Harrier) together with an apparently unstreaked orange-toned breast and belly that is most likely to draw attention to a Northern Harrier.

Plumage of juveniles

Body and underwing coverts
The key things to establish are how much streaking is present and how cinnamon or orange the underparts appear. A juvenile Northern Harrier is typically deep rufous-orange below but may be paler cinnamon on some individuals (either birds in fresh plumage or those with bleached and faded plumage later in the season). Juvenile Hen Harriers, on the other hand, usually have a creamy to warmer ochre ground colour to the breast and belly, However, richer, orangey-toned individuals are frequent so there is some overlap between the most orangey Hen Harriers and the palest Northern Harriers. Crucially though, there is less overlap in the extent of streaking on the body and underwing coverts. A Northern Harrier would be almost completely unstreaked on almost all of the breast and belly apart from some narrow and restricted streaking on the sides of the breast and, sometimes, a narrow zone of streaking immediately below the dark 'boa'. Juvenile Hen Harriers are always streaked on the breast, belly and underwing coverts, with larger, stronger and more extensive markings than

in Northern Harrier, though it is still conceivable that the most heavily marked Northern Harrier might overlap with the most lightly streaked Hen Harrier. Accurate evaluation of the strength and extent of any streaking on the underparts is vital and requires good views.

Head and neck pattern

The head and neck pattern is a useful feature for identifying ringtail harriers and this includes Northern Harrier. The neck sides of this form are more or less solid dark brown to blackish neck sides creating a dark boa recalling juvenile Pallid Harrier. On weakly marked individuals this area is less solidly dark with blotchy dark chocolate streaks on a dark rufous background but still forms a strong dark patch. On many, but not all, individuals this boa meets across the breast. In all birds it is separated from the dark ear coverts by a variable narrow pale band or collar that can extend to the nape and across the breast on some birds. Hen Harrier can sometimes show a shadowy and darker boa but it is always streaky with a rather pale ground colour that in tone either matches the rest of the underparts or is only a little darker and is therefore never as contrasting as on Northern. The difference mirrors that between Pallid and heavily marked Montagu's Harriers. Hen Harrier does share the pale collar but it tends to be less contrasting as the boa is not so dark.

The head pattern of juvenile Northern Harrier is also different from that of Hen Harrier. On Northern Harrier, the crown is chocolate-coloured and more solidly dark, the pale supercilium is warmer-toned and there is a dark line through the eye separating the pale supercilium from the shorter pale crescent below the eye. The ear coverts are usually solidly dark and concolourous with the crown. In juvenile Hen Harrier the crown and ear coverts are usually somewhat paler and more obviously streaky though the ear coverts, in particular, often form a solid-looking dark block. The supercilium is typically longer and broader sometimes reaching the forehead and joining the often larger pale crescent below the eye. Hen Harrier can often show a reduced supercilium and small pale crescent below the eye much like Northern Harrier but the latter rarely seems to have so much white around the eye as is shown by some Hen Harriers. The head patterns do vary but the best-marked birds are distinctive.

The largely dark head and solid dark boa contrasting with the largely unstreaked orange-toned body gives many Northern Harriers a striking hooded appearance. A minority are less well marked and might be hard to tell from the most rufous and plainer (least streaky) Hen Harriers especially if such birds also show a shadowy boa. Most well-marked Northern Harriers are however distinctive and not matched by any Hen Harrier.

The pattern in the primaries

The pattern of the underside of the primaries is a well-known feature for identifying juvenile harriers of the regular European species and it can also be useful for identifying Northern. The outer primary P10 in Northern Harrier shows three to four, or even five, blackish bars in addition to the black tip but Hen Harrier has only three such bars. In Northern Harrier, the longest primaries, P8 and P9, show five to six blackish bars plus the dark tip but in Hen Harrier this is usually three or four (sometimes five). There also appears to be a difference in the trailing edge of the inner primaries between the two forms. They both show a darker trailing edge to the inner hand but in Northern Harrier this tends to be paler and less contrasting than in many Hen Harriers. Some Hen Harriers, perhaps especially males, can have a very poorly marked trailing edge, though these tend to be individuals with very lightly marked primaries. Another possible feature is a tendency for Northern Harrier to show a more conspicuous pale crescent at the base of the outer primaries because the dark bars here are narrower than they are on Hen Harrier.

The pattern in the secondaries

In both forms, the underside of the secondaries is often dusky or dark overall and there is considerable overlap in the pattern of the banding. Northern Harrier typically shows three diffuse dark bands through the secondaries with the central of these bands being narrower than the others and the hint of a fourth dark bar (including the dark trailing edge) on the outer secondaries. Many Hen Harriers have 2 –3 bars on the underside of the secondaries (see illustration). There does however appear to be overlap in this feature, so it is not currently considered especially useful as a distinguishing character.

General appearance

Overall, Northern Harrier has a darker brown plumage with the paler areas more rufous while Hen Harrier is paler brown with the paler areas often colder buff or cream. The upperparts of Northern are a distinctly darker chocolate-brown with rich rufous fringes, at least when fresh. The upperparts of Hen Harrier are typically a paler mid-brown colour with paler rufous tones to feather edgings and often a paler buffy nape patch. There seems to be little or no overlap in plumage tones between the two forms when a series of skins is compared, but accurate judgement on a lone bird in the field would be much more difficult.

A vagrant juvenile Northern Harrier should only be identified using a combination of features and one of them, primary pattern, would be very difficult to judge accurately in the field and would probably depend on good-quality photographs. With the profusion of modern digital SLR cameras, recording such data has become a real possibility.

Key features of juvenile Northern Harrier

- Size and structure, including broad wings and five fingered primaries, like Hen Harrier and distinct from Pallid and Montagu's.
- Underparts rufous or cinnamon with rather fine streaking confined to the sides of the breast and just below the boa, with none in the middle of the breast and belly.
- Solid-looking dark chocolate brown or blackish boa, often extending right across the breast, recalling juvenile Pallid Harrier, with the ear coverts and crown a similar shade. These dark areas contrast strongly with the largely plain rufous or cinnamon underparts producing a strong hooded effect.
- Five or six dark bars on the longest primaries (P8-9), with three to five bars on the outer primary (P10), and a rather pale trailing edge to the inner hand (photographswould be needed to capture this detail).
- Dark chocolate-coloured upperparts with rufous fringes.
- Pale warm-toned supercilium and shorter crescent below eye, typically with dark line through eye.
- Rather dusky secondaries with the middle dark bar at least slightly narrower than the others and often with hints of a fourth dark bar (including the dark trailing edge) on the outer secondaries.

5 or 6 dark bars on
longest primaries
(3-5 on p10)

pale trailing edge
to inner hand

plain cinnamon
underparts with
limited streaking

Northern Harrier
juvenile

dark plain neck
giving hooded effect
with reduced pale
surround to eye

3-4 or 5 dark
bars on
longest
primaries
+ dark tips
(3 on p10)

extensive streaking
on underparts

Hen Harrier
juvenile

heavily streaked neck
with more pale
surround to eye

Diagram by John Martin

Summary

Northern Harrier is a very rare vagrant to Britain and perhaps most likely to occur in the autumn and winter. At least the majority of juvenile Northern Harriers should be confidently identifiable, if well documented, using a combination of features.

Acknowledgements

Thanks to Graham Etherington, Andrew Harrop and various members of BBRC for help in trying to develop these criteria and in particular to Brian Small and Chris Kehoe.

References

Cramp, S. & Simmons, K. E. L. 1980. *Birds of the Western Palearctic. Vol. 2.* Oxford.

Forsman, D. 1999. *The raptors of Europe and The Middle East - a handbook of field identification.* T & A D Poyser.

Grant, P. J. 1983. The Marsh Hawk problem. *British Birds* 76: 373-376.

Vinicombe, K. E. 2003. Travelling Circus. *Birdwatch* September 2003.

Wallace, D. I. M. 1971. American Marsh Hawk in Norfolk. *British Birds* 64: 537-542.

Wallace, D. I. M. 1998. Identification forum: Marsh Hawk - the end of a 41-year hunt? *Birding World* 11: 454-457.

Wheeler, B. K. & Clark, W. S. 1995. *A photographic guide to North American raptors.* Academic Press.

Taiga Merlin
Martin Garner

The annual banter at the Northern Ireland Christmas bird quiz in December 2000 started the ball rolling. Following some predictable ribbing about my interest in the edges and margins of birding, Willie McDowell mentioned he had seen a strange-looking Merlin on Cape Clear Island, County Cork, and asked whether I would be interested in seeing the video footage. He and Denis Weir wondered if the bird could be a Taiga Merlin, and the issue of whether the bird's identity could be secured was the main question. The intriguing dark Merlin was however pushed off centre stage a few days later when Denis located a Blue-winged Warbler, the first for the Western Palearctic! Willie very sadly died in May 2006 while birding in Venezuela with Denis and so this section is written with fond memories of him. Hey Willie, you got another first for Ireland that week!

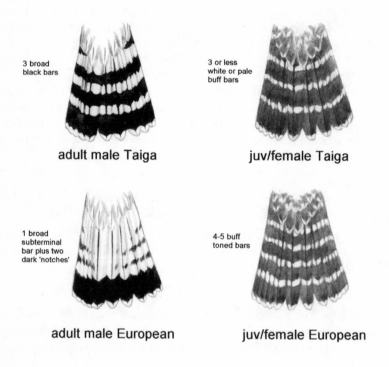

3 broad
black bars

adult male Taiga

3 or less
white or pale
buff bars

juv/female Taiga

1 broad
subterminal
bar plus two
dark 'notches'

adult male European

4-5 buff
toned bars

juv/female European

Taxonomy and geographical range

The Merlin *Falco columbarius* occurs in a range of open and semi-open habitats in the New and Old Worlds. As all Eurasian Merlins are clearly different from all American Merlins, a useful starting point in considering their taxonomy is to divide them into the two major groupings of Eurasian and American populations.

The taxonomy of North American Merlins was discussed by Temple (1972a) who suggested that all three North American forms had distinct phylogenetic histories. He suggested that they derived from a double invasion of Merlins from Asia into North America, the first giving rise to *columbarius* and *suckleyi* and the second giving rise to *richardsonii*. In total, nine forms of Merlin are currently recognised (Cramp & Simmons 1980; Palmer 1988; Ferguson-Lees & Christie 2001):

North American forms

F .c. columbarius (Taiga Merlin)
Breeds in boreal/taiga forest from Alaska to Newfoundland; highly migratory; vast winter range from Canada to northern South America. See main text for characters.

F. c. suckleyi (Black Merlin)
Breeds along the Pacific coast of North America from Alaska to Washington; mostly resident, although some migrate south to southern California and New Mexico. Averages much darker overall than *columbarius*, with the pale supercilium and tail markings reduced or absent. However, some dark female *columbarius* can appear identical to *suckleyi*. Best told by underwing pattern: in *suckleyi*, underwing all-dark in some; others have faint spotting covering less than 50% of the underwing; *columbarius* shows more obvious spotting covering at least 50% of the underwing.

F. c. richardsoni (Prairie Merlin or Richardson's Merlin)
Breeds in the Great Plains of central North America; partly resident and partly migratory, with some wintering south to New Mexico and California, and reported as far east as southern Ontario. Overall paler than *columbarius*; pale tail bands similar in number, but obviously broader in both sexes; lacks obvious moustachial marks and averages more extensive pale spotting on remiges.

Eurasian forms

F. c. subaesalon
Breeds in Iceland (birds of the Faeroe Islands and northern Britain are intermediate between *subaesalon* and *aesalon*); mostly migratory; winters south to Britain, Ireland and continental Europe. See main text for characters.

F. c. aesalon
Breeds from northern Europe (including Britain) eastwards to central Siberia, where reported to intergrade with *insignis*; partially migratory in Britain and Ireland and migratory elsewhere; winters south to the Mediterranean. See main text for characters.

F .c. insignis
Breeds in central and northeastern Siberia from east of the River Yenisey to the River Kolyma; migratory; winters south to northern India, Korea and Japan. As it performs the longest migration of any Eurasian form, it may be a potential vagrant to western Europe. Averages slightly larger and paler than *aesalon*, with less streaking below; juveniles tend to have foxy tones to broader fringes on upperparts and broader pale tail bands than *aesalon*. The difficulty of its identification is compounded, however, by its reported intergrading with *aesalon* in central Siberia and the frequent occurrence of apparent intermediates between the two in Israel (Shirihai 1995).

F. c. pacificus

Breeds in the Pacific region of northeastern Asia southwards to Sakhalin Island; migratory; winters south to Japan and northern China. Averages larger than *insignis*, with plumage apparently closer to *aesalon*.

F .c. pallidus (Steppe Merlin or Pallid Merlin)

Breeds in the steppes of south-western Siberia and northern Kazakhstan; migratory; winters southern Asia from eastern Turkey to north-western China. This form seems to be a potential vagrant to western Europe. It is also the most distinctive of the Eurasian forms and arguably a candidate for a taxonomic review. The largest and palest form, with very fine streaking on the underparts, extensively pale brown and grey barred over the upperparts with darker outer primaries, producing a somewhat Kestrel-like pattern; in juveniles, the pale tail bands are broader than the dark bands in between (unlike all other forms).

F. c. lymani

Breeds in central south-east Asia, from the Tien Shan and Altai to western China; migratory; wintering south into China. The wings are significantly longer than in other forms; plumage similar to *insignis*.

A tenth form '*bendirei*' was formerly recognised but is now considered to be a synonym for *F. c. columbarius* in western North America. While agreeing that Taiga Merlin should be regarded as a single taxon *F. c. columbarius*, Palmer (1988) does note that western birds do average paler than eastern birds, with narrower dark tail bars in adult males. 'Black' type Merlins that are recorded well away from traditional *suckleyi* range (e.g. in eastern North America) are usually considered to be darker examples of the form *columbarius* (e.g. Sibley 2000). The three American forms are quite distinct from one another, although some hybridisation occurs between *richardsonii* and *columbarius* where the ranges overlap in the central prairies, and may also occur between *suckleyi* and *columbarius* where they overlap (B. K. Wheeler pers. comm.). American Merlins are described as having differences in call from Eurasian Merlins (Ferguson-Lees *et al.* 2001).

Vagrancy potential of Taiga Merlin to Europe

Taiga Merlins are perfect candidates for transatlantic vagrancy. They are primarily long-distance migrants and the only form of Merlin that regularly crosses the equator; some travel from Canada to northern South America and vagrants have been recorded south to Brazil (Ferguson-Lees & Christie 2001). They are regular on the east coast of North America, where 92% of the birds ringed have been juveniles (Palmer 1988). One study of offshore records of American raptors in the northwest Atlantic concluded that "some individuals of these species [Osprey, Peregrine and Taiga Merlin] regularly engage in long-distance overwater flights during migration" (Kerlinger *et al.* 1983). The paper reported twenty-five records of Taiga Merlins up to 300 km offshore between Nova Scotia and North Carolina.

In the Western Palearctic there have so far been two definite records of Taiga Merlin: a juvenile male found dead in Akranes, western Iceland, in late October 1989, and a female/immature photographed on Cape Clear Island, County Cork, Ireland on 29th September 2000 (Garner 2002). An adult male Taiga Merlin, which is in the Hume Collection at the Natural History Museum, Tring, was apparently collected in Sussex in, or prior to, 1885.

Its true identity has only come to light in recent years though the data is scant and there is insufficient evidence to confirm that it was collected as a genuine vagrant.

Vagrancy potential of Eurasian Merlins to the Americas

Palmer (1988) details one record for the Pacific coast of North America (in the Commander Islands, Bering Sea) that may refer to *F. c. pacificus*. The range of *pacificus* seems to make it a highly likely candidate for vagrancy to Alaska and the Pacific coast of North America. Palmer also states that there are at least six records of Merlins from east, south and south-west Greenland, which may be *aesalon* (or more likely *subaesalon*) and one certain record of *subaesalon* from eastern Greenland (collected on 3rd July 1914). Given that *subaesalon* regularly crosses the Atlantic between Iceland and northern Europe, and that there is a record of a juvenile *subaesalon* caught on board a ship off Bahia, Brazil in November (Cramp & Simmons 1980), it seems likely that European Merlin (ssp. *subaesalon* and possibly *aesalon*) is a potential vagrant to eastern North America waiting to be discovered.

IDENTIFICATION

Taiga Merlin versus European Merlin

In Europe, the Icelandic form *F. c. subaesalon* averages larger and darker than *F. c. aesalon* and tend to show less rufous/ginger fringing and spotting to the upperparts in fresh juvenile plumage. It also sometimes has narrower, or even barely discernible, pale distal tail bands compared to *aesalon*, although this is not a constant difference. Apart from these subtle and variable differences, and bearing in mind that Merlins from the Faeroes and northern Britain are intermediate between these two forms, *aesalon* and *subaesalon* share the same basic plumage characters to distinguish them from the North American Taiga Merlin *F. c. columbarius*.

Taiga Merlins differ from European Merlins in their smaller size and, more subtly, in their plumage tones and patterns (particularly in the upperpart tones and patterning on the flight feathers), but the diagnostic difference in all plumages lies in the tail pattern. The plumage types fall into two main categories: adult males and the (very similar) juveniles/adult females.

Adult males

Uppertail pattern
Adult male Taiga Merlins have a distinct pattern of three broad black bars across the uppertail, with the distal bar about twice the width of the two basal bars, and a striking white tail-tip. The pale blue-grey bands separating these bars are narrower than the two black basal bars in eastern populations, but tend towards slightly broader than the two basal bars in western populations (Palmer 1988). Sometimes the three black bars are connected to each other by black shaft streaks giving the effect of black lines 'cutting through' the paler blue-grey bands. The longest uppertail coverts reach the basal black bar. The uppertails of European Merlins typically have a broad, blackish, distal (subterminal) bar, which is less inky-black than in Taiga Merlin, and up to three, usually incomplete and rather indistinct, dark basal bars. When present and unbroken, these dark bars are clearly narrower than the corresponding black bars of Taiga Merlins. Some evidence from museum specimens indicates that European

birds with two or three complete, narrow blackish tail bars may be younger males (second- or third-calendar-year birds). One Taiga Merlin specimen at the British Natural History Museum showed just a broad black subterminal bar and no basal dark bars, and thus a tail pattern similar to European Merlin. Although apparently not normal, such an individual would be difficult to pick out as a vagrant.

Undertail pattern

Adult male Taiga Merlins show a clear-cut, contrasting pattern of a blackish undertail with one or two conspicuous white or greyish-white bands and a broad white tip (the latter exaggerated by the shorter outer tail feathers when folded). The undertail coverts either reach the uppermost band or obscure it so often only one white band is visible. European Merlins also show a dark undertail, but it is less black and has two to three bands which are duller grey, less clear-cut and less obvious. As in Taiga Merlin, the undertail coverts either reach the uppermost band or obscure it. The blackish streaks in the undertail-coverts tend to be broader in Taiga Merlins and narrower in European Merlins, but there is overlap in this feature as well.

Upperparts

The upperparts of adult male Taiga Merlins generally appear slightly darker and richer blue than European Merlins, although there is overlap. The underparts of adult male Taiga Merlins are variable in coloration, from pale cream to rich cinnamon-orange, just as in European Merlins. However, there are differences between many individuals. Male Taiga Merlins typically have heavy, broad barring on the lower flanks clearly contrasting with fine streaking over the central underparts, whereas adult male European Merlins generally have less striking flank barring which contrasts less with the rest of the underparts giving them a more uniform appearance (although some can match Taiga Merlins).

Pale spots or bars in flight feathers

Adult male Taiga Merlins have slightly fewer and smaller, but more clearly defined, whitish spots and bars on the remiges compared to European Merlins. This is particularly true for the secondaries, where the pattern is that of neat rows of whitish spots which reach the tertials. On European Merlins, the pattern is superficially similar, but there tends to be more, slightly larger, pale marks per feather and, in particular, there tend to be pale marks on the outer webs of the remiges. These are lacking in the majority (87%) of eastern Taiga Merlins, which consequently look much plainer, less spotted, on the upperwing (Temple 1972b). The pale marks also tend to be duller and more buff-toned (rather than whitish) in European Merlins.

Summary of key features (adult male Taiga Merlin)

- Diagnostic pattern of three broad black bars across the uppertail, with the subterminal bar twice the width of the two basal bars
- Tendency to have slightly darker, richer upperparts with heavier, broader barring on the flanks
- Blackish streaks on undertail coverts average broader
- Smaller, fewer, whiter and more clearly defined spots and bars on flight feathers, particularly the secondaries

Adult females and juveniles

Uppertail
Adult female and juvenile Taiga Merlins have two or three complete, narrow greyish-white or pale buff bands across the uppertail, the distal bar usually abutting or partly obscured by the longest uppertail coverts. The dark areas between the pale bands are usually about three times wider than the pale bands. European Merlins have four or five complete pale bands on the uppertail, which tend to be duller and more buff-toned (less whitish) than those of Taiga Merlins. The dark dividing areas between the bands average a little paler and browner than in Taiga Merlins and are, at most, only twice as wide as the pale bands. In summary, Taiga Merlin has fewer tail bands, the dark bands are darker (and broader) and the pale bands are whiter so the overall impression is of a more contrasting pattern. On some juvenile European Merlins of the race *subaesalon* the uppertail can appear dark and therefore similar to the generally dark slate-coloured tone of Taiga Merlin. Occasionally, Eurasian Merlins can appear to show only three pale bands across the uppertail bands, but the pattern is still different, with the uppermost of the three most clearly visible bands being well separated from the longest uppertail-coverts, under which a fourth pale band can be slightly obscured but is still visible if looked for.

Undertail
The undertails of adult female and juvenile Taiga Merlins show up to four pale bands, but normally only one or two of these are complete and clear of the longest undertail coverts. European Merlins usually show between five and seven pale bands across the undertail, with at least two of these always well clear of the longest undertail coverts. Note that, because the undertail coverts are long and narrow, it can be difficult to read the number of pale bands in relation to them, especially when some feathers may be absent through moult.

Upperparts
The upperparts of adult female and juvenile Taiga Merlins generally have much less pale barring and feather fringing compared to European Merlins. Indeed, when perched, many individuals appear to have completely uniform, dark upperparts, an appearance never normally shown by European Merlins. The upperparts also average clearly darker in Taiga Merlin, ranging from plain chocolate-brown to slate blackish-brown, but sometimes more grey-washed, especially in fresh autumn plumage. European Merlins are typically slightly paler brown to greyish-brown, usually with obvious paler feather fringing, and with spotting and barring on the scapulars and wing-coverts (which tends to be particularly obvious in adult females). However, some juvenile European Merlins, especially *subaesalon*, can be relatively dark and less marked, although they never quite match the plain dark upperparts of typical Taiga Merlins.

Breast streaking
Adult female and juvenile Taiga Merlins tend to have narrower streaking down the centre of the breast and belly than European Merlins, contrasting with broad barring and spotting along the flanks. European Merlins typically have broader droplet-shaped streaking on the central breast (particularly in juvenile plumage), and thus have more heavily streaked underparts overall.

Pale spots or bars in flight feathers

As in adult males, adult female and juvenile Taiga Merlins tend to have slightly fewer, smaller and more clearly defined buff-coloured spots and bars in neater rows on the primaries and secondaries. Adult female and juvenile European Merlins have more marks of a larger size and irregular shape. Also as in males, the majority of eastern Taiga Merlins in female and juvenile plumage do not have pale marks on the outer webs of the remiges, whereas the majority of European Merlins do. Thus most eastern Taiga Merlins have plainer and less-spotted upper and especially underwings than European Merlins.

Summary of key features (female and juvenile Taiga Merlin)

- Diagnostic pattern of two or three complete narrow pale bars on the uppertail. Care should be taken to record feature accurately
- Often plainer and darker upperparts with less pale barring and fringing
- Less heavily streaked breast centre contrasting more with broad barring on flanks
- Buff spots and bars on flight feathers are fewer, more clearly defined and in neater rows
- Plainer, less spotted upper and underwing

Ageing and sexing of female and juvenile Taiga Merlins

Ageing and sexing of females and juveniles is even more difficult in Taiga Merlins than it is in European Merlins (see, for example, Forsman 1999). It is likely that only the very best views or trapping will secure accurate ageing and sexing of most individuals, and thus many birds will be left as indeterminate female/juvenile. Successful ageing and sexing depends on the accurate assessment of plumage tones, which can be much easier in the hand (from either live trapped or museum specimens) than in the field. The upperpart feathers of juvenile and some female Merlins tend to have a grey or slate-coloured bloom, or even a slight iridescence, over the centre of the feathers, with a plainer and browner fringe. Different light conditions can make the upperparts appear to vary from dark brown to greyish-brown or even bluish-brown. As Forsman (1999) states for juvenile European Merlins *'In fresh plumage dark brown above…but ground colour varies depending on angle of light from vinous to almost greyish'*. I am particularly grateful to Brian Wheeler and Jerry Liguori who clarified a number of the features listed below.

Adult female

The upperparts are dark brown and generally very plain, with little, if any, paler feather fringing. There can be a greyish cast to the plumage, especially when fresh but, most importantly, there is a slate-grey or even bluish-grey tone to the rump and uppertail coverts, which contrasts with the rest of the browner-toned upperparts. In contrast, juveniles are more uniformly coloured on the upperparts (Temple 1972b). The pale bands on the uppertail tend to be pale buff, but can be greyish, and are often more irregular and broken than in juveniles. Some adult females completely lack pale tail bands. In some females the underwing coverts are less buff in tone and some have more obvious dark shaft streaks on the upperparts than juveniles.

Adult females will be in obvious primary moult in August and September, with the last moulted primaries being P10 and P1. As moult nears completion, adults may appear to be in fresh plumage but can be distinguished from juveniles by their partially grown P10 and retained older wing coverts, the latter giving a patchy appearance to the upperparts in mid- to late October.

Juvenile female

The upperparts are dark brown, sometimes with a greyish cast in certain light conditions, although the rump and uppertail coverts show no contrast with the back colour. In fresh plumage during the autumn, there can be obvious tawny-buff fringes to the upperparts feathers, although these can wear off quickly after fledging and may not be apparent later. The bands on the uppertail are usually pale buff (Temple 1972b), but they can be greyer across the central tail feathers (Palmer 1988). The underwing coverts tend to be more strongly buff-washed than in adult female.

Juvenile male

Juvenile male is very similar to juvenile female. Apart from its smaller size (which is not really useful in the field) and greater tendency to have a greyish cast over the upperparts, the main difference is in the colour of the tail bands. In juvenile males theses are usually pale grey (Temple 1972b), although they can be slightly buff-toned in some individuals. By mid- winter, some have replaced their juvenile central tail feathers with grey feathers showing the adult male pattern, and, by March or April of the second calendar year, some upperparts feathers have also been replaced, these also showing the pattern of adult male.

References

Cramp, S. & Simmons, K. E. L. 1980. *The Birds of the Western Palearctic. Vol. 2*. Oxford.

Ferguson-Lees, I. J. & Christie, D. A. 2001 *Raptors of the World*. London.

Garner, M. 2002. Identification and Vagrancy of American Merlins in Europe. *Birding World*. 15: 468- 480.

Kerlinger, P., Cherry, J. D. & Powers, K. D. 1983. Records of Migrant Hawks from the North Atlantic Ocean. *Auk* 100: 488-490.

Palmer, R. 1988. *Handbook of North American birds. Vol. 5*. Yale.

Shirihai, H. 1995. *The Birds of Israel*. London.

Sibley, D. 2000. *The North American bird Guide*. East Sussex.

Temple, S. A. 1972(a). Systematics and evolution of the North American Merlins. *Auk* 89: 325–338.

Temple, S. A. 1972(b). Sex and age characteristics of the North American Merlins. *Bird Banding* 43: 191-196.

Wheeler, B. K. 2003 Raptors of eastern North America and Raptors of western North America. *The Wheeler Guides*. Princeton.

Wheeler, B. K. & Clark, W. S. 1995. *A Photographic Guide to North American Raptors*. London.